LABOR STRUGGLE
IN THE
POST
OFFICE

A HISTORY

LABOR STRUGGLE
IN THE
POST OFFICE

**From Selective Lobbying
to Collective Bargaining**

JOHN WALSH
GARTH MANGUM

M. E. Sharpe, Inc.
Armonk, New York ▪ London, England

Copyright © 1992 by M. E. Sharpe, Inc.
80 Business Park Drive, Armonk, New York 10504.

Available in the United Kingdom and Europe from M. E. Sharpe, Publishers,
3 Henrietta Street, London WC2E 8LU.

Library of Congress Cataloging-in-Publication Data

Walsh, John, 1925—
    Labor struggle in the Post Office: from selective lobbying to
collective bargaining / by John Walsh and Garth Mangum.
        p.   cm.
    Includes index.
    ISBN 1-56324-028-9 — ISBN 1-56324-146-3 (pbk.)
    1. Trade-unions—Postal service—United States—History—20th
century.   2. Collective bargaining—Postal service—United States—
History—20th Century.   3. Strikes and lockouts—Postal service—
United States—History—20th century.   4. Postal Strike, U.S.,
1970.   5. American Postal Workers Union—History.   6. United States
Postal Service—Employees—History. I. Mangum, Garth. II. Title
HE6499.W26 1992
331.88'13834973—dc20   91-43910
                                                             CIP

Printed in the United States of America

The paper used in this publication meets the minimum requirements of American
National Standard for Information Sciences—Permanence of Paper for Printed
Library Materials, ANSIZ39, 48-1984.

MV   10   9   8   7   6   5   4   3   2   1

TABLE OF CONTENTS

LIST OF PHOTOGRAPHS

Photographs follow page 144

ACKNOWLEDGMENTS

This book is the result of a desire on the part of Moe Biller, President of the American Postal Workers Union, to have an objective history written of the struggle of postal workers to form unions and deal effectively with their employer, the United States Government. President Biller gave the writers access to all the union files and to his entire staff, and never once attempted to exercise editorial control over the contents of the book. The book contains material with which he does not agree and at least one incident that he does not believe was covered in sufficient detail, but at no point did he apply pressure on the writers to change their points of view or in any way alter their conclusions. We are, therefore, grateful to President Biller, one of the outstanding labor leaders of the modern era.

The cooperation the writers received started with the president, but did not end there. William Burrus, Executive Vice President, and Douglas Holbrook, Secretary-Treasurer of the APWU, not only gave of their time, but delivered comments that were incisive and resulted in the inclusion of sections on minorities, women in the APWU, and the hearing-impaired that otherwise would have been either overlooked or treated in a less than satisfactory manner. Michael Benner, former President of the Special Delivery Messengers, and presently, Executive Assistant to President Biller, served as the liaison between the writers and the union. Our requests were answered promptly and always with good cheer. Thomas Fahey, Communications Director, and Dorothy Campbell of the Communications Department went out of their way to provide us with important materials.

John O'Donnell, General Counsel of the APWU, read the draft with an editor's gimlet eye, made valuable suggestions and even contributed a rewrite on the "Battle of the Bulk." His partner, Darryl Anderson, helped make clear an extremely complicated subject, "The Health Plan Crisis."

Much of the material in this book was obtained by way of interviews with both present and former union officials. Among the present officials interviewed were Patrick J. Nilan, Legislative Director; Kenneth D. Wilson, Director, Clerk Division; Thomas Freeman, Director, Maintenance Division; Roy Braunstein, Legislative Aide; Thomas A. Neill, Industrial Relations Director; Joyce B. Robinson, Research and Education Director; John P. Richards, President of the APWU Pittsburgh local; and David Daniel, former candidate for President of the APWU and President of the Huntington, West Virginia local.

A good deal of the history was related to us by those who lived it, including David Silvergleid, first Executive Vice President of the APWU; Philip Seligman and Milton Rosner, both officers of the Manhattan–Bronx Postal Union during the 1970 postal strike; former APWU officers Owen Schoon, Chester Parrish, Robert Kephart, Kenneth Leiner, Ben Evans and John McClelland; and Walter Noreen, former President of the St. Paul local of the National Postal Union and St. Paul Postmaster. Bernard Cushman, who negotiated the first three contracts under the Postal Reorganization Act of 1970, provided valuable insights into the inauguration of collective bargaining in the federal service.

In New York, Josie McMillian, President of the New York Metro, William Sainato, and Seymour Goltz provided unique information about the 1970 postal strike and Biller's years as President of the New York Metro. Danny Frank, also of New York, and Daniel Driscoll, former Communications Director of the APWU, brought to life the early years of Biller's presidency and his penchant for public relations. Others who were helpful to the authors were Evelyn E. Johnson, Director, APWU Library Information Center; Declan Murray, Director, APWU Information Center; Philip Tabbita, APWU Industrial Relations Division; and Betty Andrews, wife of former APWU President, Emmet Andrews.

A special note of thanks to John MacKay, former President of the National Postal Union and the man who led the "Progressive-Fed" rebellion against the leadership of the National Federation of Post Office Clerks in 1958, for his contributions regarding the history of a movement that culminated in the creation of the American Postal Workers Union in 1971.

Susan Cooper did an excellent job of preparing the manuscript for submission to the publisher, and editor Barbara Thayer managed to keep the authors honest, repair fractured prose, and improve the final product in numerous ways. Finally, our thanks to Nahid Walsh who suffered her husband's mood changes as the book was written and did everything she could to encourage her husband and see to it that all deadlines were met.

PREFACE

The intrepid riders of the Pony Express, who carried the mail through hostile territory to the most remote areas of the American frontier, are better known to most Americans than the 800,000 men and women who collect, handle, distribute, and deliver well over 166 billion pieces of mail a year to every corner of the nation and beyond. It makes no difference that the Pony Express was a private venture and lasted only nineteen months; its exploits, real and imaginary, have been drilled into the American consciousness through the romance of the Western novel and motion picture.

Yet, the nation's major communication system, a system upon which the efficient working of government and business depends, and that is vitally important to virtually every individual in the nation, might rightly be called a human express—a system driven by human beings working in environments that are far from romantic and performing tasks that require skill, accuracy, attention to detail, and plain hard labor.

This is the story of the men and women who move the mail *inside* the Post Office and their relations with their employer, the United States Government, or, more specifically, the United States Postal Service. It is the story of the world's largest postal union, the American Postal Workers Union–AFL-CIO (APWU). Relatively young as American unions go, the APWU was formed in 1971 by a merger of five older postal unions, each with a long and significant history. Thus, with its predecessors, the APWU scans the entire history of postal labor relations, including the early efforts of postal workers to form labor unions, the battle against the concept of "sovereignty," and the gradual emergence of collective bargaining in a public sector industry.

The book is divided into three parts. Part I describes the great postal strike of 1970, the first nationwide strike against the United States Government in history. That strike resulted in the reorganization of the nation's postal system and the merger that created the APWU.

Part II deals with the emergence of postal labor organizations and the government's changing labor relations policy from restraint in the early days to toleration in the 1960s. Part II is based primarily on two landmark books: the late Sterling Denhard Spero's 1927 classic case study, *The Labor Movement in a Government Industry*, and Murray B. Nesbitt's 1976 comprehensive study, *Labor Relations in the Federal Government Service*. Spero's and Nesbitt's works are pioneering contributions to a once neglected and now emerging field.

Part III concerns twenty years of collective bargaining in a government industry, the only example to date of true collective bargaining, i.e., bargaining on economic issues, in the federal government service. Prior to the Postal Reorganization Act of 1970, postal workers, like all federal workers, were dependent on Congress for the wages, fringe benefits, and working conditions that governed their employment. Beginning in 1971, postal workers became the sole federal employee group whose economic conditions were determined through collective bargaining. Thus, Part III deals with the transition from "selective lobbying" to "collective bargaining," as well as a whole host of issues that face both postal unions and the U.S. Postal Service in the 1990s, including automation, electronic mail, privatization of postal services, and the high cost of health insurance, among others.

The twenty-year history of the APWU is framed by its response to these issues.

PART I

THE STRIKE THAT SHOOK THE NATION

"Nobody ever notices the postman somehow. Yet, they have passions like other men, and even carry large bags where a small corpse can be stowed quite easily."

—G. K. Chesterton

Chapter 1

THUNDER BEFORE THE STORM

The strike that shook the nation came on the heels of one of the most tumultuous decades in the country's 195-year history—an era that began in "Camelot" with the election of the youngest man ever to become President of the United States and ended with the My Lai massacre in Vietnam. In the beginning there was Robert Frost, the nation's acknowledged poet laureate, sharing the inaugural podium with the handsome, newly elected President, Pablo Casals playing his enchanting cello at the White House, and constant news of the glitterati who were attracted like moths to the light of the Kennedy social whirl. Later, there were more somber events—the Bay of Pigs fiasco, the Cuban Missile Crisis, and the assignment of a small number of "advisors" to Vietnam. But even these inauspicious developments did not alter the jubilant mood of the nation. The change came later as the nation reeled from the assassinations of the President, Martin Luther King, Jr., Robert Kennedy, Lee Harvey Oswald, and civil rights activists Viola Liuzzo, Reverend James Reeb and Jimmy Lee Jackson, among others. The national mood became darker with the buildup in Vietnam, the bombing of black churches in the South, bra and draft card burnings, riots from Watts to Washington, D.C., and the revolt of the students who rallied around the cry, "Never trust anyone over 30," and staged endless demonstrations against the war and for "free speech," sexual freedom, women's lib, gay rights, and so on.

The plaintive strains of "We Shall Overcome" gave way to the more acid sounds of The Grateful Dead and Jefferson Airplane. Peter, Paul, and Mary were replaced by Jimi Hendrix and Janis Joplin, and the "flower children" appeared in San Francisco's Haight Ashbury district. Timothy

Leary became the guru of the drug culture. The Black Panthers, La Raza, the Students for a Democratic Society (SDS), the Weathermen, and countless other "new left" groups were born. Male hair became longer, female hair became shorter, and words such as "unisex" and "hippie" became commonly used. Daniel Berrigan and his brother, Philip, were busy pouring blood on draft records, Columbia University students were urinating on research notes, and President Lyndon Baines Johnson was being taunted with the horrible chant: "Hey, Hey LBJ! How many kids did you kill today?" When Johnson chose not to run, blood ran in the streets of Chicago during the Democratic convention that nominated Hubert Horatio Humphrey to challenge Richard Milhaus Nixon for the presidency.

It was a decade that shook up American society in a way that it had never been shaken before. Many yearned for the radicals of yore, the labor leaders who limited themselves to demanding "more" for their members (a very American demand), or even the "Commies" and "fellow travelers" who engaged in futile campaigns to rouse the masses. But the labor unions were relatively quiescent during the sixties, and the "old left" looked as much askance at the "new left" as did the Daughters of the American Revolution.

As the sixties began to fade into history, many hoped for a respite, a period of calm and deliberation, time to absorb the changes wrought during the period, time for the young perpetrators of change to reach the age of thirty and, perhaps, no longer trust themselves. But, the nation was to receive an additional jolt from a highly unlikely source, a jolt which threatened to change forever relations between the federal government and the men and women who collect, distribute, and deliver the mail.

Back in the days of Camelot, President John F. Kennedy had issued an Executive Order designed to improve relations between federal employees and management. The Kennedy Order, "Employee-Management Cooperation," provided "exclusive recognition" to unions that represented a majority of employees in a federal unit or agency. Such recognition gave the unions the right to bargain collectively with management on non-bread-and-butter-issues. After representation elections were conducted by the National Labor Relations Board, seven postal unions were certified as the exclusive representatives of their members—the only unions to gain such recognition within the federal establishment.

By 1970, after nine years of bargaining under the Kennedy Order, postal workers were far from satisfied. Their wages had not kept pace with the accelerated inflation of the Vietnam period and they had to wait twenty-one years to reach the top of their pay progression. They were far more interested in bread-and-butter issues than in noneconomic issues, thus rendering negotiations under the Kennedy Order relatively meaningless.

Nixon was in the White House. The Post Office Department itself was in shambles, the victim of years of executive neglect and a political spoils system which defied good management. Charles Whitman, in his monograph, "Selling the Organization of the Post Office," wrote, "No Department of the federal government was so shackled with vested interests, by stultifying personnel practices, by archaic regulations and equipment, by an absence of elementary management practices, and last, but not least, nowhere was the sauce of political patronage thicker than at the heart of the lavish office of the Postmaster General..."[1]

Although President Nixon acknowledged that postal workers were underpaid and undermotivated, he was determined that any pay raise granted postal workers would have to be coupled with postal reform. He intended to overhaul the entire Post Office Department.

The rank and file postal worker was not unaffected by the militancy of the 1960s. In fact, having more education than other applicants in the competitive examination recruitment system and valuing employment which interfered minimally with their chosen lifestyles, many veterans of the sixties upheavals entered the Postal Service and found themselves in a situation that was ripe for agitation. This growing militancy within the rank and file was completely overlooked, not only by the Congress and the Administration, but by the national leaders of postal unions as well. The result, in 1970, was the first major strike against the Government of the United States in history—a wildcat strike that changed forever relations between the government and the men and women who collect, distribute, and deliver the mail.

* * *

On July 6, 1775, members of the Second Continental Congress meeting at Philadelphia, agreed "...that a Postmaster General be appointed, who shall hold his office at Philadelphia, and shall be allowed a salary of $1,000 per annum..."[2] Since that date, which marked the birth of the United States Post Office Department, and up until March 1970, there had never been an organized protest on a grand scale by postal workers against their employer. Prior to the 1970 postal strike, there were indications that postal workers all over the country were on the warpath, but, as *Newsweek* noted in its story of the strike, "the workers involved, after all, were the 750,000 humble footmen who provide the average American's only regular connection with the federal government by picking up and delivering the mail every day. And never...had the docile servants of the world's largest mail service ever raised so much as a pinky in organized protest. So it was easy to understand how the beginning of the postal workers' historic uprising went completely undetected—and how the unfolding drama took almost everyone by surprise."[3]

It shouldn't have been a surprise. There were numerous demonstrations staged by postal workers across the country which were well-publicized in the media. But, who could take demonstrations by postal workers seriously? After all, they were federal workers, weren't they? They were well paid, right? They had security; it was almost impossible to fire a postal worker, right? And they could look forward to pensions in their old age. What possibly could be their beef?

Let's ask a typical postal worker of the period. We'll call him Joe Fazio.

* * *

Until 1966, Joe Fazio had been a baker, but he became worried that the small shop where he worked might have to shut down because of changes that were occurring in the neighborhood. He had a wife and three children, and he needed a job with fringe benefits, health insurance to pay the medical bills and a guarantee of steady employment. So, he took the Civil Service examination and eventually went to work as a post office distribution clerk. Yes, he found security, but little else. He worked in what Manhattan's Postmaster John Strachan called a "Postal Dungeon," the Radio City Station, located amid the squalor of tenements and bars on 52nd Street off Ninth Avenue in New York City. The facility was a poorly lit, cramped building with paint-chipped walls and floors that sagged under the weight of the workers and bulky mail bags." He sorted huge bundles of mail by hand into a pigeonhole device that had been invented by Benjamin Franklin 200 years ago, and had to put up with straw bosses who constantly prodded him on to higher and higher productivity. "Let's show a little alacrity!" was the constant cry of the pseudo-non-coms who were his supervisors. "There were ninety women employed in the building but because of a lack of toilet facilities, men and women had to share one of the rest rooms on a split-shift basis." There was no air conditioning in the summer and the heat didn't work too well in the winter. "Built in 1927, the three-story structure housed 667 employees who sorted and delivered one million pieces of mail a day."[4]

But the working conditions were not Fazio's major grievance. At bottom, he wanted more money. His salary in 1969 (counting overtime) was $8,030 a year, well below the $11,236 that the federal government said a family of four needed to maintain a "moderate" standard of living in New York City, and there were five in the Fazio family. Like many other postal workers, he moonlighted, sometimes as a bartender and sometimes as a baker. He knew, too, that not a few postal workers were receiving welfare in addition to their full-time salaries. The starting salary for postal workers was $6,176 a year and they had to wait twenty-one years before they were eligible for a raise to $8,442. It was a labor force made up primarily of buck privates who had to wait over two decades to make PFC.

The Fazios were not "poor," but they enjoyed few of the amenities. They lived in a two-bedroom apartment in lower Manhattan, where Fazio and his wife grew up. Fazio's pay, after deductions, came to $230 every two weeks. Rent was $110 per month. Even with putting in overtime—an absolute necessity—there was no cash to spare.

Fazio was one of 20,000 members of the Manhattan-Bronx Postal Union (MBPU), the largest and one of the most militant postal union locals in the world, but he was not a child of the sixties; there wasn't a radical bone in his body. He was active in the Boy Scouts, of all things, and most of his family's social activities revolved around his parish church. He had little sympathy for the "new breed" who, because of their college training were scoring high on Civil Service examinations and entering the post office in increasing numbers—veterans of the upheavals of the sixties, long-haired and sloppily dressed. These new postal workers brought their radicalism with them and they were stirring up rebellions against the entire postal establishment. The following letter, signed by "The Phantom," was circulated at the Radio City Station:

Well here we are eight months later and our fearless leaders [i.e., the leaders of the National Association of Letter Carriers] can't even remember HR 10,000, in fact, it is now HR 13,000, the Lousiest Bill of the Century. As Union leaders, they couldn't lead a pack of cub scouts. They should disgust every one of you reading this, but then nothing seems to wake up a letter carrier even when he is being shafted and paying $42 [union dues] a year for the privilege.

Meanwhile, Window Washers won themselves a $60 raise over three years, Longshoremen won $45 over three years, Private Sanitation won an immediate $20 raise plus $20 over the next two years, the President got himself a $100,000 raise, Senators and Congressmen got themselves $20,000 raises, City Employees all got themselves raises and benefits, and you can bet your boots, the Transit Authority, come January 1, is in for a Big Fat Raise, etc. etc. etc....[5]

Fazio read the letter and admitted to himself that the writer had a point. The leaders of his union were a good deal more vocal than the leadership of the Letter Carriers, but in the last analysis, what could a federal union do? But, these radicals were asking for a strike. A strike? By federal employees? Everything could be lost—jobs, pensions, everything. Still, Fazio has hopeful. He was hopeful because the President of the United States, during a visit to the Post Office Department on February 10, 1969, made the following pledge:

I would hope that as you talk to the people that you supervise, the word could get down the line, down the line, for example, to that underpaid man who Red Blount spoke to us about the other day who works in a great city and starts at $6,000 a year; if he went to the Sanitation Department, he could get $10,000 a year. Let them know that we back them. Let them know that better days are coming. Let them know that without their help and assistance, we cannot do the job that we want to do.[6]

Fazio had voted for Humphrey—though he was still voting for Franklin D. Roosevelt, the patron saint of his childhood—but he could not help but harbor the hope that the Republican President, Richard Nixon, would make good on his pledge.

*   *   *

In July 1969, postmen received a 4.1 percent pay increase as part of a two-year-old package. But, the clerks and carriers were angered rather than satisfied. Their union leaders were lobbying for a 10–15 percent increase, and they were cognizant of the fact that Congressmen had voted themselves a 41 percent raise the previous February. A 4.1 percent raise meant about $9 per pay period, $4.50 per week, before deductions—hardly a raise at all. And then came the second blow: All government employees were scheduled for a comparability raise in July 1970, but, "in order to control and contain inflation," the Nixon Administration proposed postponing the raise for six months. The Union Mail, the official organ of the Manhattan-Bronx Postal Union, put the President's picture on the front page, under the caption: "NIXON'S PLEDGE..." (here President Nixon's February pledge at the Post Office Department was repeated), followed by the caption: "PLEDGE NIXED!" and the following Nixon statement:

Because the need to control and contain the inflationary spiral is of paramount importance at this time, I recommend that the comparability pay raise (which requires Congressional action) be deferred six months beyond the recent pattern, and be made effective January 1971...[7]

Moe Biller, President of the MBPU, delivered the following statement under the headline, "BILLER BLASTS BACK":

The 1.3 billion dollar surplus that President Nixon proposed in his budget message will come out of the hides of postal and federal workers, if it is permitted to stand. His deferment of pay comparability until January, 1971, amounts to a savings of $1.4 billion on our backs.

We are tired of being considered a Silent Majority, who live and work only to serve and never complain. We're not going to complain anymore. We're going to FIGHT for our bread and butter.[8]

Fighting words, certainly. There was no doubt that the strike itch was beginning to be felt by rank and file postal workers, even if their national union leaders considered such a development unthinkable. Now, the President wanted to tie any postal pay raise into a plan developed in 1968 by a ten-man Commission on Postal Organization headed by Frederick Kappel, former Board Chairman of American Telephone and Telegraph Company. The plan recommended abolition of the Cabinet rank position of Postmaster General and the creation of a Government-owned corporation with power to set postage rates with Congressional approval. The postal unions, fearing the loss of Civil Service status and diminution of their leverage in Congress, opposed the Kappel plan. The result was that as the year 1970 approached no action was taken on postal pay rates.

While union leaders continued their ineffective lobbying efforts in Washington, rank and file postal workers were becoming increasingly restive. They had seen municipal workers go out on illegal strikes and gain pay raises and increased benefits far above the pittances handed out to postal workers by the Congress. Fazio, for example, had seen rats scurrying around the mountains of garbage that piled up during an "illegal" strike by sanitation workers in New York City, and he, himself, was inconvenienced when Mike Quill, President of the Transport Workers Union, led "illegal" walkouts on the subways, elevateds, and buses in New York and Philadelphia. Illegal or not, the strikers not only did not lose their jobs, but were now earning a good deal more than the more obedient postal workers. Indeed, public sector strikes had become more frequent after World War II and grew rapidly in the 1960s. According to Murray B. Nesbitt, "In 1966–67 alone the Bureau of Labor Statistics recorded 180 strikes involving 132,000 employees and costing 1.2 million work-days...The BLS also noted that between 1958 and 1968, government strikes rose from 15 to 254 per year; workers involved rose from 1,700 to 202,000; and work-days lost from 7,500 to 2.5 million. Assistant Secretary of Labor W. J. Usery, Jr., reported that 380 public-sector strikes affecting 250,000 workers occurred in 1969."[9] But, all of these were in state and local governments and the most militant group seemed to be traditionally docile school teachers.

These developments were not ignored by the postal unions. In 1968, the United Federation of Postal Clerks (UFPC), the National Postal Union (NPU), and the National Association of Letter Carriers (NALC) either dropped or considered dropping their no-strike clauses from their constitutions. Sidney A. Goodman, President of the National Postal Union, provided the rationale:

> But the biggest myth of all...is the prohibition on the right to strike. What is really wrong with labor-management relations in the program? There are no countervailing forces, there is no balance. It is just that simple. Before us stands an inevitable dynamic which must take the form of paternalism and it does not serve even management, if it is self-respecting, in the long run...There has not, never has been, never will be any substitute for the right of

employees to withhold their labor as a method of advancing their interests.[10]

But, it was one thing to drop no-strike clauses from union constitutions; it was something altogether different to actually call for and conduct a strike against the Government of the United States. Not one leader of the postal unions was contemplating strike action; it was the rank and file postal workers—the Joe Fazios—who were becoming more and more frustrated and alienated from their union leaders.

* * *

The establishment in Washington had ample warnings of the eruption that would occur in March 1970, but apparently they were not considered serious by the Congress, the Postmaster General, the President, or even the leaders of postal unions. It was business as usual in Washington while mutiny was brewing in the ranks.

Although demonstrations occurred in most of the nation's major cities, most of the action was centered in New York City where the first strike against the United States Government would begin. Demonstrations protesting Nixon's 4.1 percent pay raise occurred at the Manhattan General, Grand Central, and Bronx Post Offices. A total of 4,500 postal workers participated in the General Post Office and Grand Central demonstrations, and another 1,000 in the Bronx. The Nixon pay raise was branded an insult, and although the demonstrations were orderly, the anger and frustration of the protesters was quite apparent.

During the 1969 Christmas season, letter carriers at the Newark, New Jersey Post Office, working on voluntary overtime, walked off the job when carriers from other stations staged a protest because they were not offered overtime. Overtime was considered a necessity by most postal workers (how else could they make a living wage?). The local president, who called the work stoppage, was suspended for twenty-eight days for "disrupting postal service" and "bringing the agency into disrepute." However, no action was taken against the demonstrators because they were on voluntary overtime and, therefore, could leave the job if they so desired.

Eleven days after the protest against the 4.1 percent pay raise, twenty clerks and forty letter carriers at the Kingsbridge Post Office in the Bronx staged a sick-leave call in. The action, generated by the letter carrier shop steward, Bill Scott, came as a surprise to the officers of both Branch 36 of the Letter Carriers and the MBPU. When the union leaders went out to investigate, Scott had left on vacation. The "sick callers" were about to be discharged, but intercession by the leaders of both unions led to two-week suspensions instead. The MBPU paid the suspended clerks during the two-week period; the Letter Carriers did not. Despite the suspensions, sick calls spread to other stations in the city. Thus, the storm that was about to break should not have come as a surprise to dozing federal officials. Events were building toward a major eruption, but perhaps because no such eruption had ever occurred in the nation's history, their portents were not taken seriously by the politicians, bureaucrats, and the general public.

Chapter 2

THE STORM

Mrs. Margaret Lathrop of Minneapolis set off to walk the four blocks from her home to the post office on a chilly and rainy March morning in 1970. She carried an umbrella in her right hand and cradled a package under her left arm. When she arrived at the post office, she was surprised to see that there was no line and no clerks were at the desk. She tried the door. Since it opened, she walked in. A man appeared from the rear and approached the counter. Mrs. Lathrop put her package on the counter and requested the necessary stamps. The man behind the counter told her that he could not accept the package. "The Post Office is closed," he said. "There is a strike." Mrs. Lathrop looked at him blankly. "A strike?" she said, "but these are cookies for my son in Vietnam!" When her package was still refused, she shook her head in stunned disbelief.

* * *

At a Wisconsin post office, a man brought in several reels of film to be mailed to Madison. The clerk explained that such mail was embargoed. "You can't do that!" the customer exclaimed. "This is the United States Post Office!" And he dumped the containers on the counter and walked out.

* * *

A group of Brooklyn, New York letter carriers drafted a petition asking their Chicago colleagues to join the walkout, only to realize that they had no way to mail it. Not wanting to scab by sending a telegram, they decided they would keep the letter for the duration.

* * *

A New York man went out to collect his mail from a cluster mail box at 1:00 P.M. He returned to his garden apartment and said to his wife, "You won't believe this, but there was nothing in the mail box, not even the usual junk." She said, "Haven't you heard? There's a strike at the Post Office." He looked at her in amazement. "Yes, dear," she said, "we won't be getting any mail for some time now."[1]

Postal workers, federal employees, were staging the first strike against the United States Government in history. Not only that, but it was a wildcat strike—a strike against postal union leaders as well as the public, the business community, the postal union hierarchy, the Congress, the Postmaster General, and the President. While Washington fiddled, rank and file postal workers took matters into their own hands and walked off the job. Instead of the bargaining table impasse occasioning strikes in the private sector, it was an impasse between postal workers and the political system.

A Matter of Priority

The ordinary rank and file mail handlers, clerks, letter carriers, and other postal workers had one major priority—a substantial pay raise. Some, especially those in the large metropolitan areas, were also concerned about area wage differentials: A $6,000 a year postal clerk working in a small town in Alabama would be relatively well off, whereas his counterpart in New York City would be below the poverty level. They had been waiting for over a year while their union leaders lobbied unsuccessfully for a legitimate pay raise bill. They were insulted by the Administration's 4.1 percent pay raise, and angry because of the postponement of their comparability pay raise. They wanted immediate action, and they couldn't care less about so called "postal reform."

The Administration, on the other hand, was concerned primarily with problems facing the Post Office Department that required radical solutions: nineteenth-century facilities; obsolete methods of mail distribution; and the remnants of a patronage system through which many underqualified postmasters and supervisors were selected. The President and Postmaster General were not unsympathetic with the concerns of postal workers, but demanded that postal pay raise legislation, for which Congress had great sympathy, be combined with postal reorganization, for which it had little concern. Basically, what the President wanted was to change the Post Office Department from a Cabinet-level agency to a federally owned corporation. This idea was first broached in 1966 by then Postmaster General Lawrence F. O'Brien who saw his department "in a race with catastrophe."[2] The same recommendation was made by the Kappel Commission during the Johnson Administration. The proposal made by the Nixon Administration pretty much followed the Kappel Commission recommendations.

The postal unions were opposed to the idea of reducing the Cabinet status of the Post Office Department, even though the Nixon proposal would provide for collective bargaining between postal unions and the U.S. Postal Service. According to Nesbitt, the union view was that the postal service, "being the basic means of communication in the nation, should not be removed from the control of the people through their representatives in Congress."[3] Translated, this means that the unions feared the loss of the influence they had built up in Congress over the years if responsibility for post office affairs was shifted from the Post Office Department to an independent corporation.

The President's recommendations were included in a bill introduced by Representative Udall of Arizona, but, because of opposition by virtually all postal unions and the AFL-CIO Government Employees' Council, it never made it out of the House Post Office and Civil Service Committee. The unions supported a bill introduced by Representative Thaddeus Dulski of New York, which would include many of the Nixon reforms, but would retain the Cabinet-level status of the Post Office Department. The President threatened to veto the Dulski bill.

Thus, a stalemate developed, delaying pay action and increasing the agitation of rank and file postal workers.

The Administration was the first to attempt to break the stalemate. James H. Rademacher, President of the National Association of Letter Carriers, was contacted by White House aide Charles Colson. Colson invited Rademacher to work with Administration officials in developing a bill that would satisfy both the unions and the Administration. Why Colson chose to call Rademacher and not other postal labor leaders is not clear, but it may have been because Rademacher was one of the few labor leaders who endorsed Nixon in 1968, or because the letter carriers—the men and women who deliver the mail to homes and offices throughout the land—are the most visible of all postal workers. The Administration probably believed that if the support of the letter carriers could be achieved for a reform bill, the remainder of the postal unions would fall into line—a belief that soon would prove unjustified. The resulting bill, referred to as the "Rademacher Bill" in union circles (and by some post office workers as the "Rat-emacher Bill," implying that the Letter Carrier president had sold out to the Administration), was introduced by Representative David Henderson of North Carolina. Instead of a "corporation," it provided for a "Postal Authority," collective bargaining, the retaining of postal worker civil service status, and a 5.4 percent retroactive pay raise. On March 12, 1970, the Henderson (or "Rademacher") Bill was reported out of the House Post Office and Civil Service Committee by a 17 to 6 vote. The President, the Postmaster General and Rademacher were jubilant.

The action would now shift to the postal workers.

New York City

The first test of rank and file acceptance of the Rademacher Bill occurred in New York City and it was disastrous. The two largest postal union locals in the world were located in New York: the Manhattan-Bronx Postal Union (MBPU), an industrial-type union made up of clerks, mail handlers, maintenance workers, motor vehicle employees, and even some letter carriers; and Branch 36 of the National Association of Letter Carriers (NALC), a craft organization. The MBPU was affiliated with the National Postal Union (NPU), a group that had broken off from the National Federation of Post Office Clerks in 1958. Under the Kennedy Executive Order, the NPU was not one of the seven nationally recognized postal unions with the right to bargain with the Post Office Department on non-bread-and-butter issues, but the 20,000 member MBPU did have local recognition under the Order.

Relations between the two locals were not cordial. Branch 36, headed by Gustav Johnson, went all out in its support of the Rademacher Bill, whereas Moe Biller, President of the MBPU termed the bill a "sellout." When the bill was first introduced, Branch 36 issued a statement accusing the MBPU (without actually naming the union) of "attempting to 'divide and conquer' by splitting the ranks of postal workers at this crucial point in our history." The statement went on to say:

Having admitted openly that they had nothing whatsoever to do with any pay legislation that will be forthcoming from this Congress, they now find themselves in the very uncomfortable position of attempting to justify their inactivity and failure by tearing down the one union that is still instrumental in getting better pay, fringe benefits and working conditions for all postal workers. Until recently, their opposition took the form of "verbal stabs in the back." Lately, however, they have reverted to the trade they were always most proficient at—being plasterers, thus, instead of working for postal workers they are now qualified to be members of the plasterers' union with the amount of bulletin board plastering in which they have engaged.[4]

The "plastering" was a reference to a practice instituted by local President Moe Biller to inform all postal workers of the MBPU's assessment of matters affecting postal workers, such as legislation introduced in Congress. Instead of posting "News Flashes" on the bulletin boards of postal facilities, which were pretty much ignored by the rank and file, he ran off thousands of copies and had them hand delivered to postal workers all over the city. Phillip Seligman, then Executive Vice President of the MBPU, recalls participating in a demonstration in the Bronx. "The people were stopping cars on the Grand Concourse, giving them leaflets and hollering and screaming. The cops were there, and they didn't care. I came back and told Moe that we were sitting on a bomb. People are ready to go. They were really excited and upset that we were being sold out under the proposed postal reorganization action."[5]

There was no doubt that the officers of Branch 36 resented the MBPU "paper hangers." The local's Executive Board was in full support of their National President, James Rademacher, and believed that the MBPU was radicalizing their membership. In one statement, Branch 36 accused the MBPU of sending over Students for a Democratic Society (SDS) members and other radicals to be enrolled as letter carriers.[6]

When the Rademacher Bill was reported out of the House Post Office and Civil Service Committee, Branch 36 issued a news flash praising the bill and congratulating the membership for its part in its creation.[7]

On that same day, March 12, 1970, Gus Johnson received the shock of his life.

The Letter Carriers Rebel

The storm began at a regular monthly meeting of Branch 36 of the NALC at the Riverside Plaza Hotel in New York on the afternoon of March 12, 1970. Branch 36 President Gus Johnson, a tall, bearded, brooding man who was born and brought up in the Yorkville section of Manhattan and who had been a letter carrier in his home district for twenty-two years, gaveled the meeting to order and began to make some routine announcements. Finally, he looked up and announced with pride that the House Post Office and Civil Service Committee had approved the Rademacher Bill that would create a semi-independent "Postal Authority," and (here he paused) would also provide for a retroactive postal wage increase of 5.4 percent. And it was then that the storm broke. Every man in the hall rose and began to chant, "NOT ENOUGH, NOT ENOUGH, NOT ENOUGH." Someone shouted, "Strike!" and the chant changed: "STRIKE-WHEN, STRIKE-WHEN, STRIKE-WHEN." Johnson and his fellow officers on the podium were struck dumb. Storming the platform, the angry letter carriers demanded a formal meeting of the local for a strike vote. "Those bastards," one letter carrier told Johnson, "were quick enough to vote themselves a 41 percent pay raise, and they have the nerve to offer us 5 percent!"

The strike vote was set for March 17—St. Patrick's Day.

During the five-day interim, Johnson and his officers did everything in their power to push for a "no-strike" vote. Moe Biller expected Johnson to contact him, as he was instructed to do by his membership, so that the two leaders could plan for joint action in case the vote should be "yes." The only call Biller received from Johnson was to inform him of the date of the strike vote; nothing else was discussed. Rademacher made an appearance in New York and requested a meeting with Johnson, Jack Leventhal, President of the Brooklyn letter carriers local, Moe Biller, and Dave Silvergleid, President of the National Postal Union. Biller did not want to attend the meeting, but Silvergleid and Moe Kanner, MBPU Executive Secretary, convinced him to attend, arguing that because they had nothing to lose, they might as well hear what he had to say.

The meeting took place in a disco called "Wednesday" during an affair honoring Congressman Brasco of New York. Rademacher surprised Biller, Silvergleid, and Kanner by saying that he didn't want to talk about a strike; rather, he wanted to talk about a merger between the Letter Carriers and the NPU. Biller looked at him in amazement. Here they were sitting on a wildcat strike and Rademacher wanted to talk about a merger that would violate a "no-raiding" AFL-CIO constitutional provision that prohibits an affiliated union from organizing workers who belong to another affiliated union. Since the United Federation of Postal Clerks was already an AFL-CIO affiliate, it would be against the rules for the Letter Carriers to join with an unaffiliated union that also represented post office clerks. Biller told Rademacher that he was out of his mind. "You're in a foreign country! Here you are talking about a merger and a wildcat strike is about to break out!" Rademacher then said that if they didn't want to talk about merger, he didn't want to waste any more time; he had a plane to catch. As he left for the airport he told Johnson and Leventhal, "You have stuck with me all the way and I'll be with you all the way."[8]

As of March 16th, the day before the strike vote, Biller had not heard from Johnson. However, in a television interview, Johnson said that the results of a station survey he had conducted were inconclusive, and he appealed to the "silent majority" to come out and vote on the 17th. Johnson had told Rademacher that he would come through, and Rademacher had informed the Administration that all was well. Most postal officials felt sure that there would be a "no" vote because Gus Johnson and his officers were in control. Moe Biller observed: "Browning's little girl Pippa said, 'God's in his Heaven, all's right with the world.' But, that was over a century ago."[9]

St. Patrick's Day

While others were watching the pomp and pageantry of the St. Patrick's Day parade or drinking green beer in the Irish saloons along Third Avenue, the letter carriers began assembling at an old theater called the Manhattan Center to conduct a strike vote. The vote wasn't scheduled to start until 6:00 P.M. that evening, but many of the letter carriers arrived early, and soon the strident chant of "Strike, Strike, Strike" began. The mention of Gus Johnson's name brought boos. When he appeared at 8:40 P.M., as he walked down the aisle to the podium, the jeers and catcalls were thunderous. But, when Johnson told the crowd that he would abide by the vote of the membership, he was cheered.

Throughout the day, Biller waited for a call from Johnson, a call that never came. An emergency session of the MBPU Board of Officers was called late in the afternoon to prepare for the worst if it happened. Biller also sent a delegation of officers, including his Executive Vice President, Phillip Seligman, to seek out Johnson so that the two union leaders could get together and talk things over. Seligman reported that Johnson and his officers would be willing to meet with MBPU officers at about 11:00 P.M. that night. Biller replied that was not what he wanted. "I want to meet with him before the strike vote." A meeting was finally arranged at Fahey's, a saloon across the street from the Manhattan Center. Johnson, who was more or less in hiding, was represented by his top officers, including Herman Sandbank, his chief lieutenant.

Biller suggested that if the vote was "yes," he be given the opportunity to address the Carriers and propose that the strike date be postponed until the MBPU could conduct a strike vote and, thus, both unions could go out together. Sandbank and the other Branch 36 officers agreed to the suggestion, and said that they would inform Johnson. Biller and the MBPU officers felt that a deal had been made.

The entire MBPU Board of Officers was on the podium of the Manhattan Center during the strike vote. At 10:20 P.M., the vote was 1,500 "yes" and about 1,000 "no." Suddenly, Johnson banged the gavel and announced that Branch 36 was on strike as of 5:00 A.M., Wednesday, March 18th. A great roar of approval reverberated off the walls of the hall. "I will lead you!" Johnson shouted, and the assembled letter carriers cheered the new-found militancy of their president.

To the MBPU, this was a violation of an agreement which had been made half an hour earlier—an agreement that might have averted a strike since it would have given everyone a breather for a few days and time to warn legislators and the Administration for the last time. Two weeks previously, Seligman had led a delegation to Washington to warn legislators of the impending New York eruption.

Biller and the MBPU contingent felt they had been sandbagged by Johnson and left en masse through the back of the hall at 35th Street. Once outside, Biller had second thoughts. Despite the protestations of his Board, he said that he was going back. "Otherwise," he said, "the rank and file would not understand when told and would feel that the MBPU had copped out."

The MBPU contingent returned to the podium. Gus Johnson was still talking and seemed to be lost in the clouds. He had progressed from "bum" to "hero," and was now basking in the glory of his new celebrity. He asked Biller if he wanted to speak. Biller said, "Yes, but you won't like what I have to say!" Johnson told him he was free to say whatever he wanted to say. Biller told the letter carriers that they had been led down the "primrose path," and repeated the agreement that had been made at Fahey's saloon. He asked them to wait until the MBPU vote was taken, and was roundly booed. At that point, a tall, swarthy man with a shock of jet black hair and a voice like a rasp, rose and addressed a question to Biller: "This, he said is a letter carrier strike. What I want to know is whether or not the clerks will cross the picket lines?" The questioner was Vincent R. Sombrotto. In 1978, he would be elected President of the National Association of Letter Carriers. Biller answered carefully: "It is illegal for me to direct the members not to cross picket lines, but I am sure that as good union members, they will respect any picket line."[10] Biller was cheered.

The first test came at 12:05 A.M. on March 18th. The Letter Carriers had placed a two-man picket line at the Grand Central Station. The MBPU shop steward, George Applewaite, called Biller and asked what he should do. Biller asked him whether he had ever crossed a picket line. Applewaite replied in the negative and got the message. As a result, the midnight tour at Grand Central Station did not go to work.

The MBPU immediately put out a bulletin stating that good union men do not cross picket lines and that the members of the Executive Board were sure that MBPU members were good union men. Officers called shop stewards (referred to as "delegates" in the MBPU lexicon) until 4:00 A.M. to advise them accordingly. In addition, letters were hand delivered first thing the following morning to the Manhattan and Bronx Postmasters, John Strachan and Louis Cohen, advising them that the union would protect its members who observed picket lines. By Thursday, March 19, the strike in Manhattan and the Bronx was 100 percent effective.

Mania at the Statler

The stage was now set for one of the wildest meetings in postal labor union history, the regular membership meeting of the MBPU, scheduled for 7:00 P.M. on March 18th in the ballroom of the Statler-Hilton Hotel. The ballroom normally accommodated 2,000 people, but the Associated Press reported that 6,500 showed up for the meeting. Biller and his entourage arrived ten minutes late to find a surly crowd in an angry and hostile mood. Biller made his way to the podium which was surrounded by activists with raised right arms and clenched fists. The chant went up for a strike vote by hand—NOW. It was obvious to Biller that the hall had been infiltrated by at least 100 outsiders, including letter carriers, postal inspectors, the FBI, and special services detectives from the New York City Police Force. There were also militants from the SDS, the Black Panthers, and the postal services' own radical contingent. Three Young Lords in crimson berets were patrolling the platform which had been more or less surrounded by agitators. David Silvergleid, President of the NPU, vowed that he would never again show up late for a meeting where an emotional issue was involved because it gave the agitators time to stir up the crowd. At one point, the microphone was snatched from Silvergleid's hand and shoved back into his face. Several protectors pulled him back and escorted him out of the hall. Milt Rosner, Financial Secretary of the MBPU, said that chairs were being thrown off the balcony. "These were wild kids. And mean. They didn't want a secret vote."[11] It was impossible to conduct a meeting, but Biller nevertheless refused to take a strike vote by hand; he continued to insist on a vote by secret ballot supervised by the Honest Ballot Association (HBA). The crowd shouted him down. Phillip Seligman recounted that one angry member came at Biller with a knife. A huge mail handler got between Biller and the knife wielder and forced the assailant to retreat. "Power to the People," shouted the crowd (the sixties had finally arrived at the Post Office). Biller replied that he believed in power to the people through the secret ballot. In a diary Biller kept of events leading up to the strike, he wrote:

> The situation on the platform was becoming more menacing by the minute. Officers and delegates formed a protective cordon around me, but this was very difficult. Many things went through my mind and I respected and loved all who tried to protect me. What stands out most vividly was Milt Bolling, black delegate from Patron Relations Section at the General Post Office, very slight of build, always hard working, with tears rolling down his cheeks and tugging at my suit jacket, pleading with me to leave the platform. The

situation was becoming more critical by the second with well-intentioned and not well-intentioned people seizing the microphone at varying intervals. Many times it was also given back to me by people who seemed to want to ram the mike down my throat.[12]

Biller remained on the platform as long as he could. Finally, his public relations man, Tom Costigan, took him purposefully by the arm and led him out of the hall through a kitchen and a back door. It was snowing outside. If Biller had agreed to an immediate strike by hand vote, he would have been carried on shoulders through snowy streets as a hero. However, he did not yield the platform until it was made clear to everyone that the vote would be secret and supervised by the HBA.

The strike vote was conducted on Saturday, March 21st, at the Manhattan Center between 6:00 A.M. and 10:00 P.M. The results were 8,242 "for" and 940 "against." The MBPU, whose members had not crossed the Branch 36 picket lines, was now officially on strike. Thousands of MBPU members joined in a candlelight vigil around the General Post Office, and hundreds of postal workers became MBPU members during the ceremony.

The Strike Spreads

The strike was immediately effective in the New York area and soon spread to the Northeast and Pennsylvania. Later, it spread westward to Akron, Buffalo, Chicago, Cleveland, Dearborn, St. Paul, Minneapolis, Detroit, Denver, Los Angeles, and San Francisco. Altogether, approximately 200,000 workers walked off the job from coast to coast. Post Office officials, including the Postmaster General, were in a quandary; they had absolutely no experience in dealing with a strike. What could they do? They had no target; the presidents of the postal unions had not called the strike. There was even some question as to the culpability of the local leaders. Could they fire 200,000 postal workers? Not without disrupting the postal service for a long period of time. All they could do was try to ease the effects of the strike. Mail destined for affected cities and for overseas was embargoed and began piling up by the ton. At the height of the strike, 500 tons of mail destined for overseas was embargoed. Mailboxes were ordered sealed. No attempt was made to jail workers and union officials, a weapon allowed by law, because of the possibility of a more violent confrontation. A court order barring the strike was ignored by the "wildcats," despite the threat of contempt citations. There was very little violence on the picket lines, even though the mailmen were often taunted by angry members of the general public. "How am I going to get my Social Security check if you bastards are on strike?" shouted one retiree in Cleveland. "They ought to send you guys to Vietnam!" was a yell often heard by the strikers. Douglas Holbrook, then President of the Detroit local of the National Postal Union, reported that one worker who got into an argument on the picket line became so enraged that he got into his car and drove it seventy-five miles an hour down a major road and into a wall. He was killed. Holbrook also recalls that the arguments between a postal clerk and his Deputy Sheriff wife over the right of government workers to strike ended up with the Deputy Sheriff pumping seven bullets into her husband.[13] However, both because of the restraint exercised by the government and by the leadership of union officials in controlling the picket lines, the postal strike of 1970 was primarily nonviolent.

Strike Effectiveness

Few people had really understood the effect a postal strike would have on government and the business community. To the general public, the strike was indeed an inconvenience. Although many billpayers were relieved that the strike gave them a temporary reprieve, others were denied their Welfare, Social Security, and pension checks, not to mention communication with loved ones. But for government and business, a long postal strike could be catastrophic. "The strike threatened the very survival of some publishing and mail order houses, consumer credit companies, and hundreds of other firms which rely on the mails for product deliveries and cash remittances. Hundreds of millions of dollars were frozen in transit with paralyzing effects on firms and individuals. Manufacturers Hanover Trust Company President Gabriel Hague observed: 'It obviously cannot go on long. There will have to be a decision in a few days.'"[14]

Government at all levels was no less affected. Pension, Social Security, and Welfare checks had to be mailed, and if the strike lasted until April 15th, less than one month away, the IRS would have to extend its deadline for receiving income tax returns. The humble postal worker, who had remained docile for 195 years, suddenly became a person of passion.

Reaction in Washington

At first, President Nixon and Postmaster General Blount remained in the background, but as the strike spread, executive action became necessary. The problem was that the Postmaster General could not, even if he wanted to, engage in bargaining with the postal unions. Congress alone was responsible for postal wage scales and other conditions of employment. But it was the President's responsibility to protect the economy and maintain essential public services. Nixon, therefore, directed Secretary of Labor George Shultz to negotiate with the seven postal unions recognized under the Kennedy Executive Order. Shultz persuaded the union leaders to urge the striking locals to return to work. In return, he guaranteed that all worker demands would come under full negotiation. But, in meetings over the weekend, nearly all the striking locals defied their leaders; and the local in Chicago, which at first had gone out on strike and then returned to work, decided to rejoin the walkout.

This defiance brought a prompt reaction from the President. Nixon acknowledged that the postmen had legitimate grievances, but he declared that the government would not negotiate as long as the illegal walkout continued. Further, the President promised to get the mail delivered, though he did not spell out how. The tone of his remarks and the flurry of activity that occurred at the Pentagon left the strong impression that he would mobilize Army or National Guard units if necessary.

The government also applied pressure to the unions through the courts. Johnson and other officers of Branch 36 were ordered to appear in court to show cause why they should not be held in contempt of an antistrike injunction. Soon after, Biller and the officers of the MBPU would also be cited. The government asked that the Branch 36 officials be fined $1,000 for the first day of the strike, $2,000 for the second, and progressively increasing amounts for subsequent days. It also asked that the union be penalized on a similar scale, its fine starting at $10,000. Anticipating that the same fines would be levied on the MBPU, Milt Rosner, Secretary-Treasurer of the local, paid all the union's bills for a year in advance. Thus, even if the local's treasury was depleted and there would be no money to pay fines, the union could continue to operate.

President Francis S. Filbey of the United Federation of Postal Clerks filed suit in the U.S. District Court in Washington, D.C., challenging the constitutionality of the 1947 law forbidding strikes by federal employees. The suit was dismissed. Rademacher called a meeting of 300 of his branch presidents in Washington. They authorized the NALC President to start negotiations but set a five–day limit for a settlement. Secretary of Labor Shultz refused to negotiate until the locals returned to work. Once again, the union leaders urged their members to end the strike.

After a preliminary meeting with Shultz, a back-to-work movement began, but only in rural and suburban areas. Service in the majority of the urban centers remained drastically curtailed. Gradually, however, urban workers also began to return to work. On March 22, with the return to work gathering momentum in the rest of the nation, the New York City area was still tied up. It appeared that the strike which began in New York City would also end in New York City.

The Show of Force

In a national television address to the nation on March 22, 1970, President Nixon reiterated the willingness of the government to begin negotiations if the strikers returned to work, and announced troop activation to restore the postal service in New York City. He clearly implied that if necessary similar military action would be taken in other important cities. On the same day, he proclaimed a state of national emergency and by Executive Order authorized the Secretary of Defense to utilize units of the Armed Forces or National Guard as necessary to restore essential service.

On March 24, 25,000 troops entered New York City and began their postal duties. It would be an understatement to say that they were not adept at the job. MBPU attorney John O'Donnell recalled a demonstration at the General Post Office. "The troops," O'Donnell said, "were hanging out the windows waving to the demonstrators. They weren't doing anything."[15] One National Guardsman, in an *Army Magazine* article entitled "Remember Moe Biller," called his military mission "a show of farce."[16] However, no one really believed that the troops could replace skilled clerks in distributing the mail; the real purpose of the troop activation was psychological, and it worked. Postal workers on the picket lines watched glumly as soldiers took over their jobs. The general feeling was that they were beaten; that they had to give up their strike.

The Storm Recedes

At a time when postmen and women were returning to work all over the country and the troops were taking over the New York postal facilities, Gus Johnson told Moe Biller that he had heard that the following agreement had been reached between Secretary of Labor Shultz and the unions: (1) a 12 percent pay raise retroactive to October, 1969; (2) full prepaid health benefits; (3) compression of the pay raise schedule from twenty-one to eight years; (4) area wage calculations; (5) full collective bargaining; and (6) immediate amnesty for all strikers. Biller acknowledged that the "agreement" sounded good, but wanted verification before he took any action. He suggested that the strike be continued for one more day while the attempt was made to verify the agreement.

On March 24, a federal judge had given Branch 36 until 5:00 P.M. the following day before imposing fines on the local starting with $10,000 a day and increasing by an additional $10,000 for each subsequent day that the strike continued; and a personal fine on Johnson of $500, escalating in the same manner. Johnson, therefore, wanted very much to end the strike before 5:00 P.M on the 25th. He told Biller that he could not keep his members out with the kind of offer that had been made. Biller replied that he would hold the MBPU members out and expected the Letter Carriers to respect the MBPU picket lines as the MBPU had respected Letter Carriers picket lines. Johnson then proposed that Postmaster General Blount be called to verify the agreement. Biller agreed, but they were not successful in reaching the Postmaster General.

After consulting with advisors, Biller realized that he had no choice but to recommend that his members return to work. However, he would not guarantee the validity of the so-called "agreement." At a 3:00 P.M. outdoor membership meeting at the 31st Street side of the General Post Office, he made his recommendation, and said that he would go to Washington with Attorneys Eugene Victor and John O'Donnell to determine the validity of the agreement. Thus, on the afternoon of March 25, 1970, the strike was over in New York City. The storm had passed in one tumultuous week.

Chapter 3

THE AFTERMATH

In 1927, Dr. Sterling Spero wrote, "...a strike of postal employees...would cripple the postal service and could only with great difficulty be broken with the help of labor from the outside."[1] In spite of substantial provocation, such a strike did not occur until forty-three years later, but when it did occur, the strikers, acting against most of their own labor leaders, the Postmaster General, and the President of the United States, won their strike. The ordinary men and women who handle, distribute, and deliver the mail took matters into their own hands and won concessions they never could have won had they not withheld their labor.

The implications of the postal strike to federal officials were serious indeed. *Business Week*, in a special report on the strike, noted: "The wave of labor militancy that has engulfed state, county, and city employees in the last few years has now begun lapping at the ranks of federal unionists. The age of pressure-free agreements may be ended...The confrontation—illegal and the result of explosive frustration—could happen in almost any branch of government. Constitutional bars against striking are now being questioned...The tradition against walkouts on government jobs no longer is being taken for granted."[2]

On the same day that the postal strike ended, March 25, 1970, members of the Professional Air Traffic Controllers Organization (PATCO) called in "sick" or "too tired to work," creating serious airline delays. The PATCO members were engaging in concerted action—denounced as "illegal" by the Federal Aviation Administration (FAA)—to protest the transfer of three members from Baton Rouge, Louisiana the previous year, but a general dissatisfaction with work conditions and FAA policies added to their "sickness." Eleven years later, PATCO would stage the second nationwide walkout against the federal government, but the results would be disastrous for those strikers. (The reasons for PATCO's failure are discussed in Chapter 7.)

Regardless of what might happen in the future, the postal workers of 1970 had clearly won their strike. Several factors accounted for their success. First, their grievances were considered legitimate by the President, the Congress, and the general public. Second, the Administration was completely unprepared for a nationwide walkout and did not have the means to break the strike—200,000 postal workers could not be replaced with workers from the outside without causing a long-term disruption in postal services. Finally, the strike eliminated union opposition to postal reform, thereby allowing the President to push through the Post Office Reorganization Act of 1970, one of his major domestic goals.

A *New York Times* editorial placed the blame for the walkout squarely on the White House and Congress:

> ...It is clear that most of the fault for the postmen's rebellious mood lies with the White House and Congress. Inexcusable blundering in both branches of government has forced postal workers to wait month after month for the long overdue pay increases that economic justice clearly requires and everyone agrees they fully deserve. The whole issue has been snarled in the interminable battle over postal reform, another matter on which the national interest has had to mark time while Washington played politics as usual.[3]

When the postal workers returned to work, the government made good on its pledge to negotiate all worker grievances with the seven unions recognized under the Kennedy Executive Order of 1962. This, in itself, was an historic event: never before had negotiations on bread-and-butter issues taken place between federal workers and their employer, the United States Government. It would take an Act of Congress to implement the terms of whatever agreement might result, but considering the trauma of the strike, Congressional action probably would be a mere formality.

Negotiations

It was on March 25, 1970, the same day the strike ended in New York, that the Post Office Department and the seven nationally recognized unions faced each other across the bargaining table to discuss wages. The ceremonial opening round took place on the sixth floor of the Moreschi Building in Washington, home of the Laborers' International Union of North America (LIUNA), parent body of the Mail Handlers. Secretary of Labor Shultz formally opened the meeting and left the negotiations to the principles on both sides. James Gildea, top aide to President George Meany of the AFL-CIO, was the chief negotiator for the unions; his Post Office Department counterpart was Deputy Postmaster General Elmer T. Klassen. Assistant Secretary of Labor William Usery represented Secretary Shultz.

On the following day, March 26, the negotiators moved to the Hotel Sonesta at Thomas Circle where round-the-clock bargaining began. Although the media were in constant attendance at the bargaining sessions, both sides agreed to a strict news embargo concerning the negotiations and related activities.

On April 2, the Postmaster General and the seven unions signed a "Memorandum of Agreement" that included the following:

> *General Wage Increase*: A general wage increase of 6 percent retroactive to December 27, 1969 for all postal employees.
>
> *Other Post Office Provisions*: In order to meet the special needs of the unions in their representation of the Department's employees and the needs of the Department to enable adequate management of the services for which it is responsible, the parties will agree upon and jointly sponsor a reorganization of the Department which among other things will:
>
> (A) Enable collective bargaining procedures under a statutory framework establishing methods for conducting elections, providing one or more methods for solving negotiating impasses, and requiring collective bargaining over all aspects of wages, hours, and working conditions including grievance procedures, final and binding arbitration of disputes, and in general all matters which are subject to collective bargaining in the private sector.
>
> (B) Provide an additional 8% wage increase for postal workers effective as of the date the enabling legislation becomes law.
>
> (C) Provide that negotiations with the unions be immediately undertaken to establish a new wage schedule whereby an employee reaches the maximum step for his labor grade after no more than 8 years in that grade....

(D) Provide a structure for the Department so that it can operate on a self-contained basis and endow it with authority commensurate with its responsibilities to improve, manage, and maintain efficient and adequate postal services.

Administration Approval: It is the understanding of the parties that the Administration will recommend to Congress the necessary legislation to effectuate this Agreement.

Drafting: It is understood that the parties will commence at once to prepare the agreed legislation with a view to having it ready for submission not later than April 10, 1970.

Discipline: No disciplinary action will be initiated by the Post Office Department at any level against any postal employee with respect to the events of March, 1970, until discussions have taken place between the Department and such employee's union on the policy to be followed by the Department.[4]

On April 15, President Nixon signed Public Law 91-231 providing the retroactive 6 percent pay raise for all postal workers, and on April 16, the presidents of seven nationally recognized unions and AFL-CIO President George Meany signed an agreement with Postmaster General Winton M. Blount regarding postal reorganization and additional salary adjustments. The agreement was publicly endorsed by President Nixon on the same date at a White House meeting with all parties to the agreement.

It would seem with such an Administration-union consensus that the Administration bill would have had clear sailing through the Congress, but that was not to be. A bill, H.R. 17070, providing for the Administration's program was introduced by Chairman Dulski of the House Post Office and Civil Service Committee and Representatives Udall, Corbett and Derwinski. Congress appeared willing to implement the agreement, and, at first, it seemed that the bill might be ready for the President's signature by May. Two developments, however, caused a three-month delay in the bill's passage.

The first was an expansion of American military operations in South East Asia to Cambodia, causing a serious disruption in Congressional consideration of domestic matters, including Postal Reform. The second was a successful campaign by the National Right to Work Committee to prevent the possibility of the establishment of a union shop in the postal service. The unions fought hard against the inclusion of an anti-union shop provision, but the final bill that emerged from the House-Senate Joint Conference Committee contained the following clause: "Each employee ...shall have the right...to refrain from any such [union] activity, and...shall be protected in the exercise of that right."

An ironic sidelight to the Congressional debate on "compulsory unionism" occurred when Senator Paul Fannin of Arizona cited an advertisement sponsored by the Right To Work Committee that appeared in the June 15, 1970 edition of the Washington *Star*. Among the many prominent individuals and organizations listed in the ad as opposed to the union shop was Vincent R. Sombrotto, Branch 36, National Association of Letter Carriers. Senator Fannin felt obliged to explain to his colleagues the identity of Vincent Sombrotto:

> Mr. President, most of these names are quite familiar. But you...might ask, "Who is Vincent Sombrotto?" Well, Vincent Sombrotto is America, he is the worker down the street, he is the postal employee who has earned a pay increase and wants this Congress to do something about it, and he is also the postal worker who knows that the Meany-Blount deal on compulsory unionism is what is holding up postal reform and his pay raise...Only last week this man was in my office with a petition signed in one day by 900 of his fellow workers—and all union members—that says: "We the undersigned request that the provision of Executive Order No. 11491 giving postal employees the right to join or not to join a union be written into any postal 'reform' legislation; thereby expediting a just wage increase, fringe benefits and better working conditions—for all postal employees." In his own words, Mr. Sombrotto told me, "Senator, the workers don't want the union shop. They want benefits for themselves, not for the bosses...."[5]

The man described as "America, the worker down the street," was destined to become a "boss" himself. He replaced Gus Johnson as President of Branch 36 after the strike and was elected President of the National Association of Letter Carriers in 1978.

The Cambodian intervention and the Right To Work battle delayed passage of the postal reform until August 12, 1970. On that day, President Nixon signed Public Law 91-375, the Postal Reorganization Act of 1970. Its more important provisions were:

Reorganization: The reorganization of the U.S. Post Office Department into an independent agency, the U.S. Postal Service, to be governed by an eleven-member Board of Governors, nine of whom are appointed by the President. The appointment by the President of a five-member Postal Rate Commission which, after hearings and due process, submits to the Board its recommendations on postal rate changes or fees, the objective being to have rates and fees provide sufficient revenue so that income and appropriations will equal the costs of maintaining and developing the Postal Service. The establishment of a thirteen-member Advisory Committee, chaired by the Postmaster General, and made up of Presidential appointees from the sectors most vitally concerned with the mails, including four members chosen from nominees of labor unions granted exclusive bargaining rights, four members representing major mail users, and three from the general public.

Management: The removal of the Postmaster General from the Cabinet and his or her tenure to be based on performance rather than politics.

Postal Employees: The establishment of a Postal Career Service, and prohibition of the political appointment of postal employees at any level. The retention of the Civil Service Retirement System, veterans preference, and the approval of the Civil Service Commission of any changes in adverse employee actions through collective bargaining for all Postal Career Service employees. The reduction in waiting time for top pay rate in grade from twenty-one years to eight years or less, and the immediate grant of an 8 percent pay raise to all postal employees.

Collective Bargaining: The institution of collective bargaining to determine compensation, benefits, terms of employment under the same laws that apply to collective bargaining in the private sector. The introduction of arbitration procedures to settle impasses which remain unresolved 180 days after the start of bargaining. The National Labor Relations Board (NLRB) to supervise representation elections, enforce unfair labor practice provisions, and determine appropriate bargaining units.

Finances: Up to $10 billion of bonds may be issued, $2 billion of which must be purchased by the Treasury (the Department may purchase more). The authorization of annual public service subsidies to the U.S. Postal Service, amounting to 10 percent of the 1971 appropriations through fiscal year 1979, thereafter reduced by 1 percent a year from fiscal year 1980 through 1984 until the subsidies are totally discontinued. The continuation of preferred rates for Congressionally designated groups such as the blind and nonprofit organizations, with appropriations to make up deficiency in revenue.[6]

The bill did not meet all union demands, but represented all they could get. The retention of the "no strike" clause, including the requirement that all postal employees sign an affidavit swearing that they would not strike against the U.S. Government, the omission of any consideration of area wage differentials, and the prohibition against the union shop were all anathema to labor. Nevertheless, as Nesbitt notes, "its validity as a pioneering effort is unimpeachable."[7] And no one has expressed subsequent doubt that postal workers have fared much better under the Postal Reorganization Act than they did when their union leaders had to go hat-in-hand begging for handouts from Congress.

The Uninvited

The strike of 1970 never could have succeeded without the active participation of the National Postal Union. Its members constituted approximately 40 percent of those who walked off the job and, at times during the strike, including at the beginning and the end of the walkout, NPU members constituted a majority of the strikers. NPU leaders were the most militant in denouncing the inadequate legislation under consideration by Congress, including the Rademacher bill. In New York City, the only area where troops appeared, the participation of the 20,000 members of the MBPU, the largest postal union local in the world, assured that the strike would be 100 percent effective. Yet, because it was not one of the seven recognized unions under the Kennedy Executive Order, the NPU was not included in the post-strike negotiations.

Moe Biller, President of the MBPU was not about to take this omission lying down. Along with attorneys John O'Donnell and Eugene Victor and his public relations man, Tom Costigan, he descended on Washington and made his way to the Moreschi Building, the home of LIUNA, where the negotiations were being conducted. Once there, the MBPU delegation found that passes to the sixth floor were necessary, and the building guards were not about to issue passes to unauthorized personnel. That didn't stop them. They were standing in the hall close to the elevators. An elevator came down and its door opened. O'Donnell said, "Come on, let's go upstairs." The four men quickly entered the elevator and pushed the button for the sixth floor. The elevator door closed before the guards were able to prevent their ascent. Once on the sixth floor, they were barred from entering the negotiating room, but the press, which had been alerted by Costigan that an invasion was about to take place, began asking Biller questions. Biller gave them an earful. He told them that the laborers' building was a "hell of a place" to conduct an historic meeting, and that 80,000 postal workers were not being represented in the negotiations. Soon the meeting was totally disrupted and Assistant Secretary of Labor, William Usery, emerged from the room. According to Biller:

> Usery said, "Hi Moe, what are you doing here?" I said, "Never mind that crap, Bill, we want to get into the negotiations." I don't know what might have happened. They might have thrown us out physically if not for Usery. Or, they might have got people to escort us out. But, Usery mollified us and told us he would get us a meeting with Shultz in the morning.[8]

Later that evening, while eating dinner at Costin's Restaurant, Kenneth Houseman, Assistant Postmaster General for Labor Relations, came over to Biller's table and told him that Klassen, the Deputy Postmaster General and chief Post Office negotiator, wanted to see him. Biller said, "What does he want? Does he want to negotiate? If he wants to negotiate, that's fine. If he's just trying to show the press that he's a nice guy, I don't need him." Houseman said he didn't know Klassen's reason. "I'm just here as an errand boy." Biller replied, "Well, you're an awfully expensive errand boy. Get the hell out of here."[9]

The following morning the Biller entourage met with Shultz who listened patiently while Biller made his case. He insisted that the NPU deserved a voice in the current negotiations. He said that a deal could not be made with the seven so-called "exclusive unions" while ignoring the role played by the MBPU in New York and the NPU nationally. He emphasized that the NPU had 80,000 members and that no deal would work without the support of those 80,000 postal workers. Shultz made no promises, except to admit that Biller had a legitimate complaint and that he would take it under consideration. "It was," Biller remarked, "an hour of good George Shultz B.S."[10]

So, what did the Biller invasion accomplish? First, it helped hold the NPU locals together while the union's fate was being decided. Under the Postal Reorganization Act, the NPU would not be able to obtain bargaining rights; its members could not outvote the much larger United Federation of Postal Clerks. That meant that the union was on the verge of extinction. The publicity emerging from the Biller invasion proved to the men and women in the ranks that their interests were being represented, and that a solution to the union's predicament might be found.

Secondly, the Biller-Shultz meeting helped spur the move toward merger. Shultz conveyed to the seven exclusive unions that they had a problem with the NPU and that it was up to them to solve it. After all, an organization of 80,000 postal workers could not be summarily disregarded. The Shultz intervention may have motivated United Federation President Francis S. Filbey, who already favored a merger with the NPU, to work even harder to accomplish that goal.

The Birth of the American Postal Workers Union

As subsequent chapters will detail, at the time of the passage of the Postal Reorganization Act, most postal workers were organized along craft lines. There were seven nationally recognized unions: National Association of Letter Carriers, United Federation of Postal Clerks, National Association of Post Office and General Services Maintenance Employees, National Association of Post Office Mail Handlers, Watchmen, Messengers and Group Leaders (affiliated with Laborers' International Union), National Association of Special Delivery Messengers, and the Rural Letter Carriers Association. In addition, there were the NPU and the National Alliance of Postal and Federal Employees, both of which enrolled members across craft lines.

The movement for "one big postal union," composed of 800,000 postal workers, began in the 1920s when a Joint Council of Affiliated Postal Unions, made up of unions affiliated with the AFL, was formed. The move toward merger was intensified as the result of negotiations under the Kennedy Executive Order, but it wasn't until the passage of the Postal Reorganization Act of 1970 that the need for more consolidated union representation became imperative. Instead of lobbying the Congress, the unions would now be up against a quasi-corporate United States Postal Service which would employ experienced professionals to conduct negotiations. To meet that challenge, it was necessary to reduce the fragmentation of postal union representation.

The NPU had worked consistently to mend its schism with the Clerks. Early in 1966, the NPU and the Clerks worked out an agreement for merger, but the plan failed by twenty-two votes to obtain the necessary two-thirds majority at a special convention of the UFPC. At the Clerks regular convention in August 1966, despite the support of UFPC President, E. C. "Roy" Hallbeck, the delegates rejected the merger again by a far larger vote. The major problem was the NPU's insistence on proportional representation, the same issue which had caused a split between the two organizations in 1958. The smaller locals were not willing to grant the larger, big-city locals greater representation at national conventions. Hallbeck, who pushed hard but unsuccessfully for an UFPC-NPU merger, discussed the "price of disunity":

> We have paid a frightful price for disunity. It has had its effect in the Congress; it's had its effect in administrative circles. Our dealings with the Department have been something less than completely satisfactory...the Department has always had the advantage of being able to play both ends against the middle to the great disadvantage to those we represent.[11]

Francis S. Filbey, who became President of the UFPC after the death of Hallbeck, led the merger movement in 1970. Working with Monroe Crable, President of the Maintenance Employees, Chester Parrish, President of the Motor Vehicle Operators and Michael Cullen, President of the Special Delivery Messengers, merger talks were inaugurated. By December 1970, after several months of negotiations, a preliminary merger agreement was signed by the UFPC, the Maintenance Employees, and the Motor Vehicle Operators. A month later the Special Delivery Messengers signed the preliminary agreement.

Negotiations then began with the NPU. David Silvergleid, then President of the NPU, claims that the greatest obstacle to merger was Moe Biller. "I'll say this for Moe," Silvergleid said, "he was one hell of a negotiator. He wanted to get the last possible drop of blood out of them that he could. I agreed up to a point. The point was that I wasn't going to let the merger die because we would die with it." In a caucus of the NPU merger team, Biller said that he wouldn't buy the agreement. Silvergleid responded: "Moe, we have 80,000 members. I'm taking 55,000 into the merger. Where are you going to go with your 25,000? That was the end of it. Moe realized that we had no alternative. He was smart enough to know that we couldn't get any more out of them."[12]

Biller has a completely different memory of the situation. He and Vincent Sombrotto, who defeated Gus Johnson for the presidency of Branch 36 after the strike, were in the process of forming a Joint MBPU/Branch 36 bargaining committee in New York. Rademacher, who was against any local of the Letter Carriers acting in tandem with any other union, particularly Biller's MBPU, ordered Sombrotto to desist. Sombrotto refused and Rademacher put Branch 36 into trusteeship. Biller was concerned that Filbey would do the same to the MBPU if merger should occur. He refused to agree to the merger until he had assurance from Filbey that no such action would be taken against his union. When Biller became President of the APWU in 1980, he was reunited with Sombrotto, who was elected President of the Letter Carriers in 1978. Together, they formed the Joint Bargaining Committee of the APWU and Letter Carriers, representing 80 percent of all postal workers, and bargained jointly with the USPS thereafter.

After three months of negotiations, mediated by national officers of the AFL-CIO, the following issues which had to be settled before the NPU would merge, were indeed resolved:

1. National officers would be elected by referendum ballot mailed to the home of each member;
2. The new union would follow the industrial concept of a single postal union, but would maintain craft councils;
3. The provision of proportional representation at national conventions with one vote for each twenty-five members.

With these issues resolved, ratification of the merger could be sought, and a new constitution could be drafted.

The American Postal Workers Union was born, the conclusion of a long and difficult struggle. Thus, the storm which rocked the country in March of 1970 resulted in a complete overhaul of the nation's postal system and the establishment of the first major industrial union in post office history.

It is ironic to note that postal workers made monumental organizational strides during the presidency of the conservative Richard Milhous Nixon rather than during the liberal administrations of Theodore Roosevelt, Woodrow Wilson, Franklin Delano Roosevelt, John F. Kennedy, Lyndon B. Johnson, or Jimmy Carter. Never in their wildest imaginings could the men who formed the first postal unions at the end of the 19th century have predicted that postal workers would one day be able to bargain collectively with their employer, the sovereign government of the United States, or that the postal service, itself, would be set free of political patronage. The men and women who walked off the job in 1970 could not have known that their action would result in radical changes in one of the nation's largest industries, but that is exactly what happened—changes designed to preserve the dignity of both the institution and its employees.

PART II

THE LONG, HARD HAUL

"If there is no struggle, there is no progress. ...Power concedes nothing without a demand. It never did and it never will. Men may not get all they pay for in this world; but they must certainly pay for all they get."

—Frederick Douglass

Chapter 4

THE STRUGGLE

The gains won by postal workers by means of the illegal walkout of 1970 constituted a watershed in postal labor-management relations. Years of labor repression, even by the most liberal of Administrations, became a thing of the past. Postal unions were now recognized as the legitimate agents of postal workers and they had the right, by statute, to bargain with the newly formed U.S. Postal Service. For more than a century postal workers had been virtual pawns, without basic workplace rights, in one of the nation's largest industries. The attempt of the men and women in gray to gain control over their economic lives is the story of a battle against the concept of "sovereignty," a concept handed down in English common law from feudal days and based on the divine right of kings. Since the Sovereign (read "government") can do no wrong, the Sovereign's workers are denied the rights and protections granted (by government) to workers outside the Sovereign's employ (read "in the private sector").

The concept of sovereignty, however, was never evenly applied. According to Nesbitt, "the 'laborers, workmen, and mechanics' in the Navy Yards and other public works [in the 1830s] belonged to the same unions as private or municipal employees. The government resisted their demands where it was able and yielded where the pressure of labor market conditions made it expedient or necessary to do so. But it did not challenge employee rights to unionize, demonstrate, use political pressure or strike."[1] When postal workers began to organize, however, the government's reaction was not quite so benevolent. The government did not consider postal workers "laborers, workmen and mechanics"; rather, they were considered government employees and, as such, subject to the same rules and regulations that govern all government employees. Moreover, postal workers were not joining unions that already existed outside government; they were creating their own unions within government, an act which was close to sedition in the eyes of most federal officials.

Thus, when postal workers turned to the labor movement to improve their economic and working conditions, the government's reaction was either to break the fledgling organizations, or, if unsuccessful, to control them, or make them into "company unions." The latter was more successful than the former, but as postal unions succumbed to the control of management, competing organizations sprang up and challenged their more docile forerunners. When the "rebel" organizations—those that refused to succumb to the control of management—turned to the American Federation of Labor for support, a battle was joined that would not be fully resolved until the 1970 strike and the passage of the Postal Reorganization Act of 1970.

The pros and cons of the concept of sovereignty and the repression that resulted from its application to attempts by postal workers to organize into labor unions and apply pressure to both Congress and the Post Office Department will be discussed in Chapter 5. This chapter traces the evolution of the U.S. Postal Service from colonial times, summarizes the reasons why postal workers felt they had to organize, and describes the actual organizations that emerged.

In the Beginning

The first post offices in the New World were taverns or shipping offices along the Atlantic coastline. Letters destined for England were dropped off at the taverns where they would be picked up by the shipmasters of outgoing vessels. The shipmasters of incoming vessels, in turn, would drop off letters from England destined for the colonies. The first official post office in the colonies was established in 1639 when the General Court of Massachusetts designated the Richard Fairbanks tavern in Boston as the repository for all mail arriving from or being sent overseas. New York followed by establishing a post route between New York City and Boston in 1683, a trail which became known as the Boston Post Road, now part of U.S. Route 1. William Penn established the first post office in Pennsylvania in 1683, and in the south, a private messenger service made up mainly of slaves, provided mail service to the plantations.[2]

It soon became apparent that efficient and dependable communications were impossible without some sort of centralized and colonywide postal organization. In 1691, Thomas Neale received a twenty-one-year grant from the British Crown to establish a North American postal service. Neale, who never came to America, appointed Andrew Hamilton, Governor of New Jersey, as his Deputy Postmaster General. Thirty-nine years later, Alexander Spotswood, then Deputy Postmaster General for America, appointed the thirty-one-year-old editor of the Pennsylvania Gazette, Benjamin Franklin, as Postmaster for Philadelphia. Young Franklin, who was later appointed Joint Postmaster General for the colonies, was destined to become the architect of the postal service as we know it today.

As Joint Deputy Postmaster General, Franklin reorganized the entire system. By 1760, he reported his first surplus to the British Postmaster General, and when he left office in 1774, "post roads were in operation from Maine to Florida and from New York to Canada, and mail between the colonies and England operated on a regular schedule."[3] Franklin did not leave his post willingly; he was dismissed by the Crown for secessionist activities, but he would soon be back as a member of the Revolutionary Government.

The 1775 Continental Congress appointed Franklin as the Chairman of the Committee of Investigation to Establish a Postal System. The Committee recommended the appointment of a Postmaster General for the thirteen colonies. On July 26, 1775, Franklin was appointed to that position. The official history of the U.S. Postal Service concludes:

> Franklin served until November 7, 1776. America's present postal service descends in an unbroken line from the system he planned and placed in operation, and history rightfully accords him major credit for establishing the basis of a postal service which has performed magnificently for the American people.[4]

The people who manned the postal service during the colonial era and in the early days of the Republic were considered to be "government officials" rather than postal employees and were afforded the respect due to important personages. Karl Baarslag notes that in 1845, "postal workers came to work in tall beaver hats, as befitted gentlemen, and usually sported silver-topped canes"[5] (and some could even afford the costumes). Because the volume of mail was relatively light, their work was not particularly arduous, and they received free board and salaries which were surprisingly good for the period. Also, according to Baarslag:

The U.S. Official Register, which lists the office and salary of every federal official and employee from President to charwoman shows that, in 1825, postal clerks earned from $300 to $1,400 a year. Some Philadelphia clerks earned $1,200 a year, while Boston mail clerks received as little as $600. There was no uniform scale because each postmaster received a lump sum from Congress with which to operate his office. These appropriations were based on mail handled and on the political influence wielded by the respective postmasters. The salaries doled out to their assistants depended on how many clerks were employed and on each postmaster's liberality or penuriousness. The postmaster at Charleston, South Carolina received $1,400 per annum, but his son was America's most highly paid postal clerk at $1,700![6]

All this would change with the birth of the steam locomotive and the subsequent spread of railways across the nation. Baarslag notes that the railroads brought lower postage rates, and the lower postage rates, in turn, brought a tremendous increase in the mails, particularly in whole new classes of printed matter, magazines, newspapers, catalogs, etc. The voluminous amount of mail naturally meant larger clerical staffs. But salaries dropped as the lump sum appropriations had to be shared among more people. Steadily increasing mail volume also resulted in longer hours and more crowded conditions. Postal facilities soon proved inadequate to accommodate the ever-increasing volume of mail and personnel. In 1844, the Post Office handled thirty-eight million letters; seven years later, the letter volume had increased to eighty-three million.[7]

Moreover, although canceling machines were introduced in 1883, mechanization played a relatively minor role in the expansion of the postal service. The collecting, sorting, and delivery of mail continued to be done by hand. It thus became necessary to increase individual worker productivity through longer work hours and a forcibly stepped-up pace at which employees performed their jobs.

As the avalanche of mail continued to increase, postal clerks no longer wore tall beaver hats to work and could no longer afford silver-topped canes. They worked "longer hours in overcrowded, ill ventilated and poorly lit workrooms," and their pay was barely enough to sustain them and their families.[8] They had become industrial workers, laborers—a far cry from the lofty government officials they once had been.

From the Spoils System to Civil Service

From the Administration of Andrew Jackson to the passage of the Pendleton Act in 1883, post office jobs from top to bottom were bestowed on the party faithful. Local political organizations, through the appointments of postmasters, used post office jobs as payoffs to friends, relatives, and political followers. The result was that with every change in the Administration, there would be a complete change in postal personnel throughout the country. The effect on the postal service was disastrous. First, many of those who were "rewarded" with postal jobs left immediately when they discovered that they were expected to wrestle with heavy mail bags, or stand on their feet for twelve or more hours a day canceling or sorting mail. Expecting sinecures, they found only hard labor. Their replacements often were neither motivated nor qualified for exacting postal jobs. Secondly, most postal workers knew that their jobs would last only as long as the current national or local political party remained in power. There was little motivation to take their jobs seriously when they had no stake in the post office as a career.

The already overburdened postal system received another jolt when, on March 1, 1851, the Congress passed a postal act which reduced letter rates to three cents for distances up to 3,000 miles and six cents beyond that distance. Twelve years later, the distance factor was eliminated. The result was another major increase in mail volume. Postal workers who were already overworked and undermotivated reeled under the new deluge of mail, and the deterioration in the service became a matter of public concern.

The Pendleton Act

The demand for a civil service system, modeled on England's, began to receive serious attention in the United States. Civil service reform leagues came into existence, and businesses began to demand a more efficient postal service separated from politics. In 1869, Congress began considering the creation of an apolitical civil service and postal service. "The first Civil Service Commission was established in 1871, but it was not until the passage of the Pendleton Act in 1883 that a bona fide civil service was finally instituted."[9]

In the long run the attainment of civil service status was a boon to postal workers, but in the short run, the passage of the Pendleton Act had a negative effect on their employment conditions. Under the spoils system, when problems arose, postal workers could appeal to their political patrons. Whether or not the problems were resolved depended on the power and will of the patron, but at least there was a channel of appeal. Once postal workers became civil servants, the politicians lost all interest in them; they became political orphans without power. As a result, their working conditions deteriorated even further.

The Postmaster General's report for fiscal year 1906 showed that 12 percent of the nation's postal clerks had resigned during the year. The turnover rate increased to 20 percent during the succeeding year.[10] Congressman James R. Mann, representing Chicago, introduced a resolution calling for "an investigation into what was wrong with the Post Office and why employees should be quitting in such large numbers in the face of hard times and scarcity of work." In that city, 520 clerks had resigned in one year and 112 eligibles turned down appointments. Some of the latter worked for a few days and then quit.[11]

Twelve hours was considered an average day, eleven hours was getting off easy, and thirteen to fourteen hours not at all uncommon. The conveyor noise, poor ventilation, and dust from the mail sacks contributed to harder working conditions. In 1910, a shocking account of postal employee working conditions appeared in the Chicago Record Herald:

Four members of the Chicago Postal Clerks Union had died of tuberculosis contracted in the course of their employment, while four more were ill from the same cause. The doctor who investigated the ventilating system declared that it could not have been worse, while methods of dusting fell far short of the necessary requirements. Mail bags drawn over railway station platforms in all parts of the country, gathering disease germs, were never disinfected or cleaned. Yet, they were handled by hundreds of clerks. The dust from them fell in a thick coating all over the distributing cases at which the men worked. The same drinking cup was used by hundreds of persons.... The city mailing division was furnished with wooden boxes filled with sawdust for cuspidors, and no attempt was made to keep them clean. The head of the Tuberculosis Institute said that he had no hesitancy in tracing the many cases of consumption brought to his attention directly to the conditions under which the men were forced to work.[12]

It may seem anticlimactic to report that Chicago clerks were forced to work twelve hours a day, six and sometimes seven days a week, because the Post Office Department, in an economy move, would not appoint additional clerks even though the law authorized an increase of 2,000 in the clerical workforce.

If the conditions for Chicago clerks were bad, those of the Railway Mail Clerks were even worse. In 1909, the post office cars were antiquated, wooden structures that were most often placed between the engine and the baggage car, both of which, of course, were of metal construction. As a result, when a train wreck occurred, the wooden post office car was crushed between the engine and the long line of cars. Between July 1909 and July 1910, post office clerks suffered 742 casualties from train wrecks. Of these, 617 were slightly injured, 98 were seriously injured, and 27 were killed.[13] Sanitary conditions on the postal cars were scandalous:

> Toilets, not enclosed in closets, but situated in the open car, were equipped with neither flushing nor disinfecting devices. Drinking water coolers, in many instances situated above the open and all too often filthy hoppers, were left uncleaned for trip after trip.[14]

In the summer of 1909, a Texas clerk sent Harpoon (a publication edited by a tubercular ex-railway mail clerk) a bottle containing the carcass of a rat which he had found in the water tank of his car. A picture of the bottle was published in Harpoon and created somewhat of a sensation throughout the country. When the Post Office Department asked the clerk to explain why he had violated postal regulations by sending the bottle to an outside publication, he said:

> I did not report this in the prescribed way because I knew nothing would be accomplished by it. I think my method will accomplish more for the 15,000 postal clerks of the United States than any other method would have done.[15]

The clerk was dismissed from the postal service. It should also be noted that Oscar F. Nelson, President of the Chicago Post Office Clerks' Union in 1909, and the man who blew the whistle on conditions in the Chicago post office, was also dismissed from the service. However, in the Nelson case, the National Federation of Post Office Clerks fought back. He succeeded Edward B. Goltra as President of the Federation.

These working conditions were the rule rather than the exception in the early 1900s. The Pendleton Act had provided all federal workers some degree of job security. But the Post Office, which had evolved from a relatively low volume "gentleman's operation" to a giant industrial enterprise, was still managed by the recipients of political patronage who were incapable of distinguishing between the blue collar employees of an industrial-type operation and the white collar employees of the typical federal bureaucracy.

The federal government, of course, employed blue collar workers in the shipyards, Government Printing Office, and other facilities, but, as noted previously, the employees of these operations were members of unions which also operated in the private and municipal sectors, and had the support of such national labor organizations as the Knights of Labor and, later, the American Federation of Labor. Because of the unique nature of post office work, there were no existing unions postal workers could join. If they were to seek help in improving their economic and working conditions through the labor movement, they would have to form their own labor organizations.

The Postal Workers Organize

The prevailing form of organization for postal workers to model themselves on was craft rather than industry. A hundred years of U.S. labor experience had shown that against intense employer opposition and competition from a mobile work force, only hard-to-replace skilled workers had significant bargaining power. To affiliate with the unskilled along industrial lines was to invite defeat. But there were other reasons for craft organization inherent in the nature of post office employment.

At the turn of the century, there were three major categories of postal employees: city letter carriers, inside post office clerks, and railway mail clerks. Each worked in isolation from the others with no natural means of contact or communication. Since they organized from within, responding to common complaints rather than being organized from without by some preexisting labor organization, their organizations emerged in a fragmented pattern. Also, since their pay came from a single congressional appropriation, they were inevitable competitors for a share of that limited "pie."

Considerable political sophistication had to occur before they learned to jointly lobby for a larger pie.

The first to organize were the letter carriers, a homogeneous group, all of whom were engaged in the same type of work—delivering the mail. Unlike the clerks who engaged in a variety of occupations ranging from the unskilled to the highly skilled, there were few promotional opportunities available to letter carriers. Thus, as Nesbitt points out, the only improvements letter carriers could expect were those that came to the group as a whole. "This absence of the prospect of personal preferment," Nesbitt says, "saved the letter carriers from much of the factionalism that has bedeviled the organizing efforts of other postal workers, and has made them one of the most thoroughly organized occupations in the entire labor movement."[16] To this day, one of the conflicts between the letter carriers and the clerks is the method through which pay raises are bestowed. The letter carriers prefer an across-the-board increase in dollars, whereas the clerks demand a percentage so that the raises are proportionate to the various levels of clerks employed.

But, what appeared natural and even preferable in a nascent stage of organization, when cohesiveness was not a premium, became a deterrent to effectiveness when lobbying strength and, ultimately, strike potential became keys to bargaining power. By that time, eight separate unions had emerged which coalesced to four with the creation of the American Postal Workers Union in 1971. But even that degree of unity was wrenching after a century of entrenched separatism.

The Letter Carriers and the Eight-Hour Day

In 1868, Congress passed a law stipulating that eight hours constituted a day's work for "laborers, workmen and mechanics" employed by the federal government. The letter carriers who had formed local "benevolent and social associations" in several cities since the establishment of the city delivery service in 1863, sent delegations selected by the local societies to Washington primarily to lobby for the extension of the eight-hour day to letter carriers. Eventually, a permanent "legislative committee" was formed and John F. Victory became its first Secretary. He founded the *Postal Record*, which became the official organ of the National Association of Letter Carriers when it was formed in 1889.

But the Post Office Department refused to apply the eight-hour law to letter carriers on the grounds that postal workers were not laborers, workmen, or mechanics. The image of the government official lingered on, if not in the minds and paychecks of the letter carriers, then certainly in the attitudes of their superiors. The Noble Order of the Knights of Labor was on the upswing immediately after the Civil War, and led the campaign for an eight-hour day. After their failure to profit from the Eight-Hour Act of 1868, the letter carriers turned to the Knights of Labor for help. Local assemblies of the Knights were formed as ruling bodies within local letter carrier associations.[17]

With the support of the Knights, the letter carriers were finally successful in overcoming the fervent opposition of the postal authorities, and, in 1888, two years after the formation of the first Knights' Post Office assembly in New York, Congress passed a letter carriers' eight-hour law. Initially it appeared that the Act's extension to the carriers would be a Pyrrhic victory because of the vehemence of the Post Office Department's reaction:

> Organization leaders were fired for minor infractions of the rules, and employees active in the drive for the eight-hour law were harassed and suspended. Moreover, the Department, at first, ignored the law and then adopted a policy of deliberate evasion. The new law provided that "eight hours shall constitute a day's work for letter carriers...If any carrier is employed a greater number of hours a day than eight, he shall be paid extra for the same in proportion to the salary now fixed by law." The Department interpreted eight hours a day to mean 56 hours a week, so that a carrier who worked nine hours a day for six days and was off on Sunday owed the Department two hours at the end of each week.[18]

However, after five years of litigation, in 1893 the Supreme Court upheld an order of the Court of Claims rejecting the Department's interpretations and requiring the government to pay back claims for overtime totaling close to $3,500,000.

The only split that ever occurred in the ranks of the Letter Carriers Association involved the affiliation of some locals with the Knights of Labor. After the formation of the National Association of Letter Carriers in 1889, some locals elected to become affiliated with the Knights; others to remain independent. This resulted in dual locals in some areas, but with the dissolution of the Knights by the turn of the century, the two factions came together and the NALC became a strong union.

The Clerks

The road of the postal clerks to union organization was a good deal more rutted and strewn with potholes than that of the letter carriers. The major reason was that most promotions in the postal service came from the ranks of the clerks, including the railway mail clerks, and as a result, politics was an important factor in the way the clerks played the game. Spero explains that while a labor organization offered the letter carrier his only chance for improved conditions—and clerks as a whole theirs—the individual clerk "has always banked on possible political preference."[19] Thus, the clerks were always torn between maintaining good relations with the Department and risking the Department's enmity and punitive action by engaging in true labor union agitation. Thus, as Spero notes, "the history of organization among the clerks is a story of the growth of rival factions, one playing faster politics than the other, and then the formation of still other groups in protest against the whole business."[20]

The Birth of a Company Union

The attempts of the clerks to unionize was exacerbated by the failure of factions within the body of the clerks to agree on legislative priorities. The clerks in the largest and most influential group, the New York Association, wanted to push for eight-hour and vacation laws; others wanted a classification act which would rank clerks by skill level and provide for automatic salary increases. The Department, in its attempt to cripple the movement, played these factions against one another. In addition, the Department attempted to break the already formed New York Association by dismissing its officers and disciplining other active members. Those who replaced the dismissed officers tried to placate the Department by inviting supervisors to join the Association. The national officers of the newly formed (1894) National Association of Post Office Clerks (NAPOC) supported the enrollment of supervisors. This, in turn, caused many locals to secede from NAPOC and form a new union, the United Association of Post Office Clerks in 1897.

The Department, however, recognized only NAPOC. The United Association was ignored and its members gained few, if any, of the promotions and other favors bestowed by the Department. Moreover, because it never became sufficiently strong to become an effective lobbying agent, it merged back with the National Association in 1900, three years after it was founded. The result was the creation of the United National Association of Post Office Clerks (UNAPOC), a company union including supervisors which would avoid any opposition to Departmental policy until its dissolution in 1960.

Several independent associations demonstrated their lack of faith by remaining independent. Chief among these was the Chicago local which had affiliated with the Knights of Labor to protect itself from Department domination. It was in Chicago that a fateful move would be made resulting in the formation of a true postal clerks labor union, and an affiliation with the American Federation of Labor—a move that was considered both radical and dangerous at the time.

Chicago

The inciting incident seems to have occurred in October, 1899, after clerks at Chicago's Temporary Post Office had been working from 2:00 P.M. until 8:00 A.M. the following morning processing a virtual mountain of catalogs from Chicago's large mail order houses. These eighteen hours of hard labor, ten of which were uncompensated overtime, were spent in a facility which can only be described as hellish:

> Dank, foul odors rising from pools of stagnant sewage water leaking from defective pipes and collecting under the rickety wooden floor, filled the old post office with a gray, miasmatic mist. So noxious was this horrible effluvium, that old timers compared it with noisome Bubbly Creek, a dead-end canal of overpowering stench in the Stockyards district. Small wonder that a number of clerks died of typhoid fever as a result of working in the old "Temporary" Chicago Post Office. Drinking water was kept in insanitary barrels, seldom iced, and the water looked dirty and tasted vile. Poorly fitted wooden covers served little useful purpose in keeping foreign matter out of

the barrels—infrequent cleanings often revealed bottles, rags, towels, insects, and even an occasional dead rat.[21]

The situation had become intolerable, but what was to be done? The Chicago clerks were affiliated with the Knights of Labor, but the Knights were rapidly losing ground and would soon disappear from existence. The new union, UNAPOC, was too busy appeasing the Department to be of any help, and the Department itself was deaf to the entreaties of the clerks. Only the relatively new (1881) American Federation of Labor seemed to offer any possibility of meaningful external support.

The thought was a radical one for the time. If not government officials, at least the postal clerks were civil servants. Their organizations were associations, not trade unions. They sought no apprentice system nor mutual benefit schemes. They had no natural intercourse with blue collar craftsmen. The AFL itself was a conservative organization, but the image of unions to even more conservative government employees conjured up anarchism, Haymarket bombings, violent strikes and militant new organizations which would coalesce in 1905 as the Industrial Workers of the World (the Wobblies). There was an aura of socialism and unAmericanism associated with the union movement. If civil servants were to align themselves with the American Federation of Labor, many clerks believed that the Department would soon squelch such a radical movement and fire the employees involved. Affiliation with the AFL also might be illegal, but the Chicago clerks were desperate. Navy Yard workers, printers in the Government Printing Office and other groups of government workers were members of outside unions that were associated with the AFL, but they were craftsmen who only happened to apply their skills in government undertakings; they were not true civil servants.

A letter was written to Samuel Gompers, President of the AFL, asking whether the AFL would charter a federal union, and an affirmative reply was received. The AFL charter arrived on October 16, 1900; Federal Union 8703 was born. Its first President was John J. White, a bachelor who had no dependents. White volunteered for a job that nobody wanted, primarily because the president probably would be the first victim of Departmental retribution. Since most of the other leaders were married and did have dependents, John White felt that they should not put their jobs on the line.

What started in Chicago soon gathered momentum as dissident members in a number of cities broke with UNAPOC and formed AFL locals. In 1906, these unions united to form the National Federation of Post Office Clerks with a national charter from the AFL.

UNAPOC took the position that an employee association had to maintain good relations with the Post Office Department if gains were to be obtained for postal workers. The Federation was attacked by both UNAPOC and the Department as a radical group that belonged to a national organization which advocated strikes against the government. President Edward B. Goltra of the Federation responded that the organization was "in no sense antagonistic to the heads of departments or established rules," but, "if we cannot appeal to Congress in our own behalf, we must do so indirectly, and this we expect to do through the Legislative Committee of the American Federation of Labor and the various central bodies throughout the country."[22] Goltra was referring to the "gag rules," discussed in Chapter 5, which prohibited postal employees, either individually or through their associations, from petitioning Congress.

For fifty-four years the two organizations fought each other bitterly with UNAPOC gradually losing power and the National Federation emerging as the strongest agent of the postal clerks. Finally, in 1960, the two organizations merged and UNAPOC was pronounced officially "dead." The new organization, which barred supervisors from membership, was named the United Federation of Postal Clerks.

However, the National Federation had not been exempt from the factionalism which had characterized all of the organizing attempts of post office clerks. In 1958, two years before the merger, a split had occurred which would have far-reaching effects on postal unionism in general, and the eventual formation of the American Postal Workers Union.

Industrial Unionism in the Post Office

The Great Depression of the 1930s, the passage of the National Labor Relations Act, and the rise of the Congress of Industrial Organizations (CIO) are generally perceived as the key developments in the rise of labor union power in the private sector of the U.S. economy. Yet, they had little direct impact on public employee unionism. However, the Great Depression was to have a unique but long-delayed effect upon postal service unionism through the quality of individuals who entered the Postal Service during that decade of scarce opportunity.

The College Boys

John MacKay was a student at UCLA when he began his career as a substitute clerk at Los Angeles' Terminal Annex in 1936. MacKay clocked in at the night shift wearing a freshly-laundered white shirt, tie, neatly pressed slacks, and shoes that glistened. The foreman, who glared at MacKay in disbelief, assigned him to the parcel post table, surrounded by thousands of bulging sacks, dust so thick it could be tasted, and half a hundred men sweating and panting as they labored throughout the night. Eight hours later, he clocked out with a filthy white shirt, wrinkled trousers, and smudged shoes. Only his stoic expression was unchanged.[23]

The following night, MacKay reported immaculately dressed. Once again he was sent straight to the parcel post section. And so it went, night after night, until the foreman finally blinked and assigned him to another unit.

Twenty-two years later, John MacKay, a Marine veteran of World War II and the Korean War, still dressed in sartorial splendor, would lead 200 dissidents out of the convention of the National Federation of Post Office Clerks in Boston, a move that would eventually result in the formation of the Postal Service's first industrial union, the National Postal Union, and have a profound effect on the formation of the American Postal Workers Union thirteen years later.

MacKay was only one of thousands of bright, young men who entered the postal service in the 1930s. Phillip Seligman, a City College of New York student who entered the service in 1937, said that he scored 96 on the civil service exam and that there were 1124 ahead of him on the list.[24] That means that 1124 applicants in New York scored 97 or better. Teachers, lawyers, pharmacists, and other highly trained individuals, who could not find work in the depressed labor market, entered the Post Office and almost immediately encountered the hostility of supervisors who resented the "college boys." Moe Biller described his first day on the job:

I came on at 6:30 Saturday morning. Mr. Kelly was the station superintendent. Why he came in at that hour I don't know. He was a retired police captain, and he was a political guy ... The first thing we did was shape up. In other words, you hit an attendance card, indicating that you were there. That didn't put you to work. You didn't get paid for that. You got sixty-five cents an hour, no vacation, no sick leave. You were called a substitute. You could hit the attendance card, sit all day and have no work. Kelly called us over. There were twelve of us. In his New York, Irish accent, he said how many of you guys went to college. About five or six of us stepped out. He said, "You went to college, did you?" He was sarcastic, belligerent. "So, you went to college, ok, skin out them cases!" Later, I learned that he meant to sweep the mail out of the cases. We didn't know what he was talking about. So, we all looked at him. That's what he wanted. He set us up. "You went to college and you don't know how to skin a case? Ok, I'll get a stupid letter carrier in here and he'll teach you college boys how to skin out a case!" That was my orientation.[25]

The college boys entered the post office from all sections of the country and despite the antagonism of supervisors, postmasters, and their own union officers, they eventually would make their presence felt. Beside MacKay in Los Angeles and Biller in New York, there were David Silvergleid of Brooklyn, a man with a law degree who had passed the New York bar exam on his first try; Edwin Myers of Fresno, California, another Marine Corps veteran of World War II and the Korean War; Tedd Flanagan of New Jersey, who held an Accounting Certificate from Seton Hall College; James Murphy of Boston, a graduate of the Harvard Business School in Industrial Relations; John J. Pannell of Seattle; Don Johnson of Muskegon, Michigan, who flew twenty-five combat missions over Germany in World War II and later became the Mayor of Muskegon; Robert Kephart in Philadelphia, who stepped down from a supervisory position in order to become President of the Philadelphia local; Walter Noreen of St. Paul, the first postal employee ever to be elected President of the St. Paul Trade and Labor Assembly and, later, St. Paul Postmaster; Emil Dreher of Duluth; and a whole host of others, including Patrick Nilan, Emmet Andrews, Ephraim "Frank" Handman, Bernard Schwartz, Moe Kanner, Henry Berman, Otto Gottlieb, Joseph Ecker, Sidney Goodman, David Edelson, Phillip Seligman and Milton Rosner.

These were men of intelligence and ideas who in the mid-1940s would join together to form a group within the National Federation dedicated to the concepts of one big postal union and union democracy, reason enough for them to become known as the "Progressive Feds," named after Senator Robert M. LaFollette, Jr. of Wisconsin who called himself a "Progressive" and was the author of a bill liberating postal workers from the "gag rules" promulgated by Presidents Theodore Roosevelt and William Howard Taft.

McCarthy Era Repression

As the most militant group within the National Federation, inevitably the college boys became targets for the "Red hunters" of the period. In 1950, two officers of the New York local, including its President, Frank Handman, were suspended from the postal service on loyalty charges. The suspensions occurred under the Truman Executive Order relating to the Internal Security Act of 1950 that stipulated "reasonable doubt" as to the loyalty of a government employee was grounds for dismissal. After hearings, both officers were reinstated, meaning that reasonable doubt could not be proved.

Under Eisenhower, however, the reasonable doubt clause of the Executive Order was changed so that "reasonable grounds" for determining the disloyalty of a government employee was cause for dismissal. This language made it a good deal easier to discharge employees on the basis of personal associations, and, hence, the phrases "guilt by association" and "fellow traveler" became part of the American lexicon. The Internal Security Act, itself, was expressly made applicable only to the Departments of State, Commerce, Justice, Defense, Army, Navy, Air Force, Coast Guard, Atomic Energy Commission, National Security Resources Board, and the National Advisory Committee for Aeronautics. However, the Act also provided that it could be extended "to such other departments and agencies of the Government as the President may, from time to time, deem necessary in the best interests of national security."[26] Although the latter clause appeared to mean other departments and agencies that become involved in national security matters, President Eisenhower extended the Act "to *all* (emphasis added) other departments and agencies of the Government."[27] This made possible a governmentwide search for security risks, and union officers who had a tendency to rock the boat were fair game.

At the 1954 convention of the National Federation in Cincinnati, a former President of the New York local, Patrick Fitzgerald, let it be known that the officers of Local 10 (the New York local) would have security charges brought against them when they returned to New York. Fitzgerald was "cockeyed drunk"[28] when he made the statement to Walter Noreen and others. But, as it turned out, Fitzgerald knew what he was talking about because he was the prime mover in the whole affair and would be the key witness against the New York officers.

The actual suspensions did not occur until December 1955, when Handman and Biller were called to the New York Postmaster's office and informed of their suspensions on loyalty charges. The Postmaster, Robert Shaffer, was embarrassed and apologetic, but said that the suspension orders came down from Postmaster General Summerfield's office and that there was nothing he could do about it. The six officers were Frank Handman, Moe Biller, Sidney Goodman, David Edelson, Joseph Ecker, and Henry Berman. Three other members of the union, Irving Weingarten, Nathan Weisbard, and John Nicholas, were also suspended.

Patrick Fitzgerald had been President of the New York local for four years (1949–1952) and according to one of the men he accused, Moe Biller, he was a "good president."[29] He was defeated in 1953 and blamed his defeat on a coalition of officers, headed by Frank Handman. In retrospect it seems implausible that the Department would bring charges against the New York officers solely on the basis of the testimony of a man with his own axe to grind. But it was a period when the Internal Security Act was often used both vengefully and as a weapon against "troublemakers."

Postmaster General Arthur Summerfield was known as the nation's largest and richest used car dealer. The six union officers were mere postal clerks, but as union officers they had led a bitter fight against an administration Postal Reclassification Act, a bill that Summerfield very much wanted passed into law. E. C. Hallbeck, the Federation's Legislative Director, was in favor of the bill, but the progressives and some independents not only opposed the legislation, but also fought Federation endorsement of the bill. The New Yorkers organized a national rally that forced Hallbeck to back down. Later, the bill was amended (against the wishes of Summerfield) and passed into law just prior to the suspension of the New Yorkers. It is not surprising that they interpreted the Departmental action as retribution for anti-Department activities.

The six officers asked for and received hearings before an Internal Security Board. A review of the transcript of the Biller hearing reveals a nervous Fitzgerald constantly contradicting himself, a reluctant government witness who ended up weakening the government's case, and strong refutations by Biller of all the charges made against him.[30] Still, the hearing examiners could often put a witness into a no-win situation. Toward the end of the hearing, one of the examiners asked the following question: "Mr. Biller, do you know Julius and Ethel Rosenberg?" The Rosenbergs had been executed in 1953 for allegedly turning over nuclear secrets to the USSR. Biller said his heart skipped a beat when he heard that question, because he, along with hundreds of other people, lived in the same apartment building as the Rosenbergs. Did he know them? No, he didn't know the Rosenbergs, but he knew what the next question would be: "Isn't it true that you live in the same apartment building as the Rosenbergs?" And, of course, the respondent would stumble all over himself explaining that hundreds of people live in the apartment building and that not everybody who lives in the building knows everybody else, etc. But, the eyes of the examiner would remain skeptical. With all of the apartments and residents of New York City, that was an unlucky coincidence. After all, the witness's loyalty was being questioned, wasn't it?

On June 16, 1956, six months after their suspensions, the nine New Yorkers were reinstated, persuant to a Supreme Court decision concerning the application of security regulations to federal employees in nonsensitive positions. The Court concluded that the Eisenhower Executive Order had gone beyond the intent of the law when it included all departments and positions in the federal service within the scope of the security regulations. It declared that an employee in a nonsensitive position in a government department not specifically mentioned in the 1950 Act could not be removed under the security regulations.[31]

But for Frank Handman, too much was enough. Shortly after the Supreme Court decision, Handman, who had gone through the loyalty ordeal twice, resigned from the Postal Service. He had been a top officer of the New York local and the National Federation for fifteen years. He was the only member of the progressives to be elected an officer of the Federation prior to 1958 when Patrick J. Nilan, another progressive, was elected Vice President. Both the Post Office and the union lost a brilliant leader when Handman called it quits.

Later, after the reinstatement of the six New York officers, Senator Everett Dirksen of Illinois stood up on the floor of the Senate and read into the record an unsigned document alleging that the leadership of the National Postal Clerks Union is "composed of extreme left-wing elements."[32] The NPCU responded with a pamphlet entitled "These Are

The Men" refuting what was termed "unsigned libel."[33] Now, thirty years later, most people look back on the McCarthyite witch hunts as farcical aberrations; but for those who were singled out for repressive punishment, disloyalty charges were a very serious matter.

An ironic ending to the entire loyalty episode occurred in the early 1970s. While on a trip to Washington, Moe Biller, then President of the New York local, received a call from his Secretary-Treasurer, Milt Rosner. Rosner said that there was a young man in the office, a Sergeant in the Army, who claimed to be Patrick Fitzgerald's son. The son informed Rosner that his father had died and wondered whether the union would contribute to the funeral. Rosner, who had not been charged with disloyalty, but who knew how much the charges disrupted Biller's life, suggested that he refuse the son. "No," said Biller, "Fitzgerald was a member of this union for many years and its President for four years. Tell the kid we will contribute."[34] That put a period to the whole security episode.

The Progressive Feds

Edward B. Goltra, the first President of the National Federation of Post Office Clerks said in 1908: "...the new-born Federation—formed by the larger cities—wisely decided to limit the voting strength of the larger cities."[35] Fifty years later, J. Cline House, then President of the National Federation, used this quote to justify the union's basis for representation at national conventions. House, a resident of Oklahoma, nicknamed "The Wooden Indian," succeeded Leo George who had led the union with an iron hand for thirty-three years.

Goltra's reasoning may have been valid in 1908 when there were few small locals, but in 1958 when there were enough small locals to offset the strength of the big locals, the situation was reversed and a big city movement began to change the rules. After more than fifty years of relatively conservative leadership, however, a power structure had been created which fought all attempts at reform. This led to the formation of a group within the union, made up of the "college boys" and others, who called themselves the "Progressive Feds," published their own national and local newspapers, and engaged in pitched battles against the union leadership.

Philosophically, the Progressive Feds favored industrial over craft unionism and were unalterably opposed to dual black and white locals which still existed in some areas of the country, including the nation's capital. But their immediate goal was to create a more democratic union. Under the rules that existed in the 1950s, national officers were elected by the delegates to national conventions, but no one local could have more than ten votes. This meant that eleven small locals with only three members each, or a total of thirty-three members, could outvote the New York local with ten thousand members. The sixteen members of the Executive Board, each of whom had one vote, could also outvote the largest local in the country. District vice presidents did not have to reside in the areas they represented; thus, the district vice president for New England might very well reside in Florida or Arizona. These rules made it difficult for national officers to be elected from the big cities, or for the concerns of the progressives to receive any consideration at national conventions. They were rules designed to maintain the status quo—to keep the machine in power.

Formed in 1946, under the Chairmanship of John MacKay, the Progressives strove for twelve years to gain concessions from the union leadership. Specifically, their program called for:

1. Selection of officers by referendum ballot mailed to the homes of union members;
2. Proportional representation at national conventions;
3. District vice presidents to be selected from members who reside in the districts;
4. Elimination of dual black and white unions; and
5. The promotion of one big postal union.

At every convention, from 1948 to 1958, the Progressives tried mightily to push their program, but they were up against a system that was stacked against them; they could not win even a single concession. As the 1958 convention approached, a meeting was held in Washington, D.C. between President House, Secretary-Treasurer John Bowen, and two Progressive leaders, John MacKay and James Murphy. House and Bowen listened, but made no comments on the MacKay-Murphy proposals. Later in the week, four Progressives met with Francis S. Filbey, the President of the Baltimore local and a supporter of the administration. Filbey, who often was referred to as "House's waterboy," was playing the role of mediator between the Progressives and the union hierarchy. Filbey listened sympathetically to the proposals and agreed to discuss them with the NFPOC resident officers. Later, he reported back to MacKay and Murphy that "he could get nowhere." This prompted MacKay to issue the following statement:

> It is now quite apparent that our national officers are not willing to meet us even half-way on any suggestion for the good of the Federation. Considering that it was President House himself, who almost two years ago made an appeal in the Union Postal Clerk entitled, "Come, let us reason together," in which he claimed there were no differences between us that could not be talked over and straightened out, I leave to our members the responsibility of confirming the irony and futility of trying to reason with our national officers.[36]

The stage was now set for the Thirtieth Convention of the National Federation of Post Office Clerks which would be held in Boston, August 25–30, 1958.

The Boston Tea Party

The cry was "taxation without representation" and the walkout by the Progressive Feds from the 30th Convention of the National Federation was termed "The Boston Tea Party." The progressives, led by John MacKay, David Silvergleid, James Murphy, Tedd Flanagan, and Walter Noreen, made one last attempt to gain concessions from the administration, but they suffered one defeat after another and were constantly ridiculed and jeered by the majority who classified themselves as the "Independent Caucus." Herman R. Berlowe, then President of the Arizona State Federation and, later, Postmaster of Tucson, wrote: "Twelve years of frustration, twelve years of bitter, costly efforts to democratize the Federation, to ignite the spark of true trade unionism, had culminated in a solid week of cruelly, arbitrary rulings from the chair and lack of achievement from the convention floor. So, the bubble burst. It had to. How long could it go on?"[37]

Two of the convention's major issues were a raise in the per-capita tax and an increase in salaries for the Federation's officers, both of which were opposed by the Progressives unless changes were made in the union's basis for representation at national conventions. John MacKay rose and told the delegates that it would be a "great pleasure" for him to support a pay raise for his officers, but that he would oppose such a resolution "as long as you deny our members the right to vote." Then, he made clear the intention of the Progressives: "You may be interested to know that today a delegation of members of this organization met, constituting over one-third of the delegates to this convention, and they went on record to consider the withholding of further per-capita tax until they have had a chance to reevaluate the value of their continued affiliation with the Federation." He concluded:

> Now, my friends, this is the day of decision. This is the day of reckoning. Our members, each and every one of them that pay their dues, expect to have the right to vote on their Local Officers and they have come to realize that it is time that they have the right to vote on their National Officers and, until they get their democratic rights, they will oppose any increase in salaries for National Officers, any increase in the National per-capita tax, and any of the other resolutions that are being made to perpetuate the leadership in the Federation as it exists today.[38]

Federation President J. Cline House struck back. "I have never played in a game," he said, "where I took the attitude if I couldn't announce the rules of the game that I would pick up my marbles and go home." Referring to union dues and local representation, he said:

> Much has been said about taxation without representation. In my home town in Oklahoma, I have a good friend and neighbor who is a multi-millionaire who pays more than a half million dollars in taxes each month. I pay a very small amount. Yet, in all the years I have known that good neighbor of mine, he has cast one vote in the ballot box and I have cast one...I have never heard him complain about taxation without representation.[39]

The Progressives were not impressed. They had played the game for twelve years according to the administration's rules and were never successful in gaining concessions which would give them at least an equal chance to "win." The comparison of one Oklahoma multimillionaire to 10,000 members of a local union was not persuasive. Thus, at the Saturday, August 30, morning session, John MacKay rose for the purpose of making an announcement:

> We wish to announce that there will be a meeting of the supporting Locals of the National Progressive Federation Committee...and at this time we regret to announce since we feel we have completed our assignment and have attended to everything to preserve democratic ideals and operation in the National Federation of Post Office Clerks, that supporting Locals of this National Progressive Federation Committee discontinue in any further participation in this convention....[40]

MacKay then led two hundred delegates out of the hall, one-third of all the convention's delegates, and, as it eventually turned out, out of the National Federation of Post Office Clerks. The Federation responded immediately. First, a committee was named to meet with the Progressives and urge them to return to the convention floor. But the committee had no authority to offer the Progressives a single concession, so the walkout continued. The battle lines were then drawn. A constitutional amendment was introduced by Francis S. Filbey who acted as the floor whip for the administration throughout the entire convention:

> No local affiliated with this National Federation can dissolve, disaffiliate or secede while three (3) or more members desire to continue the local in existence, and all funds, assets and properties, real and personal, of the local remain in the local as long as it continues in existence. In the event of the complete dissolution of any local or its disaffiliation or secession by unanimous vote, all the funds, assets and properties, real and personal, of the local shall revert to the National Federation to be held in trust for the purpose of forming a new local.[41]

The motion was passed by standing vote. John MacKay's "day of reckoning" had indeed arrived.

The National Postal Union

The Progressives met in New York one week after the convention and served notice that unless measures were taken by January 1, 1959 to correct the system of representation at national conventions, Progressive-Fed locals would leave the National Federation of Post Office Clerks. The decision was qualified, however, by possibilities that either the AFL-CIO or an "arbitration" committee, headed by President William Cady of Local 67, Kansas City, Missouri, might avert the split. A protest against the "undemocratic" system of convention representation was filed with the Ethical Practices Committee of the AFL-CIO.

In October, however, President House rebuffed Cady, saying that he didn't believe anything would be gained by meeting with the Progressives. He added that he would "wait and see what they would do." No response was received from the AFL-CIO Ethical Practices Committee. At that point, the Staten Island, New York local seceded from the Federation and House responded by suspending the officers of the local and placing the union under the trusteeship of a member, Louis J. Isola. On November 18, Walter Noreen's St. Paul local followed suit.

The Progressives were still reluctant to secede en masse. At a November meeting in Philadelphia, they deferred any withdrawals from the Federation until at least February 15, 1959, so as to permit further exploratory peace overtures. Nine days later, House suspended eight Progressive-Fed locals, including New York, Philadelphia, Brooklyn, Boston, Los Angeles, Detroit, Minneapolis, and Newark. The Minneapolis local, headed by Patrick J. Nilan, was reinstated after Nilan, once a leader of the Progressives, was elected Vice President of the Federation at the Boston convention and dropped out of the Progressive movement. Nilan claims that the Minneapolis local was the only Progressive local that was given the opportunity to vote on whether to secede or remain in the Federation. The members elected not to secede. Nilan was reelected Vice President in 1960 and 1962, and in 1964, he was elected Legislative Representative, a post he held with the APWU until his retirement in April 1992.

All of the suspended locals immediately set about creating their own independent unions and in February 1959 they joined together to form the National Postal Clerks Union. At the new union's first convention, held in Washington, D.C. in April 1959, officers were nominated and a constitution drafted. The constitution called for elections by referendum, proportional representation at national conventions, the elimination of all forms of discrimination (including dual locals), and the election of district representatives from members who were residents of the districts to be represented. John MacKay became the first President and David Silvergleid was elected Secretary-Treasurer.

The word "Clerks" in the name of the new union belied the intent of its founders to be an industrial union, a union enrolling all post office occupations. Moe Biller, who became President of the newly formed Manhattan-Bronx Postal Clerks Union in 1959, entered into discussions with Philip Lepper, President of Branch 36 of the Letter Carriers, at Lepper's request, about the possibility of MBPCU members becoming associate members of Branch 36. An inducement to the MBPCU for establishing that relationship was eligibility in the Letter Carrier's health plan—a participant in the newly enacted Federal Employees Health Benefits Program (FEHBP). (The FEHBP authorized the government to pay 40 percent and, later, 60 percent of health insurance costs.) However, Biller placed higher priority on the formation of a single postal union in New York than on the health plan, and decided against the move. He wasn't foregoing much. His local already had a health plan and a credit union, both of which the Federation tried unsuccessfully to take over, in fact, after the break. His discussions with Lepper finally ended in an agreement that the MBPCU would not "raid" the Letter Carriers, but would attempt to organize all other postal occupations.

However, in order for the MBPCU health plan to be eligible for participation in the FEHBP, it had to be national in scope. The National Postal Clerks Union did not have a health plan, though the New York local did. It was for that reason Lepper had offered associate membership to the MBPCU. Instead, the members of the MBPCU local hospital plan turned over $60,000 in their equity to the National Postal Clerks Union to enable the NPCU to begin a national plan, and therefore be recognized by the Civil Service Commission under the FEHBP. That completed, Biller wired John MacKay and David Silvergleid that henceforth the Manhattan-Bronx Postal Clerks Union would drop the "Clerks" and be known as the Manhattan Bronx Postal Union. The National followed suit and, in 1960, the National Postal Union became industrial by declared ambition if not yet by membership.

Meanwhile, the defection of the Progressive Feds cost the National Federation approximately 25,632 members and $154 thousand in annual per-capita tax. Eventually, the National Postal Union grew to 80,000 members; thus, the per-capita tax loss grew proportionately. The merger with UNAPOC in 1960 helped the Federation overcome both the loss of membership and the consequent per-capita tax.

From Eight Unions to Four

In addition to the National Postal Union and the United Federation of Post Office Clerks, the three smaller unions that merged to form the APWU in 1971 were the National Association of Post Office and General Services Maintenance Employees, the National Federation of Motor Vehicle Employees, and the National Association of Special Delivery Messengers. The Maintenance Employees Association was formed in 1947 as the result of a merger between the National Association of Mechanics and the National Association of Custodial Employees. The Special Delivery Messengers received a charter from the AFL in 1937. The Motor Vehicle Federation, originally called the National Association of Chauffeurs and Mechanics, was founded in 1924. All three would maintain separate craft divisions within the APWU.

The Railway Mail Association, later renamed the Postal Transport Association, eventually joined the National Federation when the railway mail service was discontinued in the 1950s. One of the most conservative of postal unions, the RMA was primarily responsible for the formation of the National Alliance of Post Office and Federal Employees in 1913. The Alliance, an industrial union made up primarily of black federal employees, was established because blacks were barred from RMA membership. The majority of its members are postal workers, and its membership cuts across craft lines. Not recognized as a bargaining agent by the Postal Service, the prime function of the Alliance is to serve as a civil rights watchdog for minority employees.

But, despite all the restructuring and merging, one big postal union was still a dream. Once, in the 1950s, the Letter Carriers passed a resolution calling for one postal union, but at the time, the Clerks Federation was not interested. Later, it was the Letter Carriers who resisted amalgamation. The formation of the National Postal Union gave impetus to the industrial union concept, and the merger of 1971 greatly reduced the union fragmentation that previously existed. In 1991, four unions are officially recognized by the U.S. Postal Service: the American Postal Workers Union, the National Association of Letter Carriers, the National Association of Post Office Mail Handlers, and the Rural Letter Carriers Association. The APWU and the NALC account for over 80 percent of all postal workers and bargain jointly with the U.S. Postal Service.

*　*　*

At this writing, a full century has passed since the formation of the National Association of Letter Carriers in 1889—one-hundred years of agitation and struggle, of intra- and interunion struggle and confrontation with the postal authorities, the arm of the federal sovereign. But the organizing efforts of postal employees tell only half the story. The attempts by the sovereign to break, control, or gag postal unions is the subject of Chapter 5. The one hundred years of history thus far summarized is unique in that it concerns the unionization of federal employees engaged in an industrial enterprise, and, as such, is quite different from similar efforts in the private sector.

The importance of the Progressive-Fed movement within the National Federation of Post Office Clerks and the eventual formation of the National Postal Union in bringing about the merger which created the APWU cannot be underestimated. The democratic constitution adopted by the merged American Postal Workers Union in 1971 was based on the constitution adopted by the National Postal Union in 1959, and in 1980, ten years after the merger, the top officers of the APWU were all drawn from the ranks of the NPU. The emphasis on industrial unionism and the elimination of racial discrimination were important contributions of the Progressive-Feds and the NPU.

Finally, the strike of 1970 which brought about dramatic improvements in the wages and working conditions of postal workers could not have succeeded without the participation of the NPU. Although the New York Letter Carriers triggered the strike by being the first to walk out, at the height of the strike, 48 percent of the men and women who walked off the job were clerks, and of this figure, the vast majority were members of NPU locals. Only 38 percent were Letter Carriers, and an additional 14 percent were employees from other crafts, many of whom were also members of the NPU.[42] Thus, the NPU played a key role not only in bringing about the merger which formed the American Postal Workers Union in 1971, but also in influencing the creation of a "truly democratic and modern" constitution.

Chapter 5

FROM REPRESSION TO COOPERATION

The postal unions, from their formation in the late 1800s, suffered some basic disabilities shared by all public sector unions of the time. They had very little bargaining power and few areas where pressure could be applied to the United States Post Office Department. Their sole recourse was to the Congress which established the rules governing postal employment, including wages, hours, fringe benefits, and working conditions. They were hampered by restrictive rules governing political activity, could not bargain collectively with the Department, and did not have the right to strike. The philosophy of government upon which these restrictive policies were based was stated succinctly by Spero in 1927:

> The feeling [is] that those who earn their living in the service of the state owe their governmental employer a special obligation of loyalty and a peculiar duty of obedience different and distinct from the obligations of ordinary wage earners to their employers, which make it improper to agitate their grievances by methods generally approved for others.[1]

The view that government workers are not entitled to rights granted to workers in the private sector is based on the concept of "sovereignty" handed down through the centuries from the feudal system's "divine right of kings." When postal workers first tried to organize, they were confronted by a deep hostility that was rooted in the philosophy that government, as an employer, had special immunity. Employees of government were expected to devote themselves with utter loyalty to their "sovereign."[2] This made attempts at organizing among postal workers particularly difficult. And any attempts by unions to agitate (much less achieve) amelioration of the intolerable working conditions met with formidable repression. To counter this, antirepression measures were introduced in the Congress and one such measure, the Lloyd-LaFollette bill, was passed into law. From that point on, labor relations in the post office depended to a great extent on each successive Administration's emphasis on "service" or "surplus," that is, whether the post office was primarily a government service that should, at best, break even, or whether it was a profitable enterprise that should return a surplus to the Treasury. Although the latter question was never fully resolved, the repression of the early years gradually gave way to more enlightened views of federal labor-management relations, leading eventually to the era of Employee-Management Cooperation in the Kennedy Administration. The latter lasted until the strike of 1970. Then began the era of collective bargaining.

The Case for Sovereignty

In April 1920, Senator Myers of Montana, in a speech urging the passage of an Act which would forbid federal employees from affiliating with the AFL, said:

> I claim that employees who work for the Federal Government are analogous to soldiers in the army. They should owe their entire allegiance and loyalty and affiliation to the Government for which they work. They should not enter into any movement of affiliation or association which might put them into an attitude of antagonism to the Government for which they work, because the general welfare is at stake, the welfare of the entire body politic, of the entire people, of the Government itself is at stake, and I do not believe that any Federal employee should be permitted innocently or otherwise, to join any association or affiliation which might by any chance lead him, in association with others, to take a position or a stand which might be antagonistic to the true interest of the government which

employs him, feeds him, and upon which we are all dependent for our peace, tranquility, and welfare.[3]

The soldier analogy was put forth even more forcefully by President Nicholas Murray Butler of Columbia University. Commenting on a strike by French postal workers in 1909, he said:

In my judgement the fundamental issue is perfectly clear. Servants of the State in any capacity—military, naval or civil—are in our Government there by their own choice and not of necessity. Their sole obligation is to the State and its interests. There is no analogy between a servant or employee of the State on the one hand, and the laborer and private or corporate capitalist on the other...In my judgement loyalty and treason ought to mean the same thing in the civil service as they do in the military or naval services...Indeed, I am not sure that as civilization progresses, loyalty and treason in the civil services will not become more important than loyalty and treason in the military and naval services. The happiness of the community might be more easily wrecked by the paralysis of its postal and telegraph services, for example, than by a mutiny on shipboard...To me the situation which this problem presents is, beyond comparison, the most serious which modern democracies have to face. It will become more insistent and more difficult as Government activities multiply and as the number of civil service employees increases. Now is the time to settle right principles once and for all.[4]

If the concept of sovereignty still largely prevailed near the end of the twentieth century, it was unchallenged at the century's beginning. No distinction was made between "the government as the instrument of public authority and government as employer of its civil servants."[5] Federal workers accepted as a given that they were denied certain rights granted to workers in the private sector, including the right to strike and the right to engage in partisan political activities. However, they did believe that they had the right to petition Congress, as a class, regarding their own wages and working conditions. The government's position, on the other hand, was that the employee organizations should be free to function only under the supervision of the administration. In 1912, Second Assistant Postmaster General Joseph Stewart put it this way:

> The executive branch is responsible for the conduct of the service under the laws and conditions as they may exist. The regular, proper, and orderly procedure with respect to recommendations emanating from the executive branch concerning the service is that they should be suggested by the officers in charge of the service and transmitted to Congress by the executive or head of the department...The necessary corollary to this proposition is that Federal employees who are not charged with the direct responsibility for the service should volunteer representation or statements to the Congress only through the head of their department, *and this applies to organizations of Federal employees as well as to the employees individually* (emphasis added).[6]

Some seventeen years prior to the Stewart statement, President Cleveland's Postmaster General, William L. Wilson, issued the first order designed to restrict employee activities in their own behalf:

> That hereafter no Postmaster, Post-Office Clerk, Letter Carrier, Railway Postal Clerk, or other postal employee, shall visit Washington, whether on leave with or without pay, for the purpose of influencing legislation before Congress.
>
> Any such employee of the Postal Service who violates this order shall be liable to removal.
>
> Postmasters and other employees of the Postal Service are paid by the Government for attending to the respective duties assigned to them, which do not include efforts to secure legislation. That duty is assigned to the representatives of the people elected for that purpose.
>
> If bills are introduced in either branch of Congress affecting the Postal Service, upon which any information or recommendation is desired, I am ready at all times to submit such as lies in my power and province.[7]

The rule was never very effectively enforced and soon came to be ignored completely, but it did set a precedent which would be applied later, not only to individuals, but also to employee associations.

A Decade of Gag Orders

The gag orders were the result of an intensive 1901 lobbying campaign by both the Letter Carriers and the Clerks—an effort that backfired and led to a decade of repression. The major bill under consideration concerned reclassification and automatic promotions which were firmly opposed by Representative Eugene F. Loud of California, Chairman of the House Committee on Post Office and Roads. The campaign included letters, telegrams, and petitions to President Theodore Roosevelt. Roosevelt's response was to issue an Executive Order on January 2, 1903, which became known as the first "gag order":

> All officers and employees of the United States of every description, serving in or under any of the executive departments, and whether so serving in or out of Washington, are hereby forbidden, individually or through associations, to solicit an increase of pay or to influence or attempt to influence in their own interest any other legislation whatever, either before Congress or its Committees, or in any way save through the heads of the Departments in or under which they serve, on penalty of dismissal from the Government service.[8]

Organized opposition to the Roosevelt gag order began with the formation of the National Federation of Post Office Clerks which was affiliated with the AFL. If the gag order prevented the Clerks from petitioning Congress either individually or as an association, their grievances could be presented through legislative committees of the AFL. Thus, the formation of the Federation "had a profound effect on the whole future history of the organized movement among public employees. It definitely lined up the official labor movement with the government worker, and it stood as an example and invitation to other public employees to line themselves up with labor."[9] Moreover, the battle against the gag order had the full support of the AFL. In 1906 the Federation presented to the President and the Congress a document called "Labor's Bill of Grievances," that included a statement to the effect that as long as the gag order stood, "the constitutional right of citizens to petition must be surrendered by the government employee in order to retain his employment."[10]

However, the AFL Bill of Grievances had little effect on the President. In that same year, because his gag order had not always been obeyed by postal workers or enforced vigorously by the Department, President Roosevelt issued a revised and strengthened order:

> All officers and employees of the United States of every description, serving in or under any of the executive departments or independent Government establishments, and whether so serving in or out of Washington, are hereby forbidden, either directly or indirectly, individually or through associations, to solicit an increase of pay or to influence or attempt to influence in their own interest any other legislation whatever, either before Congress or its Committees, or in any way save through the heads of Departments or individual Government establishments, in or under which they serve, on penalty of dismissal from the Government service.[11]

Prior to issuing his revised order, President Roosevelt changed the Civil Service rules to permit the President or any Department to dismiss employees without notice.[12] The sovereign had spoken and had made his intentions perfectly clear.

President William Howard Taft, who succeeded Theodore Roosevelt, went even further. His Order prohibited federal employees from answering Congressional requests for information:

> It is hereby ordered that no bureau, office, or division chief, or subordinate in any part of the Government, and no officer of the army, navy or marine corps stationed in Washington, shall apply to either House of Congress, or to any members of Congress, for legislation, or for appropriations, or for Congressional action of any kind, except with the consent and knowledge of the head of the department; *nor shall any such person respond to any request for information from either House of Congress, except through, or as authorized by, the head of his department* (emphasis added).[13]

The Taft Order, which added very little to the Roosevelt rule, only served to increase the discontent of postal workers, and even irritated some members of Congress who looked upon the order as an unnecessary and possibly illegal attempt to interfere with the business of Congress.[14]

The Lloyd-LaFollette Act

The unrest caused by the gag orders was most severe in the railway mail service. Standards of safety and sanitation had declined to a scandalous state. When attempts were made to call these conditions to the attention of the public, the Department issued what became known as the "Wreck Gag," forbidding employees from making any public comments on accidents, or to say anything which might disturb the Department's "respectful relations with the railroads."[15] The Department also fired the editor of the Bundy Post Office Recorder, a paper published by the Seattle local of the National Federation of Post Office Clerks, that questioned the legality of the gag order and other civil service regulations tending to limit the political freedom of federal employees. Then, in 1910, Postmaster General Frank Hitchcock, acting on suggestions made by President Taft's efficiency commission, issued "take up the slack orders" in the railway mail service. Work was speeded up, routes combined, layover periods reduced, crews cut, and the filling of vacancies forbidden—all on the eve of the Christmas rush. Spero describes what happened next:

> The slack order was the last straw. The morale of the force and its prided efficiency went to pieces. Conservative, hard working, and loyal clerks who used to boast that they "never went stuck" (failed to finish their distribution) now openly grumbled that they didn't care whether they "cleaned up" or not. Tons of Christmas mail remained unworked for days at a time. Some of this had to be carried back and forth on the "stuck lines" until the crews could find time to work it. Thousands of sacks were transferred to cars sidetracked for the purpose to be worked by men called from their rest periods. In the Northwest where the situation was especially bad, anywhere from 10 to 160 sacks per train of unworked mail would come into the terminals....[16]

There were acts of blatant insubordination within the Tracy (Minnesota)-Pierre (South Dakota) Railway Post Office, and threats of mass resignations in St. Paul, Minneapolis, and in South Dakota.

The Harpoon

The gag orders, of course, were not totally enforceable; there was no way to stop postal workers from talking to their congressman, if not in Washington, at least in their home towns. But they were effective in preventing postal workers and their unions from publicizing postal conditions through the media. Occasional stories appeared in the newspapers, such as the story about conditions in the Chicago post office, but for the most part the public remained uninformed about intolerable working conditions in the Postal Service. All this would change with the emergence of a small magazine, Harpoon, edited by a former railway mail clerk, Urban A. Walter. Walter contracted tuberculosis and was forced to quit work and move to Phoenix, Arizona. He had been on unpaid leave from the Department for eight months when he sent the following letter to Postmaster General Hitchcock:

> Please find enclosed, under registered mail, an advance copy of the first issue of the Harpoon. Permit me to say that it will be well worth your while to carefully peruse this issue. I wish especially that you would study the cartoon, and also read the opposite page, entitled "Silenced." Don't forget to read the article entitled "Tank and Can" and, if there be any libel in any of the articles contained in this issue, I trust that you will not neglect to take the matter up at once.[17]

The Department's reaction to the letter was an order informing Walter that his resignation (which he had never submitted) was accepted.

Harpoon advertised itself as "A Magazine that Hurts" and emblazoned across its inner title page was a headline "Strike? NO!—Publicity? YES!" Its method was sensational and feisty, but underneath it all, highly intelligent. It published pictures of train wrecks with crushed mail cars and dead clerks, the unsanitary conditions existing on railway mail cars, and stacks of unprocessed mail that resulted from the "take up the slack" orders. Underneath all the sensationalism, however, was its announced purpose to "kill the gag orders." From its first issue, its circulation grew to 200,000, and among its subscribers were some of the nation's leading newspapers.

The effect of Walter's efforts was truly amazing. He aroused the bureaucracy in a way it had never been aroused before. He shook up the super-respectful Railway Mail Association and eventually caused a break within that organization and the formation of the progressive Brotherhood of Railway Postal Clerks. Most important, he got the news of the conditions affecting the postal service out to the general public and the Congress. "In its third month, [Harpoon] received more than 1,000 favorable newspaper notices. At the height of the anti-gag fight, it had 12,000 Railway Mail Service subscribers and another 12,000 outside the service."[18] Eventually the "take up the slack" order was modified and a bill was passed by Congress in 1911 which specified that railway mail cars must be sound in construction and equipped with sanitary drinking water containers and toilet facilities.

Congress Acts

The stage was now set for the fight against the gag orders. Republican Senator Robert M. LaFollette, Jr. of Wisconsin conducted his own investigation into the antilabor activities of the Department. He sent a letter to every railway postal clerk in the country. In his letter, Senator LaFollette stated:

I desire to secure direct statements from railway postal clerks as to whether, in any way, they have been...threatened or intimidated. If you have been approached and an effort made to prevent you from joining or to force you to withdraw from a union or to cease your activities as a union man, state fully the circumstances...

The railway mail clerks have the right to organize. If the officers of the Department are endeavoring to prevent them from so doing by threats of discharge, such action is without legal authority or moral right. If I find conditions in the railway postal service to be generally such as have been represented, I shall introduce and do everything in my power to pass a bill to prevent the continuation of such unAmerican practices and to preserve to all government employees the right of petition which belongs to every citizen, and the right to form or join labor organizations for the improvement of their conditions...

Your answer will be held confidential except as to the facts stated, as it is my purpose merely to collect the information and present it to Congress without disclosing the names or any circumstances which would lead to the identification of my informants.[19]

Despite Taft's Order precluding government employees from responding to requests for information from Congress, the Senator received thousands of replies which indicated, he said, that conditions in the Railway Mail Service "were probably more arbitrary than in any other branch of the civil service." He also charged that letters addressed to him were opened in violation of postal laws, and that he "was subjected to an espionage almost Russian in character."[20]

Despite united opposition from the White House, the Post Office Department and the National Association of Manufacturers, a milestone bill, the Lloyd-LaFollette Act, was passed by Congress on August 24, 1912. It guaranteed postal workers the right to join associations which did not obligate them to engage in strikes, and the right of postal workers, either individually or collectively, to petition Congress. Samuel Gompers, President of the AFL, participated in the drafting of the bill, especially the clause which guaranteed postal workers the right to join outside associations as long as the associations did not obligate them to engage in strikes. The Lloyd-LaFollette Act ushered in a new era of postal labor-management relations, and served as the legal underpinning of that relationship for half a century, until the Kennedy Executive Order of 1962.

The Burleson Years

The passage of a law, however, is one thing; enforcement of the law is quite another. Six months after the passage of the Lloyd-LaFollette Act, President Woodrow Wilson appointed Albert B. Burleson Postmaster General of the United States. Rather than reverse the Department's traditional antilabor policy, Burleson took it several steps further. Burleson's sole purpose was to cut costs as much as possible, not merely to make the service self-sustaining, but to yield a surplus that could be turned back into the Treasury. His attitude toward his employees was colored by this policy, and his attitude toward employee associations was downright hostile. He waged a relentless war against postal unions, refusing to meet with their leaders or even acknowledge their right to exist.

An archconservative from Texas in an Administration that generally was considered liberal, Burleson attacked postal labor legislation enacted as the result of the gag fight. He reduced salaries, opposed employee efforts to win pay increases to meet rising wartime prices ("they are receiving three times as much as those fighting in the trenches"), attacked affiliation with the AFL, and demanded immediate repeal of the Lloyd-LaFollette Act. One of his most misdirected acts was to remove all of the national officers of the postal unions (with the exception of the company union, UNAPOC) from their jobs. Far from weakening the organizations, this move actually strengthened them by forcing the unions to employ their officers on a full-time basis, thus removing them from the authority of the Department and allowing them to devote full-time to union business. Though delaying the expected benefits of the Lloyd-LaFollette legislation, the long-run impact of Burleson's actions was to strengthen postal unions and increase union militancy.

When Burleson left office in 1921, the Union Postal Worker, official publication of the National Federation of Post Office Clerks, ran his picture over the following:

A citizen of Austin—Mr. Burleson of Austin, Texas Who Almost Succeeded in Finishing What Ben Franklin Started—our Postal Service. If His Involuntary Retirement Brings Him the Joy it Brings Us He is a Happy Mortal.[21]

The Roaring Twenties

The 1920's began on an upbeat note when President Harding's Postmaster General, Will H. Hays, announced that Burleson's policies would be "completely reversed":

The postal establishment is not an institution for profit or politics; it is an institution for service; and it is the President's purpose that every effort shall be made to improve that service.

Every effort shall be made to humanize the industry. Labor is not a commodity. The idea was abandoned 1,921 years ago last Easter. There are 300,000 employees. They have the brain and they have the hand to do the job well. We propose to approach this matter so that they shall be partners with us in this business. It is a great human institution touching every individual in the country. I know that with 300,000 men and women pledged to serve all the people and discharging that duty, fairly treated, properly appreciated, all partners with us here in this great enterprise, we can do the job. It is going to be done.[22]

Unfortunately, however, Postmaster General Hays was faced with a postal deficit of $84 million, a deficit, however, that did not take into account the millions of dollars of penalty or free-mail matter, and other nonpostal expenditures. Regardless of how exaggerated the postal deficit may have been, the new Postmaster was forced to issue an economy order similar to the Hitchcock "take up the slack" order.

Nevertheless, Hays pressed forward with his attempt to "humanize" the postal service. He announced his intention to create a "Welfare Department" through which employees could submit their grievances and suggestions for a better postal service. The first such organization was the National Welfare Council, headed by a "Director of Welfare," and composed of two delegates from each of eight postal associations. Local councils were established in all first- and second-class offices. The name was later changed to the National Service Relations Council and representatives of the National Association of Supervisory Post Office Employees were added to the council.

The "regular" unions—those that were affiliated with the AFL—were suspicious of Hays' motives. The membership of the Council was heavily weighted in favor of management, primarily because all but three of the employee organizations represented on the national and local councils were associations that seldom opposed management policies. The National Association of Supervisory Post Office Employees, of course, was composed of political appointees who owed their positions to management. Hays himself added to the suspicion when, in a speech before UNAPOC, he declared: "We shall treat all alike, but shall cooperate so closely together that there will be no need of affiliations," that is to say, no need of legitimate postal unions.

Regardless of Hays' motives, he actually did reverse Burleson's policies, and although he may have been as opposed to postal unions as any of his predecessors, he nevertheless made the effort to bring about closer cooperation and better understanding between Department officials and post office employees. The National Service Relations Council was purely advisory and accomplished very little during its fourteen-year history, but it was a step in the right direction. The Council died of inertia in 1934.

Under three successive conservative Administrations (Harding, Coolidge, and Hoover), postal workers and their unions gained very little but experience. However, postal unions did demonstrate their potential power when, in 1924, they obtained the passage of a salary bill increasing wages above the levels desired by the Administration. President Coolidge vetoed the bill, but Congress adjourned before the veto message was received. When the House met again, after the President's overwhelming victory in the 1924 election, the veto was sustained by only one vote. Later, in 1925, Coolidge's veto of a night differential bill was overridden. The political potential of postal unionism was beginning to be felt. But that potential would meet its greatest test in the following decade—the decade of the Great Depression.

The Depression

The stock market crash of 1929 ushered in the Great Depression, putting a forceful end to the era of Coolidge-Hoover economics and the Wall Street-Brisbane promise of "sky without end and prosperity without limit." Bread and soup lines appeared throughout the country, and twenty-five million Americans became unemployed, about one-quarter of the labor force. With government revenues down, President Herbert Hoover ordered the first wage reductions in the federal service in the form of payless furloughs. Those ordered for the postal service amounted to a salary reduction of about 8.3 percent. However, if there had to be a wage reduction, the postal unions favored the furlough method, because statutory wage rates would be maintained.

The 1932 landslide victory of Franklin Delano Roosevelt over Herbert Hoover brought in the New Deal and, arguably, the most pro-labor administration in the history of the country to that time. The National Industrial Recovery Act of 1934 and (after that Act was declared unconstitutional) the National Labor Relations Act of 1935 supported the organization of labor unions. As World War II neared, employment expanded, resulting in an unprecedented rise in labor union membership. The New Deal also brought about an expansion of government services and a resultant increase in federal employment, from 600,000 in 1932 to one million in 1940, a war-swollen 3.2 million by 1945, and a more steady state of two million by 1950. The newcomers were primarily young and enthusiastic supporters of both the New Deal and the growing labor movement.

All of this should have boded well for postal unions, but such was not to be the case. Franklin D. Roosevelt had campaigned with the promise to balance the federal budget. One of Roosevelt's first acts as President was to cut postal salaries by a straight 15 percent. Thus, one of the most pro-labor presidents in history outdid the conservative Hoover, who never did directly cut statutory postal wage rates. In 1933 the Postmaster General, James A. Farley, declared a $5 million dollar surplus, but rather than use the money to improve conditions for postal workers—especially for substitutes who were not receiving enough work to make a living wage—Farley attempted to increase the surplus by instituting payless vacations for regular postal employees, a four-day payless furlough, and an even greater curtailment of the employment of substitutes.[23]

These acts led to attacks on union leadership by organized insurgents within the unions. Their leaders were accused of "supinely surrendering to the economizers," and militant splinter groups organized demonstrations, marches, and increasingly aggressive verbal assaults on the Administration. Much of the action revolved around post office substitutes.[24]

Substitutes were civil service employees, appointed after passing civil service examinations, who were given work only when regulars were off duty or when the mails were too heavy to be handled by regulars alone. They were on call at all times, but were paid only for those hours that they worked. Their wage rate was sixty-five cents an hour, a substantial hourly wage rate for the time, but they received no vacation or sick leave. Because of the depression-induced decline in postal business, substitute employment fell on hard times. In many large cities, substitutes on call for a week earned as little as six dollars.[25]

The substitutes in several cities became impatient with the postal unions for what they felt was a neglect of their grievances, and formed their own union, the National Association of Substitute Postal Employees (NASPOE). The new union which enrolled members across craft lines, turned to militant tactics. They staged a March on Washington demanding a "job for every substitute." Following Farley's equivalent of the "take up the slack" order, another March on Washington took place. The established unions entered the fray and Farley eventually was forced to rescind his economy orders.

The campaign for Administration recognition of federal unions became intensive in the mid-1930s simultaneous with the creation of NASPOE and a CIO movement for one big postal union. A "Committee for One" was established which developed into the "Postal Workers of America," made up primarily of mail handlers, motor vehicle employees, and substitutes. The Postal Workers of America, was accused of Communist domination, an accusation based primarily on the fact that the union was affiliated with the CIO and supported by *The Red Write-Up*, a communist publication which was openly distributed in front of all the large post offices. Militant mass demonstrations and picketing were conducted and the statements of union leaders became increasingly aggressive, including demands for collective bargaining in the federal government, and a strengthening of the Lloyd-LaFollette Act. Some congressman became alarmed and there were moves to suppress such militancy and to make collective bargaining in the civil service illegal.[26]

In the midst of all this controversy, President Roosevelt was issued an invitation to speak before the Twentieth Jubilee Convention of the National Federation of Government Employees (NFGE). In a letter to NFGE President Luther C. Steward, Roosevelt regretted that he was unable to attend, but nevertheless set forth his views on federal employee-management relations.

"According to Otto S. Beyer, presidential labor advisor, the letter was intended to strengthen the leadership of the established unions by approving their methods and objectives and decrying the militant tactics of the challenging newcomers," e.g., the National Association of Substitute Post Office Clerks.[27] The President's put-down of federal union militancy allegedly was intended primarily to block threatened congressional action that he felt, might hamper the Administration's control over personnel policy. Although the letter succeeded in that purpose, it nevertheless erected a barrier against collective bargaining which would stand until the Kennedy Order of 1962. The President wrote:

All government employees should realize that the process of collective bargaining, as usually understood, cannot be transplanted into the public service. It has its distinct and insurmountable limitations when applied to public personnel management. The very nature and purposes of government make it impossible to bind the employer in mutual discussions with employee organizations. The employer is the whole people, who speak by means of laws enacted by their representatives in Congress. Accordingly, administrative officers and employees alike are governed and guided, and in many cases restricted by laws which establish policies, procedures and rules in personnel matters.[28]

This section of the Roosevelt letter would be cited in personnel manuals for years to come as a statement of Presidential policy declaring that collective bargaining in the federal service was "impossible." According to Nesbitt, it became "the most influential official pronouncement on federal labor relations between the Lloyd-LaFollette Act and the Kennedy order."[29]

The Roosevelt letter was published in 1937, the same year that he received the report of his Committee of Administrative Management. The Committee noted that not only were administration officials "reluctant to recognize and confer with representatives of employee groups," but also that such groups "frequently appear to encounter passive if not active opposition." Despite his strong support of trade unionism in the private sector, Roosevelt not only took no action to change the situation that the report called to his attention, but also ignored the proposal in the report:

> The majority of employees in any group or craft or other appropriate unit should have the right to determine the organization, person, or persons to represent the group, craft, or unit in joint conference with administrative officials or representatives of such officials.[30]

Nesbitt concluded that had this recommendation been implemented, "a program along the lines of the Kennedy Order might have had a quarter-century head start. What actually happened...was that the great majority of the employees continued to turn to Congress for improvement, and employing officials continued to point to the [Roosevelt] letter...to justify their refusal to enter into negotiated arrangements with their employees."[31]

Gains and Losses

Harry S. Truman proved to be a better friend of postal workers than the man he succeeded. During the Truman Administration, several bills were passed regarding substitutes, readjustment of salaries, overtime, pay raises, veterans' preference, reclassification, compensation for injury, and retirement—all in all, a substantial pro-public employee record. Truman was also applauded for his appointments of two career employees of the Postal Service, Jesse Donaldson and Vincent Burke, as Postmaster General and First Assistant Postmaster General respectively. The initial love affair between the postal workers and their unions and the Donaldson-Burke appointments was not a lasting one, but Truman continues to be credited as the first President to choose postal service experience and expertise over political involvement. Another important development which occurred during the Truman years was the creation of the Government Employees' Council of the AFL, composed of all state, local and federal employee unions. Its purpose was to improve the economic conditions of civil service workers and to intensify efforts to organize public employees.

From the point of view of the American labor movement, the most negative development of the late 1940s was the enactment, over Truman's veto, of the Taft-Hartley Act in 1947. Its primary impact was on private sector labor-management relations, but Section 207 of that Act gave statutory authority to a long-assumed taboo that had never before been set down in legislation, that is, the prohibition against the right of federal employees to strike:

> SEC. 207. It shall be unlawful for any employee of the United States or any agency of instrumentality thereof to participate in any strike or to encourage anyone to strike. Any employee of the United States or of any such agency or instrumentality who strikes or participates in striking or who encourages others to strike shall be discharged immediately from his employment and shall forfeit all rights of reemployment, and shall forfeit his civil service status, if any, and shall also forfeit all benefits and privileges which he may have acquired by virtue of his government employment.[32]

The constitutionality of Section 207 has been unsuccessfully challenged in the courts several times, and the right of postal workers to strike continues as one of the major goals of the American Postal Workers Union. The right to strike, along with amendment of the 1939 Hatch Act, which forbids all forms of partisan political activity by federal workers, are seen by the union as the two major goals to provide economic and political freedom for federal employees.

Although President Truman did not give away the store, postal workers did quite well during his Administration. The same cannot be said of the Eisenhower Administration. Three pay raise bills were vetoed by the President, and Postmaster General Summerfield's reclassification bill was passed over much union opposition. Summerfield even attempted to insert into the Postal Manual a gag rule reminiscent of pre-Lloyd-Lafollette days:

(a) Information relating to the policies and decisions of the Post

Office Department will be released only through official channels. Employees shall not actively engage in campaigns for or against changes in the service or furnish information to be used in such campaigns unless prior approval has been attained from higher authority.

(b) If an employee has justifiable reasons for favoring or opposing changes in the Postal Service, he shall contact the proper officials and await specific instructions before engaging in local hearings or activities.[33]

Thus, forty years after the passage of the Lloyd-LaFollette Act, the attempt to gag postal workers continued. The order, it turned out, was not successful; that portion of the manual was ignored with impunity.

The Winds of Change

There were four great landmarks in postal labor-management relations, the last of which was the Postal Reorganization Act of 1970, that brought effective collective bargaining rights to postal employees. The three others were, first, the Pendleton Act of 1883, giving postal workers civil service status; second, the Lloyd-LaFollette bill of 1912, outlawing the gag orders and providing for union recognition; and third, the Kennedy Executive Order of 1962, providing for union recognition and limited form of collective bargaining. The Kennedy Order ushered in nine years of "Employee-Management Cooperation," a period that ended with the great postal strike of 1970.

The Kennedy Order did not just happen; it followed a great deal of both administrative and Congressional maneuvering. Neither managers nor employees were satisfied with the federal personnel system as it was operating since the tremendous growth in civil service employment that occurred during and after the 1930s. Management complained about the system's inflexibility and employees about its disregard of employee input, or its "unilateralism." Organizations as diverse as the National Civil Service League (NCSL), the American Bar Association, and two Hoover Commissions made recommendations for improvements—recommendations which were generally ignored by both the Truman and Eisenhower Administrations. For example, in 1946 the National Civil Service League, in a report on Employee Organization in the Civil Service, stated as follows:

> The head of a public agency must at all times be free to accept petitions or requests for conferences from any source, but he should reserve any "agreements" for conference with the group representing the majority.[34]

Fourteen years later, the NCSL issued a similar statement which no doubt had an effect on the new policy initiated by President Kennedy. During the years between the two NCSL statements, two Hoover Commissions declared that "the federal government had lagged behind other organizations in recognizing the value of providing formal means for employee-management consultation,"[35] and in 1955 the American Bar Association stated flatly:

> A government which imposes on other employers certain obligations in dealing with their employees may not in good faith refuse to deal with its own public servants on a reasonably similar favorable basis, modified, of course, to meet the exigencies of the public service. It should set the example for industry by being perhaps more considerate than the law requires in private enterprise.[36]

The pressure for change was not limited to outside organizations; there was also a good deal of action on the legislative front. The first bill calling for union recognition was introduced in 1949, the same year as the first Hoover Report. Between 1949 and 1962, the year of the Kennedy Order, dozens of bills requiring union recognition and collective bargaining in the federal service were introduced, but of these, only one, the Rhodes-Johnston bill, received serious consideration.

The 1962 version of the bill, which had been in the Congressional hopper since 1952, recognized "the right...of a union of government employees to present grievances on behalf of their members without restraint...or reprisal," and required conferences upon union request regarding "matters of policy affecting working conditions, work procedures, automation, safety, in-service training, labor-management cooperation, methods of adjusting grievances, transfers, appeals, granting of leave, promotions, demotions, rates of pay and reduction in force."[37] The bill also provided procedures for resolving grievances and collective bargaining impasses.

When John F. Kennedy was a Senator, he was one of the most vigorous supporters of the Rhodes-Johnston bill. He gave testimony favoring the bill at committee hearings, and, as a candidate for President, Kennedy, in a letter to John W. Ames, Publicity Director, Illinois Federation of Postal Clerks, declared that he "always believed that the right of federal employees to deal collectively with the federal departments and agencies...should be protected." He expressed his "regret that the Congress had adjourned without acting on Senator Johnston's bill," and concluded: "I should think that a Democratic 87th Congress with Democratic leadership from the White House could deal effectively with the proposal."[38]

Once he became President, however, Kennedy's perspective changed. The same Rhodes-Johnston bill that had his full support as a Senator and as a candidate, was pending before the Congress. But the President proceeded to cut the rug out from under the bill by appointing a Task Force on Employee-Management Cooperation to review and make recommendations on federal employment relations. The Kennedy Order would be based on the recommendations of the Task Force.[39]

Executive Order 10988

The Task Force on Employee-Management Cooperation was, in effect, a committee of federal employers, composed of the Secretary of Labor (Chairman), Secretary of Defense, Postmaster General, Director of the Bureau of the Budget, Chairman of the Civil Service Commission, and Special Counsel to the President. Its mandate was to study the broad range of issues relating to federal employee-management relations, including, but not limited to, definition of appropriate employee organizations, matters upon which employee organizations might be properly consulted, and the participation of employees and employee representatives in grievances and appeals. The Task Force, which was convened on June 22, 1961 was to report its findings to the President not later than November 30, 1961. The report recommended official recognition of "bona-fide organizations of federal employees which are free of practices denying membership because of race, color, creed or national origin; which are free of corrupt influences and do not assert the right to strike or advocate the overthrow of the Government of the United States." Three types of recognition were suggested: Informal, Formal, and Exclusive:

> *Informal*: Would permit any organization to be heard on matters of interest to its members.
> *Formal*: Would be granted to any organization with 10 percent of the employees in a unit or activity of a Government agency, where no organization has been granted exclusive recognition.
> *Exclusive*: Would be granted to any organization chosen by a majority of the employees in an appropriate unit.[40]

Informal recognition, according to the Task Force, was simply an extension of the right of any government employee to be heard. The prime advantage of formal recognition was that it granted the right to broad consultation. While the organization did not have the right to act on behalf of the entire unit, it was granted the opportunity to raise issues with management and to present its views in writing for management's required consideration.

Exclusive recognition gave an organization the right to bargain collectively with management and to negotiate an agreement covering all employees in the unit. Negotiations could cover working conditions, promotion standards, grievance procedures, safety, transfers, demotions, reductions in force, and other matters consistent with merit system principles.

The report did not recommend arbitration as a terminal point in settlement of disputes. It provided that methods for helping to bring about settlement should be devised and agreed to on an agency basis, and that such techniques themselves be the subject of negotiations with each Department and agency.

On January 17, 1962 President Kennedy issued Executive Order 10988, Employee-Management Cooperation in the Federal Service, thus putting into effect the recommendations of the Task Force.

The Post Office representation election took place from June 1 to July 16, 1962. In this unique and historic election, ballots were mailed to the homes of 520,000 eligible employees. The complexity of the operation staggered even old hands at the National Labor Relations Board. In this one election some 93,000 voting units were involved in 35,000 post offices from coast to coast. In all the seventeen years since World War II, NLRB elections had involved only 94,000 units.

Significance of Kennedy Order

Though subsequently hailed as a landmark, the significance of the Kennedy Order must be appraised in comparison to the Rhodes-Johnston legislation, a bill which would have become law had it been given the presidential stamp of approval. Wilson R. Hart, writing in the Industrial and Labor Relations Review, charged that the Kennedy Order "pulled the rug out from under the government unions just as they were about to pluck the golden apple. It not only deprived them of the prize, but made them like it."[41] Hart was referring to the fact that Kennedy's appointment of the Task Force on Employee-Management Cooperation rendered moot the pending Rhodes-Johnston bill, which would have provided union recognition and collective bargaining by law, rather than by executive discretion. Judging from the reaction of union officials, the substitution of executive action for legislation was not a cause for concern. John A. McCart, Operations Director of the AFL Government Employees Council, called the Executive Order "the most momentous development in the history of [government] labor relations since the enactment of the Lloyd-LaFollette Act in 1912."[42]

McCart, of course, was correct, but it would have been even more "momentous" if union recognition and unlimited collective bargaining had been achieved by statute. Still, the Kennedy Order was an inevitable step in the evolution of federal labor-management relations. Limited collective bargaining began in the postal service as a result and continued right up to the strike of 1970. Following Kennedy, Task Forces were appointed by Presidents Johnson and Nixon and modifications were made in the Kennedy order. Johnson's Executive Order eliminated "informal" recognition and maintained "formal" recognition only at the local level. Nixon's Order eliminated formal recognition entirely, thus maintaining only "exclusive" recognition.

However, before the Nixon Order could be put into effect, the strike of 1970 and its aftermath rendered all of the Executive Orders and the entire Employee-Management Cooperation Program obsolete, at least in so far as postal employees were concerned. Labor relations in the federal government, and especially in the postal service, had evolved from gag orders preventing postal employees, either individually or through associations, from petitioning Congress to "cooperation" under the Kennedy, Johnson, and Nixon Orders. All of this development was codified in the Civil Service Reform Act of 1978 during the Carter Administration, but by then, the issues were moot as far as postal employees were concerned.

With the passage of the Postal Reorganization Act of 1970, a new era in postal labor-management relations began—an era of true statutory collective bargaining which, in 1991, is still unavailable to other employees of the federal government. But prohibition of the right to strike still kept the reality of joint decision-making problematical.

PART III

THE ERA OF COLLECTIVE BARGAINING

"At the banquet table of nature, there are no reserved seats. You get what you can take and you keep what you can hold. If you can't take anything, you won't get anything. And you can't take anything without organization."

—A. Philip Randolph

Chapter 6

THE FIRST DECADE

The American Postal Workers Union (APWU) met for its first biennial convention at the Rivergate Convention Center, New Orleans, Louisiana, August 12–16, 1972. The new union was born out of eighty-one years of trial and error, of inter- and intra-union conflict, and of persistent battles for union recognition. A new era of postal employer-employee relations lay before the nascent union that represented the first significant experiment at collective bargaining on economic issues in federal employment. The President of the APWU, elected by referendum, was Francis S. Filbey, former President of the United Federation of Postal Clerks, and the General Executive Vice President was David Silvergleid, former President of the National Postal Union. Owen Schoon, Secretary-Treasurer of the United Federation, became the Secretary-Treasurer of the APWU, and the Presidents of the three craft unions assumed the presidencies of their respective craft divisions within the APWU.

Five out of six of the APWU's top officers and thirty-five members of the forty-eight-person Executive Board were from the craft union tradition. It was not altogether certain that the craft and industrial factions would be able to get along with each other. When President Filbey called the 1972 convention to order, the craft unions were the dominant faction. But the inclusion of 80,000 members of the National Postal Union out of a total of 300,000 members, created an unresolved tension within the organization. It was not until 1980 that a slate of NPU candidates defeated craft candidates for the top positions in the APWU.

The eventual triumph of the NPU faction was perhaps inevitable. The politics of the craft unions were based primarily on the manipulation of power centers (the presidents of local and state unions) whereas the NPU directed its appeals to the rank and file. Officers of the craft unions were elected by the delegates to conventions who, in turn, were selected by the presidents of local and state organizations; officers of the NPU were selected by ballots sent to the homes of all union members. When the United Federation agreed to the election of officers by referendum, the advantage inevitably swung to the NPU faction.

Equally important was the NPU's sense of public relations and willingness to engage in activities which were considered eccentric, bizarre, and dangerous to the conservative craft union faction. Robert Kephart, former Secretary-Treasurer of the NPU, who was trained in public relations, said that he often talked to Filbey about improving communications with the rank and file and with the public, but could get nowhere. "He was too conservative, too staid...he didn't think public relations was dignified."[1] The NPU faction had no such "scruples" regarding public relations and, as a result, their leaders became well known both to the rank and file and to the general public.

Roy Hallbeck, President of the United Federation of Postal Clerks, had tried hard to bring the NPU back into the Federation, but could not convince the power structure to agree to the NPU demands. Chester Parrish, former President of the Motor Vehicle Union and later Secretary-Treasurer of the APWU, said that the reason Hallbeck failed was because he was dealing with the local and state presidents, not with the rank and file.[2] When the rank and file was asked in 1971 by Filbey to approve the merger, the agreement was approved by a ratio of two-to-one. On the other hand, Owen Schoon believes that the reason the merger agreement was approved by such an overwhelming margin was simply because the NPU demands were written in such fine print that most of the members "did not know what they were voting for."[3] Regardless of the reason, Francis S. Filbey, one of the most active opponents of the Progressive Feds, was primarily responsible for bringing about the merger that created the APWU and he proved to be an highly effective steward of the new organization until he died of cancer in 1977.

Francis Stuart Filbey

Francis Stuart "Stu" Filbey was the last President of the United Federation of Postal Clerks and the first President of the APWU. The cigar-chomping

Filbey, who affected a brusque personal style that masked a sensitive personality, was enormously popular with his own membership and respected by the press. Some newsmen in Washington professed to believe that they could judge the progress or lack of it in his negotiations with management by the tilt of Filbey's cigar as he left the bargaining sessions.

Although born in Wrightsville, Pennsylvania, he spent his childhood and most of his life in Baltimore, Maryland, where he started his career as a postal clerk in 1926. Filbey was an officer of his home local for over twenty years, nine of them as President.

In the mid-1940s, Filbey joined the Progressive-Fed movement within the National Federation of Post Office Clerks, but soon dropped out to become a leader of the so-called "Independent Caucus" and a strong supporter of the administration. When President J. Cline House suspended the New York and Brooklyn locals in December 1958 after the Boston Tea Party, Filbey was named trustee for the two locals. From 1959 to 1962 he also served as President of the Baltimore Labor Council of AFL-CIO unions and for five years before that was President of the Baltimore Federation of Labor.

It was at the St. Louis national convention in 1960 which elected Roy Hallbeck as the National President, that Filbey moved for the first time into the national limelight by defeating Sidney Lindenberg of Pennsylvania for the office of National Vice Presdient. He came to Washington two years later, after his election as National Administrative Aide at the Portland, Oregon national convention. When Hallbeck died, in 1969, Filbey was elected President of the United Federation of Postal Clerks.

The move was a difficult one for Filbey, whose ties with Baltimore were strong and deep. He had served there on countless civic as well as labor bodies, including the Baltimore Equal Employment Opportunity Commission, the Mayor's Advisory Committee on Civil Defense, the Mayor's Advisory Comittee on Housing and Enforcement of Urban Renewal, the Maryland Commission for Prevention of Juvenile Delinquency, and the Board of Directors of the Red Cross Regional Chapter.

Through all the subsequent years in Washington, reading the *Baltimore Sun* was always his first order of business. He had two hobbies: playing poker with his colleagues one night a week, and reading. He steeped himself in books on history and governmental philosophy and was also a master of Robert's Rules of Order. Few union leaders were his equal in presiding over large conventions, especially when the going got rough.

At one APWU convention several delegates accused him of being confused when he paused to have a brief consultation with the parliamentarian. Filbey restored order by booming out with a straight face: "No one confuses the chair, but just once in a while he seeks advice from other than the Good Lord!"

Filbey was Vice President of the AFL-CIO, and a member of the AFL-CIO's Executive Council. He was also a member of the Executive Committee of the Postal Telephone and Telegraph International, and traveled widely on international postal affairs.

He remained based in Washington until his death in 1977. Then Postmaster General Benjamin Bailar, future Postmaster General William F. Bolger, and AFL-CIO President George Meany attended Filbey's funeral. The eulogy was delivered by Filbey's close friend, Orrin Bradshaw, who at the time was Secretary Treasurer of the APWU Benefit Association. Mr. Bradshaw said:

> His success was not limited to any one area of life, but it included all the facets of his relationships as a husband, as a father, and as a man. Stu Filbey was also a great human being, oftentimes full of bravado to cover disappointments in his fellowmen, giving generously of himself and his goods to all those in need...the kind of friend to whom you could pour out all the contents of your heart and know it remained with him...

Listening in an adjoining anteroom were his widow, Evelyn, with whom Filbey celebrated his fiftieth anniversary a year before his death; his daughter Elizabeth and her two children, and his sister Lucille.

The Merger Movement

Filbey, fresh from his success in bringing about the merger that created the APWU, began thinking about an even larger merger—a merger which would bring together not only all postal unions, but also the 650,000 member Communications Workers of America, headed by Joseph Beirne. The rationale was industrywide bargaining for a private-public communications industry. Beirne addressed the APWU's first convention and expressed his full support of exploring merger possibilities. Filbey, who made it clear that the chance for merger with the Letter Carriers was not good, nevertheless entertained a resolution directing the "National President to approach and expedite the proposition of merger of APWU, the National Alliance of Federal Postal Workers, the National Association of Letter Carriers, the Mail Handlers of LIUNA, the Communication Workers of America, and the Rural Carriers."[4] The motion was passed, but despite Filbey's subsequent efforts, the proposed merger never came to fruition; twenty years later, the union lineup remained the same.

The chief stumbling block to merger was the National Association of Letter Carriers. Despite statements to the effect that the Letter Carriers were open to merger, the Rademacher administration was concerned about the extensive assets the NALC would bring to a merger. "NALC has millions of dollars of assets in real estate and insurance," Rademacher declared, "which we are not about to turn over to a merged group of unions without something substantial in return." He concluded: "As the oldest and most respected of all unions representing government workers, we do not intend to turn our assets, our membership and our prestige over to any group or groups until we are confident that in so doing, we would be acting in total support of the welfare of our membership."[5]

If the APWU and the NALC merged, the possibility of a CWA, Mail Handler and Rural Letter Carrier merger would be greatly enhanced, although the Rural Carriers have always maintained a separatist policy. Chester Parrish believes that the NALC's version of merger was to have all postal workers join the NALC—or in other words, absorption rather than merger.[6] William Burrus, Executive Vice President of the APWU, says that the NALC "pursues the philosophy of the old AFL. The Letter Carriers are a craft union; they represent a single group of employees. That's their whole history and philosophy; they have no interest in the industrial concept."[7] Thus far the obstacles and objections have precluded an APWU-NALC merger. The concept of one big communications union still remains no more than a dream.

Convention Jitters

The first convention of the APWU brought together five unions accustomed to operating as separate units, and it was quite apparent that a certain nervousness existed when they all got together for the first time. Michael Benner, Executive Assistant to the APWU President and former President of the Special Delivery Messengers, said that the delegates from each of the five unions stayed at different hotels in New Orleans,[8] and Chester Parrish felt compelled to rise early in the convention and recommend that the delegates "refrain from making references to our former unions."[9] Parrish's point was that the APWU was now one union, and that the delegates should act accordingly.

Not only was there tension between the old NPU faction and those in the Federation who had consistently voted against merger, but also between the anti- and pro-Filbey factions. Joseph F. Thomas, former Federation Director of Organization and the last President of the old company union, UNAPOC, was defeated by Filbey for President of the APWU. Prior to the election, Thomas had approached Moe Biller, President of the powerful New York local, and asked for his support against Filbey. Biller turned him down flat and became a Filbey ally. "Filbey may not have been my kind of a union guy," Biller says, "and maybe I wasn't Filbey's kind of a union guy, but at least Filbey knew what a union was. Joe Thomas wouldn't know a union if it stared him right in the face."[10] When Biller got up at the convention to speak, the boos and hisses from the Thomas faction made it difficult for him to be heard. Filbey brought Biller up to the podium, but when the New York leader started to speak, somebody set off a cherry bomb.

However, things eventually calmed down and the delegates got down to business. A Rank and File Bargaining Advisory Committee was established, and it was moved and passed that all collective bargaining contracts would be subject to ratification by the membership. After much debate pro and con, George McGovern received the convention's endorsement for President of the United States, and three major legislative goals were established: (1) Hatch Act Reform; (2) Right to Strike; and (3) Union Security. The same legislative goals have been set at subsequent conventions, but not one has yet been realized. Hatch Act reform made it through both Houses of Congress twice, only to be vetoed by Presidents Ford and Bush. George McGovern, perhaps reacting to the APWU endorsement, introduced the first Senate bill in history designed to give federal workers the right to strike, but it died in committee. No action has occurred authorizing the union shop.

The Farah Strike

Although postal unions were affiliated with the AFL-CIO and were represented, along with other federal unions, on the AFL-CIO's Government Employees Council, they remained aloof from the larger labor movement. The postal unions had been reared within the constraints of the federal structure and, thus, operated in a different environment from the private sector unions—unions which enjoyed full political freedom and the right to strike. There had never been a case, for example, where postal workers showed their solidarity with the general labor movement by joining nonpostal strikers on the picket line. All that would change at the 1972 New Orleans convention.

On July 19, 1972, the AFL-CIO Executive Council voted to launch a nationwide boycott of Farah Manufacturing Company products until a satisfactory settlement of a strike against the Texas-based clothing company was reached. The AFL-CIO contended that Farah was employing vicious tactics in an attempt to break a strike by nearly three thousand workers, many of them Mexican-American, who wanted to join the Amalgamated Clothing and Textile Workers of America. According to the AFL-CIO, "these tactics included plant patrolling by vicious attack dogs, court orders barring peaceful and legal picketing, arrests in the middle of the night, unlawful discharges of workers for union activity, and personal intimidation and coercion of workers."[11]

John O'Donnell, General Counsel of the Manhattan-Bronx Postal Union, and his grandson, who accompanied Moe Biller to New Orleans, saw on television a news segment showing dogs attacking the Farah strikers. O'Donnell suggested to Biller that the APWU had a wonderful opportunity to show its solidarity with a group of exploited workers by picketing the two New Orleans Department Stores which, on the previous Sunday, had sponsored full-page advertisements for Farah slacks in the New Orleans Times Picayune. Biller, who needed no pep talk from O'Donnell, immediately suggested the idea to Filbey. But Filbey demurred, saying "these guys have never picketed before in their lives." However, he said he would talk it over with his counsel and get back to Biller. Later, Filbey said that if Biller could get a police permit, he would okay the demonstration. When Biller mentioned a police permit to O'Donnell, O'Donnell told him that if he applied for a police permit, he wouldn't get it until long after the convention adjourned. "If you're going to picket,"

O'Donnell said, "forget the police permit and go ahead and picket." Biller suggested that if Jacob Potofsky, President of the Amalgamated Clothing and Textile Workers, would send a telegram requesting APWU support, Filbey would be forced to okay the idea. O'Donnell responded, "If you need a telegram from Potofsky, I'll get it for you."[12] O'Donnell and his grandson, Neil Sheehan, worked long into the night preparing picket signs for the planned demonstration.

The next day, Filbey did indeed receive a telegram from Potofsky and immediately authorized the demonstration. Thus, at 12:00 noon, two thousand APWU delegates descended on the Maison Blanche and Holmes Godchaux department stores armed with the signs made by O'Donnell and his grandson. Young Sheehan marched beside Biller at the head of the picket line with a sign that read, "I told my mother that I would not wear Farah slacks." Biller asked O'Donnell how he was able to get a telegram from Potofsky so quickly. "It was easy," O'Donnell replied, "I sent the telegram myself and signed Jake's name." To the day he died, Filbey never knew that the "Potofsky" telegram was actually a forgery.[13] The demonstration received wide coverage in the New Orleans newspapers, including pictures of Moe Biller, John O'Donnell, and his grandson leading 2,000 postal workers in the demonstration.

John O'Donnell believes that the Farah demonstration was an extremely significant incident in the history of the APWU. "It was the first time in their lives that many of those postal workers ever carried a picket sign or ever thought or recognized themselves to be part of the national labor movement in this country. After all, you have to remember that while most big city postal workers make a fair wage, postal workers in Arkansas and Mississippi make the same wage. Down there they are paid more than the school principal; they are middle-class people. I don't think they ever thought they would be seen carrying a picket sign. In other words, I think it was a very significant development and I also think it did quite a bit to give Biller status as an aggressive leader who wasn't afraid to marshal support for other working people."[14] Similar demonstrations would occur at APWU conventions in San Francisco, Chicago, and Las Vegas.

The APWU emerged from New Orleans a much stronger union than it had been prior to the convention. The animosities between various factions within the union were eased and, despite the show of nerves and the "cherry bomb attack," the delegates banded together into one, united union. The Farah demonstration helped unify the delegates, as well as promote solidarity between postal workers and the larger labor movement. In subsequent conventions, the delegates would no longer segregate themselves by craft in different hotels, and their former affiliations would no longer interfere with their identification as members of a united APWU.

The First Contract

Winton M. "Red" Blount, the 62nd Postmaster General of the United States, was a highly successful contractor, builder, and civic leader of Montgomery, Alabama. At the time that he was appointed Postmaster General, he was also President of the United State Chamber of Commerce. During the twenty years prior to his appointment he had been responsible for building multimillion dollar projects ranging from huge industrial plants to missile and space installations. Blount, who was in office during the strike of 1970 and who became the first Postmaster General of the U.S. Postal Service, would be responsible for the first collective bargaining session under the Postal Reorganization Act. He had been forced to stand by more or less helplessly when postal workers gained a 14 percent pay raise after the strike—the largest pay raise ever received by postal workers before or since—but he was determined that he would be far from helpless at the bargaining table.

One week before the 1971 negotiations were scheduled to begin, Blount surprised everybody by defying history and issuing a new "gag rule" barring postal employees from any contact with Congress on postal affairs, or vice versa. On March 11, 1971, in a hostile confrontation with members of the House Post Office and Civil Service Committee, Blount insisted that he would not retreat one inch from the controversial rule. However, Representative William D. Ford of Michigan was successful in attaching a rider to the Fiscal 1972 Postal Appropriation Act which prohibited salary payments to any postal official, including the Postmaster General, who may try, in any way, to interfere with a postal worker contacting his Congressman or United States Senators. No postal official has attempted to issue a gag rule since.

The first collective bargaining session took place before the merger and before the official transfer of Post Office Department resources to the U.S. Postal Service, so the negotiations were between the seven exclusive unions and the Post Office Department. In January 1971, a Federal panel of three judges ruled against the National Postal Union and the National Alliance of Federal and Postal Employees on their plea for a temporary injunction to stop postal collective bargaining, to which they were not parties. The decision gave a green light to the negotiations which were scheduled to begin on January 20, 1971. Blount hired James Blaisdell, a lawyer and experienced management negotiator in the West Coast longshore industry, to be the chief negotiator for the U.S. Postal Service. The seven exclusive unions formed the Council of American Postal Employees (CAPE) and hired attorney Bernard Cushman, who had represented unions in transit, railroad, airline, and electric power negotiations.

Ninety days after the commencement of negotiations, the two sides found themselves at an impasse. The unions had placed sixty-three issues on the table, but according to President Filbey the only counterproposals made by management "were designed to take away protections already enjoyed by employees and to set up a system by which all phases of a new contract would be subject to arbitrary decisions of management."[15] Management asked for an extension of bargaining beyond the April 19 deadline, but after Blaisdell declined to say whether the Department would make any counterproposals to the union wage and money demands, the unions refused to grant the extension. Cushman said that in his thirty years of negotiating experience he had never encountered "a situation where management refused to make even a token offer on wages and fringe benefits."[16]

Under the Postal Reorganization Act the stalemate automatically triggered the fact-finding procedures of the law, which call for the establishment of a three-member panel appointed by the Director of the Federal Mediation and Conciliation Service to hold hearings and investigate the facts during the succeeding forty-five days. A panel was selected, but after one-and-a-half months of enormous effort it was unable or unwilling to make a substantive recommendation on the issues. The panelists cataloged the differences between labor and management, emphasized the transitional problems, and proposed ways and means of isolating some of the issues, but failed to come up with a single finding of fact or recommendation.

Bernard Cushman maintains that the panel did the right thing:

It was almost impossible, within the time allotted, for a fact-finding board to get a grasp on all the elements involved. There were a web of statutes and regulations that had to be understood, health and welfare programs, and how all this would affect collective bargaining...Beside the general overall issues, you had each craft...with its own special work rules and problems...Much of my time really was spent mediating between the various groups that picked me, where the lines were shadowed, what went where, who did what, etc. I thought the panel made the best recommendation it could by making no recommendation.[17]

Both sides realized that an arbitration panel would face the same problems experienced by the fact-finding panel; a base had to be created before fact-finding or arbitration would work, and that base could be established only by the parties involved, that is, the Post Office Department and the seven unions. As a result, crisis bargaining ensued which eventually produced the first collective bargaining agreement on bread-and-butter issues in the history of the federal government. On July 20, 1971, the Department and the seven unions signed a two-year agreement for the following:

1. A pay package that provided for five $250 wage increases at prescribed intervals in the life of the contract, plus a $300 bonus;
2. Cost-Of-Living Adjustment (COLA) of one cent an hour for each 0.4 increase in the Consumer Price Index (CPI) up to $160 a year;
3. Total job security by outlawing layoffs during the life of the contract; and
4. Creation of grievance arbitration machinery, including the establishment of a shop steward system requiring counseling in disciplinary actions, as well as notice of such actions and 30 days on-the-clock before removal, and binding arbitration, if needed.

The contract marked the first time that cost-of-living adjustments had been applied to the wages of federal workers. It was not the best COLA that was ever negotiated—it didn't gain as much in relation to increases in the CPI as would future COLA provisions, and it was capped at $160—but it was a beginning. Cushman considered the "no layoff clause" a real achievement. He also felt that the grievance arbitration system "contained all the necessary elements...it has been refined over the years, but the base was established in 1971."[18]

The Outlaws

Most union officials and postal workers considered the first pact between postal management and labor to be the best that could be expected under the circumstances, but a militant faction of the Letter Carriers and of the MBPU in New York denounced the agreement and demanded a strike. Damon Stetson, writing in the New York Times, reported that a meeting of more than 3,000 members of the Manhattan-Bronx Postal Union and Branch 36 of the Letter Carriers at New York's Manhattan Center "erupted into a shouting, brawling melee as the rebellious group expressed their dissatisfaction with the agreement." The two union Presidents, Moe Biller and Vincent Sombrotto, could not control the meeting and finally were forced to leave "but two hundred of the angry dissidents followed them down 33rd Street to Eighth Avenue shouting 'Sell Out,' 'Chicken,' 'We don't need you anymore,'" and other somewhat harsher epithets. When Biller and Sombrotto climbed into a cab, "some of the dissidents banged on the roof and windows before it was able to move ahead in the minor traffic jam caused by the shouting clerks and letter carriers."[19]

Moe Biller, generally characterized as the most militant of all postal union officials, was having trouble with a well-organized left-wing group within his own local. Biller, who had fought for union democracy ever since he joined the Postal Service, was being accused of the very thing he fought against—undemocratic practices, including the staging of vendettas against union members who challenged his rule. The center of anti-Biller sentiment was at the New York Bulk and Foreign Mail Center in Jersey City. When the New Jersey workers voted to join the Manhattan-Bronx Postal Union, the local's name was changed to the New York Metropolitan Area Postal Union, or the "New York Metro." A group calling themselves "The Outlaws" gained control of the New Jersey shop. Composed primarily of young men and women, some Vietnam veterans, but mainly 1960s-style radicals, The Outlaws fought the Biller administration by disrupting meetings, staging mini-strikes, and disseminating antiadministration literature. It was The Outlaws who broke up the Biller-Sombrotto meeting, and they continued to cause problems in New York and, later, California and Washington, until the early 1980s.

Actually, The Outlaws' challenge to Biller was a study in irony. When the "college boys" entered the postal service in the 1930s, they were considered the radicals. It was the college boys who disrupted union meetings, demanded union democracy, and generally comported themselves in an aggressive, antiestablishment manner. One generation later, the radicals of the thirties found themselves to be the establishment, and were being challenged by a new group of radicals, forged during the hectic sixties, who used tactics similar to those of their predecessors. But there were differences between the two groups: The "outlaws" of the thirties—even most of the college boys—came from the working poor, many of them the children of immigrants from Eastern Europe, Italy, and Ireland, who entered the post office as a last resort. The sixties version were children of the middle class who "dropped out," not out of economic necessity, but to show their contempt for the society that nurtured them. It was the "old left" against the "new left."

The major tactic of The Outlaws was to pack union meetings, especially when issues that would have an effect on their status were being considered. They capitalized on the fact that less than five percent of union members attend local meetings. The Outlaws would arrive in force prepared to vote down anything proposed by the administration. One such issue was a constitutional amendment that provided for the election of vice presidents citywide rather than by post office station. If passed by the required two-thirds majority, it would mean that Kenneth Leiner, the Director (chief shop steward) of the New Jersey bulk facility, who was elected by the bulk workers, would be voted out of office. The twenty-three-year-old Leiner was a leader of The Outlaws and one of their chief strategists. He believed, as did most of the bulk workers, that the constitutional amendment was a deliberate attempt by the administration to "get him." Biller called for a voice vote on the amendment and declared that the "Ayes" had it, and that the amendment was adopted. The dissidents called for a "division," or a standing vote, but Biller refused to grant a division. The reaction of the "bulkers" was to create a mini-riot—chairs were thrown, tables upset, and the shouting dissidents prevented any further business from being conducted.

At another meeting, approximately two hundred bulk workers appeared armed with a petition, signed by the majority of the workers at the bulk center, demanding that Leiner be sent as a delegate to the APWU's second convention in Miami, Florida. Biller refused to accept the petition, so the bulkers locked arms and formed a line around the hall which prevented anyone from leaving without crashing through the line. The police were called, but instead of going after the bulkers—who were predominately white—they began harassing the peaceful black delegates attending the meeting. Josie McMillian, President of the New York Metro, remembers hollering: "Hey! You're going after the wrong people!"[20]

It appears that the "old left" had learned a good deal about how to control a meeting from the "old right," and that the "new left" experienced the same frustration experienced by the old left years earlier.

Another Freeze

One month after the first collective bargaining agreement was signed by the Post Office Department and the seven unions, President Nixon imposed a wage-price freeze—freezing the wages of federal workers for ninety days, and thereby wiping out the first $250 wage increase negotiated for postal workers due on October 20. The President's attempts to cool the Vietnam war economy by tightening the money supply and reducing expenditures were not working. By 1970, the inflation rate had risen to 5.9 percent and was still climbing; thus, Nixon turned to wage-price constraints.

The postal unions, on August 20, notified Postmaster General Blount that they expected the U.S. Postal Service to fulfill its contractual obligations by paying both scheduled step increases and the $250 wage increase, regardless of the so-called "wage-price freeze." On August 26, the Postmaster General rejected the union demand. The unions filed suit in federal court on August 31, charging the Postal Service with violations of contract agreements. The suit further requested an injunction to compel payment of wage increments on schedule and challenged the legality of the Nixon wage freeze. The court case was dismissed. The judge held that the Economic Stabilization Act of 1970 gave the President wide discretionary powers to combat inflation, and superseded the Postal Reorganization Act's stipulation which held that no other law should govern postal wages.

However, wholehearted backing by the AFL-CIO accomplished what court action could not. President Nixon had placed administration of his wage and price controls under a cabinet-level Cost of Living Council advised by a Presidential Pay Board composed of corporate CEOs and union presidents. Heartened by the judicial response to the postal union's protest, the Council, backed by the management members of the Pay Board, resolved to extend the freeze for an additonal two months, disallow retroactive pay boosts and require renegotiation of deferred increases, and impose a 5 percent ceiling on future pay raises.

Already concerned that the freeze on prices was mushier than that on wages, the union members flatly rejected the concept that any person or agency had the power to abrogate any legal collective bargaining agreement or any other contract voluntarily and legally entered into by American citizens or their representatives.

To dramatize that commitment, the AFL-CIO members of the Pay Board walked out, destroying the advisory body's bipartisan credibility. President Nixon's response was a retroactive defrosting of the wage freeze.

Are Postal Workers Federal Employees?

The first contract did not provide for improvements in postal worker fringe benefits, but the unions had every reason to believe that their members would be covered by a bill introduced by Representative Jerome Waldie of California which would progressively increase the Government's share of its contributions to health benefit costs from the existing 40 percent to an ultimate 75 percent. However, the U.S. Postal Service suddenly announced that its employees would not be covered by the pending legislation. Waldie immediately proposed an amendment to the measure which specifically included postal workers and the bill, as amended, passed the House in April 1972.

The Senate passed a different version of the Waldie bill which excluded postal workers and provided for a much smaller government contribution. The adamant position of the Chairman of the Senate Post Office and Civil Service Committee, Gale McGee of Wyoming opposing the inclusion of postal workers doomed any House-Senate conference agreement prior to adjournment.

The Waldie bill controversy led to Congressional debates regarding the status of postal workers. Waldie and others argued that if postal workers are federal employees, they should be included in bills covering federal employees. If they are not federal employees, then they should be given the right to strike, the right to a union shop, and political freedom. The opposition argued that although postal workers are federal employees, their wages and benefits are determined by collective bargaining, not through legislation enacted by Congress. The substance of this issue is still a continuing controversy. Postal workers were not included in the bill that eventually was signed into law. However, as we shall see, they gained more through collective bargaining than they would have gained had they been included in the Waldie bill.

100,000 Impasses

In addition to fringe benefits, another issue not covered in the first agreement had to do with local level implementation of the national agreement. When issues that the union believed should be resolved at the local level were raised, management took the position that the union demands were inconsistent with the provisions of the national agreement. On this basis management would not agree to bargain or even discuss the demands. The issues included wash-up periods, the establishment of a regular five-day work week with either fixed or rotating days off, guidelines for the curtailment or termination of postal operations due to local conditions, formulation of local leave programs, methods of selecting employees to work on holidays, among many others. Local management's refusal to bargain on these issues resulted in over 100,000 impasses throughout the country, and led the unions to stage nationwide protest rallies. In addition to the 100,000 impasses, the unions were protesting the lack of Congressional action on Hatch Act reform and the right to strike.

Informational picket lines were established in fifty cities and 2500 postal workers rallied in Washington, marching on the U.S. Postal Service. In New York, Moe Biller and Vincent Sombrotto staged an eight-hour sitdown in the office of Regional Postmaster General Harold Larsen. The result was that management unfroze local negotiations and some of the problems were resolved. But the overall issue would not be completely settled until local implementation was spelled out in detail in the 1973 contract. All of this occurred after the APWU conducted its first conference and workshop on the national agreement (November 1971), and established a Committee on Political Action (COPA) in March, 1972.

The Mail Handler Question

In 1968, when the smaller independent postal unions were contemplating merger with the larger unions, it was expected that the National Association of Post Office Mail Handlers would join either with the Clerks or the Letter Carriers. But at a special convention in April, the delegates surprised everybody by voting to join the Laborers International Union of North America (LIUNA). LIUNA had approximately 500,000 members, about 30,000 of whom were state- and local-level government workers. The merger was plagued with difficulties, but eventually withstood challenges to the constitutionality of the special convention and an attempt by the Mail Handler President McAvoy, just prior to his death, to void the merger.

In New York, however, the vast majority of mail handlers belonged to the Manhattan-Bronx Postal Union, now a local of the APWU; Local 1, Mail Handlers Division of LIUNA, had few members. Thus, the APWU and LIUNA agreed to permit MBPU and Local 1 to jointly represent all the mail handlers in New York. A local agreement was reached which stipulated "no raiding," and applied to negotiations concerning local working conditions and participation in labor-management, Health and Safety Committee, and Employee Recreation and Welfare Committee meetings.

A joint statement by MBPU President Biller and Sam Mason of Local 1 noted that Manhattan and Bronx are the only two post offices in the United States where such an agreement exists and expressed the hope that "if we can work this out successfully in our area, it will set an example for development of true unity on a much broader scale."[21] The hope, of course, was that the New York agreement would eventually lead to a national agreement between the APWU and the Mail Handlers, but that hope was never realized. In 1980 the APWU tried (unsuccessfully) to decertify LIUNA as the representative of the Mail Handlers. Again, in 1985, Lonnie Johnson, the President of the Mail Handlers Division of LIUNA, tried—also unsuccessfully—to disaffiliate from the laborers' group. Right down to the present day, relations between the Mail Handlers and the APWU/NALC have been, to put it mildly, contentious.

The Second and Third Contracts

Elmer T. Klassen, formerly the President of the American Can Company and Deputy Postmaster General under Blount, was elected the sixty-third Postmaster General by his fellow governors on December 7, 1971. In March 1972, Klassen announced a freeze on hiring which he hoped would reduce the payroll sufficiently to avert a $450 million rate increase. Five months later the work force had been reduced by 33,000 and the financial picture improved. However, by February 1973, Klassen was forced to concede that the freeze had resulted in a serious deterioration in service.

The APWU at its second convention in Miami established goals for the 1975 negotiations, including maintenance of the "no layoff" clause and adopted a "no contract no work" resolution. Biller, with a keen nose for the value of public relations, hired a plane to fly above the convention hall trailing a banner emblazoned with the motto: "NO CONTRACT NO WORK."

The Postal Service, for its part, put out press releases claiming that postal workers were well paid and cited as proof the long waiting lists throughout the country for postal service jobs. According to Jeffrey Keefe, "the unions responded by contacting the large business mailers and telling them that there was a strong possibility of a strike on July 21 unless a new contract was signed and ratified. The large mailers, in turn, put pressure on management, saying that if there was a strike, they would seek permanent alternative methods of getting their material to the public."[22] CAPE was replaced by the Postal Coordinated Bargaining Committee (PCBC) consisting of the APWU, NALC, Mail Handlers Division of LIUNA, and the Rural Letter Carriers Association. Bernard Cushman was again retained as chief negotiator for the unions. Darrell Brown, Senior Assistant Postmaster General for Labor Relations, replaced James Blaisdell as management's chief negotiator.

An agreement was reached a month before the July 20th deadline. The APWU Rank and File Bargaining Advisory Committee endorsed the contract by a nine-vote margin, and 85 percent of the rank and file members, voting by referendum, approved the agreement. Wages were increased by $700 in the first year and $400 in the second. The cap on the COLA was removed with four adjustments scheduled during the life of the agreement. The Postal Service assumed full payment of life insurance, and added a staged increase in contributions to health insurance from 40 percent to 65 percent. In addition, twenty-two specific items were listed as subjects for local negotiations, finally eliminating the long-standing local impasse problem.

The Battle of the Bulk

In January, 1974, a strike or a lock out, depending on whether the work stoppage is viewed from the labor or management side of the table, took place at the "Bulk"—the New York Bulk and Foreign Mail facility in

Jersey City, New Jersey. When the Postal Service was about to open the Bulk, the workers at the old Brooklyn Army Terminal and one or two other facilities were invited to bid on the new jobs. They were offered attractive schedules, mostly day work.

The new facility was not long in operation when its manager discovered that the work schedules and the flow of mail were incompatible. Most of the mail processed in the Bulk originated in Manhattan. The peak mailing period was around three in the afternoon. Consequently, most of the mail arrived at the Bulk after four o'clock. By that time, the day workers were going home. During the day, when there was a surplus of workers, comparatively little mail came through. The manager of the Bulk, who was new to the Postal Service, reacted precipitously. Without any advance notice to the union or to the workers, he posted new schedules assigning the majority of employees to work between 4:00 P.M. and midnight.

The workers were up in arms. They felt they had been misled by management into picking jobs in New Jersey because of convenient schedules and once the jobs were filled the work schedules were changed. The site of the Bulk was isolated with little or no public transportation after midnight. The problem was exacerbated by the fact that most of the Bulk employees were women for whom the travel situation and late shift hours were impossible. The APWU's shop stewards at the Bulk called Biller who immediately visited the site. He told the manager that he had no right to change the schedule without first negotiating with the union. Then he told the employees to disregard the new schedules and report for work in accordance with their original schedules. On the following morning, the workers began arriving at seven o'clock only to find the gates locked. The manager called the police and, as more workers lined up at the gates, the Postal Service approached the Federal District Court in Newark seeking an injunction against what they called an illegal strike. It also asked the judge to impose a $100,000 fine on the New York Metro with an additional $100,000 fine for each day the Bulk workers remained off the job.

John O'Donnell, arguing the case for the union before Judge Lawrence Whipple, asserted that a plaintiff seeking an injunction in a court of equity has to come to court with "clean hands," a prerequisite that the Postal Service could not satisfy. They had misrepresented to the workers the types of schedules to which they would be assigned and therefore were not entitled to any relief from the court. Judge Whipple ordered the parties to negotiate the schedule problem and gave them a week to resolve it.

A week later, the Postal Service was represented by its top trial counsel from Washington whose arrogance did not find favor with Judge Whipple. By contrast, O'Donnell presented a picture of injured innocence. Whipple ordered the parties to arbitrate the dispute and said that if they could not agree on an arbitrator, he would appoint one.

Eventually, a pre-arbitration settlement was reached and executed by James Gildea (for the Postal Service), and Francis S. Filbey (President of the APWU), and Moe Biller (President of the New York Metro). Gildea, formerly Executive Assistant to AFL-CIO President George Meany, was the same person who negotiated for the union after the 1970 strike. He had gone from the AFL-CIO to the Labor Relations Department of the Postal Service and was not unfamiliar with the employees' viewpoint.

The agreement assigned 511 clerks and 306 mailhandlers to late shifts (7:00 P.M. and 11:00 P.M.), but specified that no one who worked at the Bulk as of January 1, 1974 could be assigned involuntarily to a late tour. Thus, new Bulk workers could be assigned to the new tours, but the original workers could work the late shifts only if they volunteered to do so.

AFL-CIO Public Employee Department

In November, 1974, the former Government Employees Council of the AFL-CIO was replaced with a Public Employee Department, composed of twenty-four unions representing two million federal, state and city employees. George Meany, President of the AFL-CIO, in announcing the new department, said: "Public employees have got to fight for what is theirs, what is just and proper, using the same methods as workers in the private sector. While the whole question of the rights of employees, as spelled out by law, is still to be determined, militancy is the key to success in the fast growing field of public employee unionism."[23]

The Third Contract

On January 8, 1975, Postmaster General Klassen announced that he was stepping aside on February 15th. The Board of Governors selected Klassen's Deputy, Benjamin Franklin Bailar, to succeed him. Bailar, forty years of age, was a native of Champaign, Illinois, who held a Geology degree from Colorado and a Master's degree from the Harvard Business School. He entered the federal service from the American Can Company, where he was Vice President in New York. He had worked closely with Klassen both in private industry and in the Postal Service. The man named after the country's first Postmaster General delighted postal workers when, in one of his first statements, he came out in opposition to President Ford's "selective sacrifice" concept of a 5 percent ceiling on federal wages, saying that government workers buy their groceries at the same store as everyone else. But, Bailar, who was faced with a record $800 million dollar deficit, and a potential $1.6 billion deficit by the end of the next fiscal year, insisted that this huge deficit could not be ignored in the negotiations. The unions, on the other hand, pointed out that the CPI was 11 percent higher than the 1974 level, and this, too, could not be ignored.

The settlement was mediated by William Usery, then Director of the Federal Mediation and Conciliation Service. The contract was written for three years. It provided for 12 percent wage increases over the period, in addition to the same uncapped COLA, as existed in the prior contract and an increase to 75 percent (from the previous 65 percent) of the Postal Service's contribution to health insurance.

A Women's Movement

During the 1960s and 1970s, the number of women entering the postal service increased substantially. This was a direct result of the Kennedy Executive Order which struck down the practice of having separate employment lists for men and women. The Order stipulated that all candidates for postal service jobs, both men and women, be registered, in order, on the same list. Prior to the Kennedy Order, women would not be selected until the "male list" had been exhausted. The new rule gave women an equal opportunity to obtain postal jobs. The number of women entering the postal service grew rapidly.

The first move toward a women's organization within the APWU, other than the auxiliary which had already existed, began in New York. Moe Biller sent Josie McMillian, Fanny Harrigan, and Shirley Hardin to a meeting of women in labor organizations that was being held in Philadelphia. The three women, all officers, were to represent the New York Metro at the meeting. The Coalition of Labor Union Women (CLUW), whose President, Joyce Miller, now serves on the National Executive Board of the AFL-CIO, was formed at that 1974 meeting.

Upon their return from the Philadelphia meeting, the three women recommended the establishment of a women's committee within the local. Biller agreed, the committee was formed, and began holding monthly meetings. Josie McMillian emphasizes that the meetings did not deal with "how to sew an apron, serve tea, or make an apple pie...we dealt with how women can get more actively involved in union affairs, motivating women to become involved in the union, effective speaking, and parliamentary procedures. We wanted women to go to union meetings and not be afraid to speak, to let their feelings be known."[24] The women's committee was well received by both men and women in New York and a move to create a similar organization within the APWU began. At the 1978 convention, a resolution introduced by the women's caucus that would bar the APWU from holding its 1980 convention in any state which had failed to ratify the Equal Rights Amendment was defeated. The women attributed the defeat to their lack of knowledge of parliamentary procedures, and resolved to create their own organization. The first meeting was held on April 28, 1979 in St. Louis where the organization was named Post Office Women for Equal Rights (POWER). At the 1980 convention, POWER became an official APWU organization.

Constitutional Convention

The merger of the five unions resulted in an APWU superstructure that needed streamlining. The first convention in New Orleans adopted a resolution establishing a Restructuring Committee that was to appraise the needs of the national union and draw up a resolution to be presented at the 1974 convention changing the sections of the constitution to be more in line with the union's need and its financial ability to meet its responsibilities.

The committee, chaired by Douglas Holbrook of Detroit, attempted to present its report to the 1974 convention, but whenever Holbrook rose to present his report, the Chairman moved on to other business. It was finally decided to assign the streamlining problem to a Constitutional Convention to be convened in mid-1975 with full powers of its own to consider recommendations of a new Select Committee of Restructuring. The new committee, chaired by Ransom Erskine, was to have several advantages over its predecessor, particularly in the areas of professional counseling and technical assistance.

The Constitutional Convention was convened in Kansas City, Missouri on June 2–5, 1975. The Report of the Select Committee, however, was so amended by the convention delegates that instead of slimming the union's structural profile, it was fattened to the estimated tune of $400,000 in salaries alone, requiring a minimum increase in the per capita tax of thirteen cents to fund the changes.

On the fourth and final day, the delegates failed by 1,120 votes to achieve the two-thirds majority needed to ratify the changes. Apparently, the time was not right. When restructuring eventually did occur in the 1980s, most of the recommendations made by the original Holbrook committee, including a reduction in the size of the National Executive Board, were adopted.

Postal Study Commission

By 1976, the Postal Service faced an operating deficit of more than $4 billion, along with a $3.2 billion bond debt. Clearly, something had gone wrong since postal reorganization. Senator Gale McGee of Wyoming introduced a bill providing that 10 percent of the total operating budget of the U.S. Postal Service be appropriated as a subsidy for each of the succeeding three years. A blue-ribbon committee was to be appointed to study what had happened in the Postal Service since reorganization and to determine what should be paid for by the mailer and what should be paid for as a public service by the taxpayer.

Because of opposition from the Ford White House and the Office of Management and Budget, the McGee bill went nowhere. Instead, the Senate took an earlier House bill and substituted new provisions agreed to by the Ford Administration, the Postal Service, the House Post Office and Civil Service Committees, and the Senate Governmental Affairs Committee. The bill provided an additional one billion dollar subsidy for one year, and the establishment of a seven-person Postal Study Commission.

The Commission's mandate was to study the public service aspects of the Postal Service, estimate their costs, and identify the differences between the costs which the Postal Service should bear and the revenues the Service was likely to receive. Beyond those goals, the Commission was also to decide whether the Postal Rate Commission should be abolished or altered, develop rate-making criteria, review the appropriateness of service levels, assess the long-range impact of electronic transfer and communications techniques and analyze the feasibility of the Postal Service operating such systems. The Commission had only six months to come up with their findings and recommendations. James Rademacher, retiring President of the National Association of Letter Carriers, and David Johnson, Executive Vice President of the APWU, were appointed to the Commission.

Among the recommendations made by the Commission were an increase in public service appropriations to ten percent of the postal expenses per year, permanent limitations on post office closings, a five-day delivery scheme and amendment of the private express statutes to allow delivery by private couriers under certain conditions. The Commission emphasized the low priority given to postal research and suggested joint ventures with private industry to determine within the succeeding two years whether the Postal Service had a future in electronic communications. With respect to the latter, there were dire predictions regarding a decline in postal volume because of increased use of electronics. Sixteen years later, Time Magazine asked Postmaster General Anthony Frank whether in the computer age there should be less paper mail in the future. Frank replied: "The Postal Service said in 1975 that volume was going to go down because of electronics. Since then, there have been fourteen consecutive years of up volume, each year higher than the last. The Postal Service seems to continue to be doubling about every twenty years in volume. We don't see any interruption."[25]

The Battle Royal

On May 17, 1977, Francis S. Filbey died after a year-long battle with cancer. During the six years that he led the first industrial union of postal workers, an organization of which he was the principle architect, he presided over three consecutive collective bargaining agreements without resort to interest arbitration, and the expansion of the APWU's jurisdiction to include the Postal Data Centers (1973) and Mail Equipment Shops (1974). Perhaps even more important, Filbey was able to hold together the warring factions within the APWU, to bring together natural enemies, and therefore, to keep the union operating on a fairly even keel. His passing would mark a turning point in the history of the APWU. A brief period of discord ensued, followed by a substantial change in the union's leadership.

Emmet Andrews

Emmet Andrews, the Director of Industrial Relations, was elected by the Executive Board to fill out Filbey's term. Andrews, a native of San Francisco's Mission District and one of the bright young men who entered the Postal Service in the 1930s, began his union career in Local 2 (San Francisco) of what was then the National Federation of Post Office Clerks, later the United Federation of Postal Clerks. Born in 1916, he was the grandson of a shipbuilder who was the first person to design a ferry boat that was equipped with rails. His father died when he was very young and as a result he was forced to enter the labor force immediately after his graduation from Mission High School.

Andrews, an excellent speaker and raconteur (his wife, Betty, describes him as very "Irish") entered the Postal Service in 1936 and rose quickly in the postal union movement. At various times, he was Secretary, Legislative Director, First and Second Vice President of the local, and eventually was the first Local President to serve two consecutive terms.

He came to Washington in 1966 when he was elected Executive Aide. He became Administrative Aide when Filbey assumed the office of President. At the time of the merger in 1972, he became Administrative Aide in the Clerk Craft of the newly formed American Postal Workers Union. In 1972, he was elected Director of Industrial Relations and was reelected to that position in 1974 and 1976. Andrews was elected President of the APWU in 1978.

A tough competitor with an earthy sense of humor, Andrews was an excellent golfer—a game he learned to play on the municipal courses of San Francisco. Mike Benner recalls one Saturday afternoon when he was playing with Andrews and Forrest "Frostie" Newman, then APWU Director of Industrial Relations. At one point, Newman found himself in a sand trap and after trying unsuccessfully to extricate himself, let go with a stream of frustrated profanity. Andrews, who was on the green with Benner, leaned over and remarked, "Somebody's talking Chinese over there."

Andrews and his wife, Betty, had one daughter, Cathy Maurer, and two grandchildren.

His first full term as APWU President was a stormy one. Andrews was the last of the APWU leaders from the craft union tradition, and had the misfortune to ascend to the APWU presidency at a time when the industrial faction was making its bid for power. In 1980 he would be defeated by Moe Biller of New York, the same man who nominated him for President after Filbey's death. At the same time, J. Joseph Vacca replaced the retiring James H. Rademacher as President of the National Association of Letter Carriers. Neither Andrews nor Vacca had the leadership abilities of their predecessors and that fact would be brought out forcefully in the 1978 negotiations which turned into something of a free for all.

Another personnel change instrumental in bringing about the 1978 fiasco was the appointment of William F. Bolger, as the 65th Postmaster General, to replace Benjamin Franklin Bailar, who resigned to become Vice President of the American Gypsum Company. The initial union reaction to Bolger's appointment was favorable. A career postal employee, Bolger had been Bailar's deputy at the time of his appointment. He began his postal career as a financial clerk, and, after service in World War II, moved up through the ranks, working in district offices in Maine and New Hampshire and later in top management jobs in the New England Region. He was Director of the Boston Region when the United States Postal Service was created and was Regional Postmaster General for the Northeast before he became Deputy Postmaster General.

He was the second career postal employee to be named Postmaster General. Although the unions were happy to see one of their own achieve that exalted position, Bolger would soon change their minds. On the day of his appointment, he spoke before a postal management meeting in Cleveland:

You know, it's commonly charged that in our greater emphasis on efficiency and productivity, we've forgotten the great people tradition of the Post Office Department. Well, let's face it. It's easy to make this charge when in so many places we have an adversary relationship between craft employees and supervisors, between supervisors and postmasters, between postmasters and sectional center managers, and yes, between the associations and headquarters.

I want that to end.

Such divisiveness is fruitless and counterproductive. There are times, such as with the upcoming collective bargaining, when post office people must sit down across the table from one another. But, even in those times, acrimony serves no purpose whatsoever. If we must be adversaries, let us be friendly adversaries.[26]

The 1978 negotiations turned out to be the most acrimonious before or since, and the adversaries definitely were not friendly. Eighteen months before negotiations began, the Postal Service inaugurated a public relations campaign designed to blame "overpaid and underworked" postal workers for the sad financial plight of the U.S. Postal Service. Columnist Bob Williams wrote: "Adding to labor woes was the realization by most outsiders that the USPS was a sinking ship on a sea of rapidly breaking technological advances. A long standing pattern of postal service mismanagement, which saw billions of dollars wasted on grandiose schemes, and steady increases in postal rates, unfairly were laid in the collective lap of union workers."[27] Postal workers were portrayed as snails and slugs in cartoons and as a selfish group always clamoring for "more" at the public trough. This was the era of California's Proposition 13, an era when public disenchantment with high taxes caused public resentment of all government workers.

As the 1978 negotiations were about to begin, Bolger announced a major cost-cutting campaign. Since labor costs account for 85 percent of the USPS operating costs, cost cutting immediately translates into labor cost reductions. Thus, one of Bolger's major goals was to get rid of the "no layoff clause" in the current contract and to hold any wage increases down to the bare minimum.

The unions organized themselves into the Postal Labor Negotiating Committee (PLNC) consisting of James J. La Penta, Mail Handlers Union, and Andrews and Vacca of the APWU and Letter Carriers. The Rural Carriers decided to negotiate separately. As a result, yet another change in personnel negatively affected the negotiation process. Bernard Cushman, who had negotiated three straight contracts without resort to interest arbitration, was replaced by James La Penta, who was named Secretary of the PLNC, and Deputy Postmaster General, James Conway, became the chief negotiator for the Postal Service.

When the two sides faced each other across the bargaining table, it was clear that the unions were in an extraordinarily tough position. They had lost the bargaining momentum before they even came to the table, and their new bargaining team (the PLNC) was inexperienced and ill-prepared to face the confident USPS negotiating team. But, if the count was no balls and two strikes on the unions as bargaining was about to begin, a statement by the President of the United States made certain that the unions would do nothing more than either pop up to the infield, or strike out altogether.

President Carter Intervenes

The 1978 Democratic sweep that brought Jimmy Carter to the White House and overwhelming Democtratic majorities to both Houses of Congress should have boded well for postal workers. But the oil crisis and subsequent inflation became of paramount concern. Postal workers' salaries fell victim to efforts to control inflation.

On June 13, Postmaster General Bolger gained a powerful ally when President Carter urged wage restraint in the postal negotiations in order to control inflation. Carter wanted postal workers to take the same 5.5 percent wage increase that he had recommended for all federal workers. Andrews, Vacca, and AFL-CIO President George Meany issued statements blasting the President. But the two New York "power brokers," Moe Biller and Vincent Sombrotto, organized a demonstration intended to protest the slow pace of negotiations, Carter's intervention in the collective bargaining process, and to counteract Postal Service attacks on postal workers.

On July 12, 6,000 postal workers, led by Biller and Sombrotto, staged a march from the Washington Monument to USPS headquarters at L'Enfant Plaza and then to the White House. Signs carried by the demonstrators said:

> They call higher interest rates sound fiscal policy.
> They call higher wages inflation.
> I'm a postal orphan. My father works 60 hours a week.
> The CIA permits OSHA [Occupational Safety and Health
> Administration] inspections. Why not the Postal Service?
> No more mandatory overtime.
> We won't accept peanuts from Carter.
> Carter should butt out of negotiations.
> The no-layoff stays.

In what was one of the largest and noisiest displays that postal executives could recall, the marchers chanted, "No contract, no work," and in a press conference at the U.S. Postal Service headquarters, both Moe Biller and Vincent Sombrotto warned that their members would strike if the national unions and Postal Service were unable to negotiate a contract by July 20. Very much in the background, and obviously embarrassed, were Emmet Andrews, President of the APWU and J. Joseph Vacca, President of the

Letter Carriers. Although the demonstration was billed as a joint PLNC effort, the march was actually led by Biller and Sombrotto, both of whom expressed surprise that Andrews and Vacca played only secondary roles in the demonstration.

A Civil Service Contrast

Mike Causey, writing in the July 13, 1978 edition of *The Washington Post*, contrasted postal workers with their white collar brethren:

> Civil servants who take what they can get, and postal workers who get what they can take, met briefly yesterday right in the middle of Independence Avenue.
>
> There was plenty of symbolism in the "confrontation" between the two groups of government employees who have almost nothing except the same Uncle Sam in common.
>
> The more docile white collar workers, who by law and tradition depend on Congress and the White House to hand out pay and fringe benefits, stood aside. They watched from the street or from airconditioned offices as nearly 4,000 militant mailmen and women marched on the U.S. Postal Service's plush, futuristic building at L'Enfant Plaza.
>
> While the white collar employees watched, some applauding, some embarrassed, some grim-faced, the postal union members chanted "no contract, no work," and threatened to shut down the mail service unless they get a substantial pay raise and lifetime job guarantees. Joggers from the Agriculture Department, Defense agencies and AMTRAK ran by the postal people...wondering what it was all about.
>
> What it was about, in effect, is the tremendous difference between the way white collar federal workers and military personnel view the government and are treated by it, compared to the simpler, get tough approach of the postals....[28]

Causey brought into bold relief the difference between federal "factory workers" and federal "bureaucrats," and recalled the Congressional battles of the early seventies regarding whether postal workers are or are not federal workers. In the days ahead, a wildcat strike and its aftermath would make this question even more pertinent.

A New Contract—Perhaps?

With the unions threatening a strike unless there was a new contract by the July 20th deadline, and the USPS publicly issuing a plan to deal with a strike that included the use of troops to deliver the mail, an agreement was reached one hour after the deadline. The new contract called for a 2 percent wage increase and six cost-of-living adjustments with a cap of $1,518 (or 73 cents per hour). The previous COLA was rolled in and the no layoff provision was maintained. Just two days before bargaining was concluded, Bolger, at the cost of more than $100,000, signed his name to a letter that warned postal workers that they would be fired and permanently barred from future government employment if they went on strike. Columnist Bob Williams commented: "The letter is reflective of appalling bad judgment and, coming as it did in the crunch of things, only exacerbated an already tense situation. One would have expected more of Bolger."[29]

Andrews declined to give his stamp of approval to the pact. Instead, he said that he would send the contract to his members without comment. Vacca made no comment whatsoever. Only James La Penta of the Mail Handlers gave a positive assessment of the new contract. He characterized the pact as a "very honorable agreement,"[30] Later he would be accused, as Secretary of the Postal Labor Negotiating Committee, of leading Andrews and Vacca into a "dishonorable settlement." The ambivalent position of the union leaders was due mainly to the cap placed on the COLA, and a failure to meet union demands regarding wages and the elimination of mandatory overtime. The annual wage increase was lower than the 7 percent rise in postal productivity, and to put a cap on the COLA when inflation was rising at double digit rates, and interest rates were hovering around 20 percent was resented by the rank and file.

The Outlaws "Strike" Again

On June 13, 1978 the General Accounting Office (GAO) issued a highly critical report of the billion dollar investment the Blount administration poured into twenty-one Bulk Mail Centers in an abortive effort to recapture a portion of the market taken by the United Parcel Service (UPS).

The bulk centers failed in their challenge to UPS, primarily because their costs were so high that it was impossible to set competitive rates. These huge "mail factories" were totally mechanized and, according to the men and women who worked in them, not only unsafe, but also dehumanizing. Their installation caused a massive migration from other post office stations. The most radical of post office employees, the so-called "Outlaws," figured prominently among those migrants. Hard to control under any circumstances, this faction of the New York Metro and their counterparts in other areas of the country—especially those at the San Francisco Bulk and Foreign Mail facility in Richmond, California—were ready to explode. They had participated in the Washington demonstration and had been revved up by the strike talk at the USPS L'Enfant Plaza headquarters. They were not merely prepared for a fight, they wanted a fight.

When the new contract was announced on July 21st, The Outlaws struck. Four thousand workers at the Bulk Centers in New Jersey and Richmond, California walked off the job and established picket lines around the facilities. Although the strike was not authorized by either the locals or the national union, strike talk was so strident during the negotiations that the super-sensitive bulkers thought that their locals would not only back the walkout, but go out on strike in their support. Moe Biller, who was in Washington putting the heat on Andrews, says that the strike never would have occurred if he had been in New York. "Until today," Biller says, "I have not mastered how to be in two different places at the same time. My determination was, and Sombrotto's, too, that we better be down there in Washington where things were getting hairy and these guys (Andrews, Vacca and La Penta) were getting scary."[31] At the request of the USPS, an injunction was issued against the walkout and Bolger fired 200 of the 4,000 strikers. The "fired workers" claimed that Biller did absolutely nothing to help them until it was too late. He was accused of talking a great game, but failing to come through in the pinch. Biller countered that he should have called a strike as soon as the workers were fired, but that he was busy in Washington, and didn't ask the New York Metro Executive Board for a strike vote until after his return. By that time it was too late; Biller's strike proposal was voted down. That didn't stop the bulkers from accusing Biller of talking strike continually, constantly chanting "no contract, no work," flying an airplane around the Miami convention, but when the time came to strike, backing down and leaving the bulkers out on a limb.[32] In a television documentary of the 1978 bulk strike, Biller admitted that he should have called a strike, that he made a mistake and that he regretted his error.[33]

Bolger's Home Picketed

When Biller did come to the aid of the fired workers, he pulled out all the stops. His public relations man, Danny Frank, was given a free hand and instructed to do everything he could to put the pressure on Bolger. Frank had his own firm and the New York Metro was just one of his clients. That made it possible for him to do certain things that he could not have done had he been an employee of the post office or of the New York Metro.

On a cold and snowy December day in 1978, Frank led several busloads of fired workers down to Washington, D.C. to stage a protest at the L'Enfant Plaza headquarters of the USPS. Josie McMillian, who was the titular leader of the delegation, demanded that Bolger meet with the fired workers. She was told that Bolger was not in the office. After picketing in front of the USPS for a couple of hours, Frank suggested that the delegation drive over to Bolger's home in suburban Virginia, and, of course, he made certain that the media knew what was occurring.

The buses made their way into a pleasant suburban cul-de-sac and about 200 people stepped out of the buses with their anti-Bolger signs and placards. Josie McMillian rang the front door bell and Bolger's wife came to the door. Mrs. Bolger said that her husband was not at home. "Thank you very much," said McMillian, "we'll just sit out here and wait for him." Soon the police and postal inspectors arrived and told the demonstrators that they could not walk around outside the buses. If they were waiting for Bolger, they would have to remain on the buses. Says Josie McMillian:

We were having a peaceful thing. We just sat there, the buses lined up in front of Bolger's house. Then, the neighbors came out to see what was happening, they read all the signs and, lo and behold, they began to applaud us! There were a couple of little kids that lived in the neighborhood, little guys, they must have been about seven or eight years old, they came on our bus and we told them that the Postmaster General had fired these people, and that it was Christmas time, and that the fired workers were family people. Those little guys were on television that night saying that they thought it was terrible that it was Christmas time and that Mr. Bolger won't give the workers their jobs back.[34]

The demonstration made a very good human interest story on TV and in the newspapers, but it did nothing to soften Bolger's position. If anything, it made him even more recalcitrant and a lifelong enemy of Moe Biller. In addition, David Johnson, Executive Vice President of the APWU, wrote a scathing article in the official APWU periodical, *The American Postal Worker*, criticizing Biller for disrupting Bolger's family who had nothing to do with the firing of the bulk strikers. But, to the union rank and file Biller appeared to be a union leader fighting for the rights of his members, while the national leaders appeared to assume the position of the proverbial ostrich.

The demonstration outside Bolger's house lasted six hours, and when the buses finally pulled out and began the trip back to Washington, D.C., the angered postal inspectors allegedly tried to run the buses off the road. According to Josie McMillian, "the drivers had to pull in at a depot, way out somewhere, and call the police to get us some protection."[35]

The Postal Forum Demonstration

The public relations effort did not stop with the picketing of Bolger's home. When the Postmaster General was scheduled to speak at a September 1979 Postal Forum luncheon at the New York Hilton Hotel, Danny Frank planned a two-pronged event. First, in the name of his own company, he rented a booth and loaded it with anti-Bolger propaganda. The booth, staffed by Dorothy Campbell and Sonyia Leggett, was paid for in advance and set up the day before the luncheon that would be attended by approximately 1,000 people. When Frank arrived on the day of the luncheon he found that the booth had been dismantled and all of its literature removed. Frank, however, did not complain. He had already planned for a demonstration either during or after Bolger completed his speech. As a booth holder, he was entitled to several tickets to the luncheon, and he figured that if he complained too much about the booth, he might lose his tickets.

About an hour before the luncheon began, Frank dressed a postal worker as a waiter and had him place anti-Bolger literature on all the plates in the ballroom. As the guests began to arrive, the postal inspectors discovered what had been done and went scurrying around the ballroom in an attempt to remove the literature. They were too late; the diners had begun to arrive en masse and it became impossible to remove the New York Metro "hors d'oeuvres."

Frank, Biller, and Josie McMillian took seats right below the head table directly in front of where Bolger was to sit. When Bolger arrived, all three got up to greet him. In the meantime, Frank had secreted sixty union members in one of the hotel's large suites. When Bolger got up to speak he sensed that something was about to happen and began to cut his speech short. This alarmed Frank who was afraid that Bolger might finish before the sixty union members made their entrance into the ballroom. According to Frank:

> There was tension in the whole room. They didn't know what to expect. Bolger's getting to the end of his speech...I said oh my God this isn't going to work because the people are up in the room, and they were set to come down at a certain time. I go out of the room. A couple of postal inspectors follow me. I couldn't go up to the room or use the house phone because that would have been a tip-off. So I go outside the building to a pay phone on the corner. Now these inspectors are outside with me wondering who in the hell I'm calling. Well, I call the room and tell them to get down there and hurry up! I run back into the room just as Bolger's speech is ending.[36]

Suddenly, while the guests were applauding, sixty people led by Wilma Alexander, a tall, handsome woman, and Bill Sainato, who looked about half the size of Alexander, came charging into the ballroom hollering and screaming about the fired workers. The postal inspectors tried to intercept them, but the demonstrators just sat down on the floor. The inspectors started pulling them up and trying to get them out of the ballroom. Biller, who had got hit in the back by a walkie-talkie carried by a postal inspector, pretended that the walkie-talkie was a gun. "Put your guns away," he yelled, and when the people in the crowded room heard that, they fled, racing out of the ballroom. Says Frank: "Moe kept yelling about guns. There was complete chaos. The guests didn't know what to expect. We, in effect, ruined the occasion for them."[37]

The next day Frank wrote a letter to the Postal Forum threatening to sue unless his company was paid for the closing down of its booth. The Postal Forum acquiesced. "They paid for everything," Frank says, "our rooms, everything we had printed up and designed, anything I had a bill for. They sent us a check for a couple of thousand dollars without protest...We really did a number on them and got them to pay for it besides."[38]

All of this did very little to help the fired workers. Their case eventually went to arbitration. Those who struck "on the clock," that is, while they were on duty, lost, but one of the fired workers, Kenneth Leiner, was elected APWU Vice President, Mail Handler Division, in the 1978 elections.

The Death of Michael McDermott

The bulk mail centers were designed to handle large volumes of mail as rapidly as possible. Safety devices hampered speed, so they were more often than not disconnected or, if defective, left unrepaired. Workers at the New Jersey bulk facility complained constantly about the unsafe conditions existing in the facility, but their complaints were ignored. Clyde Dinkins, a foreman at the New Jersey facility, after reporting the unsafe conditions to management several times without ever receiving a reply, closed down sixty "bays" on his own for safety reasons. He was rewarded by being demoted from supervisor to clerk. Dinkins wrote to President Carter and received the following reply from Carter aide, Landon Kite: "The results of the investigation to date substantiate a number of your charges, either in full or in part, and Postmaster General Bolger's staff has initiated necessary corrective action."[39]

On Saturday, December 15, 1979, mail handler Michael McDermott, age twenty-five, married and the father of an eight-month-old baby girl, was killed while working on an extendable conveyor belt. According to David Neustadt:

McDermott was alone on one of the bays—a high volume loading dock, filling a trailer with parcels and sacks headed for Atlanta. Throughout the Christmas rush, he and other workers at the bulk mail center had been working eleven-hour days, six days a week of mandatory overtime on the noisy docks. After sorting by destination, mail came down on thirty-foot extendable conveyor belts which moved into the trailers and gradually retracted as the trailers were filled. Mail handlers like McDermott took mail off the belt and stacked it in the trailer...McDermott's death was painful and probably not immediate....[40]

He was sucked into the belt and, with all safety devices inoperative, was unable to fight off the machine. Mail handlers usually worked alone at the center, despite postal regulations which required at least two men at each bay. Neustadt reported: "With the constant noise, nobody could hear if he screamed, nor could they see him struggling. By the time the belt's thick metal chain broke, McDermott's right hand and right ear were virtually torn off, his skull had multiple fractures, his chest was crushed, and his internal organs [were] cut and bleeding."[41]

The death of Michael McDermott set off an uproar. Although the USPS was not covered under the Occupational Safety and Health Act (OSHA), postal management was forced to invite OSHA technicians in to inspect the center. OSHA listed twelve major violations of safety standards and recommended immediate correction. The frequency rate for reportable accidents at the center was 31.9 per hundred workers per year. Only three other industrial classifications in the United States had a similar rate. "In other words," said Neustadt, "working [at the bulk mail center] is more likely to lead to an accident than working in a coal mine."[42]

Hearings on the accident were held in Jersey City by a Joint Congressional Committee on January 7–8. Congressman Frank Guarini of New Jersey, who arranged the hearing, requested Postmaster General Bolger to be present, but he declined and sent Regional Postmaster James Jellison to represent him instead. Neither Jellison nor Alexander Gallione, General Superintendent of the bulk facility, was able to justify safety conditions at the center; in fact, they both proved to be extremely weak apologists for the USPS. One month after the investigation, Alexander Gallione resigned.

Moe Biller called the retirement of Gallione "inadequate. He is merely a scapegoat."[43] In his testimony at the hearing, Biller noted, "the Postmaster General is not here today. He fired over 100 workers of this unsafe facility...One worker has been killed. Ten days later, another worker, Frank McGhee, narrowly escaped a similar fate and is here today. Yet, the Postmaster General is permitted to carry on."[44]

McDermott's widow testified at the hearing. Crying throughout her testimony, but nevertheless very articulate, she asked whether a mail sack is more important than a human being and said that she hoped her husband "did not die in vain."[45] On February 26, 1980, President Carter issued Executive Order 12196 which brought federal agencies under the health and safety standards imposed on private industry by OSHA. Safety conditions at the bulk centers definitely were improved after the death of Michael McDermott. Most of the fired workers never regained their jobs, but their walkout did call attention to serious problems that otherwise would have gone unnoticed. Several years later, in a ceremony that included McDermott's widow and daughter, the street leading to the bulk facility was renamed Michael McDermott Place.

Contract Rejected

Meanwhile Biller and his Letter Carrier colleague, Sombrotto, were busy in Washington. Both men lacked confidence in the La Penta-Andrews-Vacca triumvirate and, thus, felt that they had to be on the scene to keep the pressure on a relatively weak bargaining team. On the eve of the contract deadline, July 20, the APWU Executive Board met all day, waiting to see whether or not there would be a contract. At eleven in the morning, Chester Parrish made a motion that the Board adjourn until five the next morning. His motion was seconded and approved, but Biller argued so forcefully that the Board had no business adjourning when the contract deadline was at midnight that night, that the Board reluctantly reconvened. The Board sat and waited all day long.

At 6:30 P.M., Andrews called Biller to his suite and told him that he was being called over to the Federal Mediation and Conciliation Service. Biller responded that it would be a mistake for him to go, because he would be a captive in that environment. Andrews responded that he had no choice; he had to go. Andrews told Biller that he was worried about New York and nothing else. Biller told him to hang tough and we will support you. "If we go out on strike," Biller said, "we will be there side-by-side with you."[46] Andrews did not want a strike. But he knew that the officers of the New York Metro and Branch 36 of the Letter Carriers were meeting in New York and awaiting word from Biller and Sombrotto as to whether or not a contract existed. Before he left, Andrews gave Biller the number of the Federal Mediation and Conciliation Service.

When the deadline passed at midnight, Biller called the FMCS, but there was no answer. Biller received calls from Seligman in New York at 1:30 and 2:30 in the morning, but he had nothing to report. At 4:00 A.M. Andrews called and said that an agreement had been reached, but that he couldn't talk about it because he was being bothered by the press. Biller called Seligman and told him that an agreement may have been reached, but that he didn't have any idea as to what was in it. He asked Seligman to hold everything.

At about 4:30 in the morning, Andrews met with the APWU Executive Board and described the new contract. A motion was made to strike, but it was voted down. Biller called New York at 6:00 in the morning and told Seligman that the Executive Board had voted against a strike. He said that the Letter Carriers also had decided against a strike, and that if the New York Metro were to do anything now, it would be making a big mistake. "The only chance we have now," Biller said, "is to reject this contract."[47]

Later, James La Penta had scathing criticism for the "power brokers," Biller and Sombrotto. "And let's not forget...the Sombrottos and Billers," La Penta said, "who began to set strike issues even before bargaining began. They horribly manipulated the strike as an issue and then lost their credibility by not calling their own walkouts July 21...They committed fratricide on their own organizations rather than fight the real adversary: namely the employer."[48] The two New Yorkers, in turn, accused La Penta of leading the lambs (Andrews and Vacca) to slaughter.

The First Rejection

The APWU's forty-nine-member Rank and File Bargaining Advisory Committee met to consider the new contract. Under the APWU constitution, each member of the National Executive Board appoints one member of the committee, which has full veto power over any proposed national agreement. Late in July the committee rejected the contract by a 29–15 vote, then directed, on a 30–9 vote, the national officers to conduct a mail referendum of the entire membership anyway. John P. Richards, President of the Pittsburgh APWU local, filed suit in U.S. District Court to prohibit the mail referendum and send APWU negotiators back to the bargaining table.

Richards maintained that the national union leaders were violating the APWU constitution by initiating the mail referendum without approval of the new contract by the Rank and File Bargaining Advisory Committee. In an opinion from the bench, Judge Barrington D. Parker ruled against Richards. He said that it would be disenfranchisement for those few members of the advisory council to block the right of thousands of ordinary members from voting on any proposed contract. Immediately after the ruling, ballots were sent out to the APWU membership.

The Denver Convention

The APWU gathered for its fourth biennial convention in Denver, Colorado on August 14, 1978 in the midst of the referendum, and it turned out to be the most divisive of the union's conventions before or since. Just prior to the convention, AFL-CIO President, George Meany, told a national press conference that he thought the postal union negotiators "could have done better." Meany's statement angered Andrews, Vacca, and La Penta, and played right into the hands of Biller and Sombrotto, who were pushing for rejection of the contract. Said Joe Vacca of the Letter Carriers: "He (Meany) can no longer criticize Barry Bosworth (President Carter's chief inflation fighter) now that he is guilty of the same interference in the collective bargaining process."[49]

Meany's statement was just one of the sparks that set the Denver convention aflame. The fired workers arrived and proceeded to blast both the national (Andrews and company) and local (Biller and company) leaderships. The major issue on everybody's mind, of course, was the contract. All the elements were present for an all-out brawl.

When Andrews was introduced he was greeted with a chorus of boos, and when he shouted over the mike, "I am not a quitter!" he set off a two-hour demonstration of derision against him and the other national officers for caving in to postal management. Led by the Pennsylvania and New Jersey delegations, delegates from locals throughout the country eventually joined in haranguing their national leaders. Signs brandished by the demonstrators read:

"We repudiate the gutless negotiators."
"Nuts to the contract."
"Two percent is a disgrace."
"We were sold out by our negotiators."

The demonstrators banged on tin cans and demanded support for George Meany's denouncement of the contract. Biller got into a shoving match with a delegate who accused him and other New York delegates of threatening his life. There was little Andrews could do to restore order. at one point, Andrews showed his scorn for a delegate who shouted at him on the platform by giving him the finger. A photographer caught Andrews in the act, and, later, Biller held up the picture and called out to the delegates: "This is what he thinks of you!" Andrews replied that the gesture was meant for only one person, not the entire delegation.

When things calmed down, William Burrus, President of the Cleveland local, made a motion that the delegates go on record as totally rejecting the tentative agreement negotiated between the United States Postal Service and the American Postal Workers Union. On a roll call vote that took most of the afternoon, the Burrus motion was approved.

Later, Burrus rose again to make the following motion:

> If a majority of the membership voting for a national contract rejects a tentative agreement, the APWU negotiators shall inform the USPS demanding to reopen negotiations. If the negotiations are not opened within five days after the vote is tallied, the General President shall be mandated to call a nationwide strike. Such negotiations shall terminate no longer than sixteen days after negotiations begin...
>
> If such negotiations do not result in the tentative agreement which improves substantially on the initial agreement, the General President shall be mandated to call a nationwide strike within five days.[50]

The second Burrus motion was carried as well.

Next came the question of amnesty for the fired workers. The delegates defeated a rather mild amnesty motion introduced by Andrews and backed by the other national officers. Instead, they chose to support a much more sweeping resolution introduced by Biller, providing financial aid to the fired workers. Biller, in defending his substitute motion, said that the APWU must not pay "lip service" only to the fired workers, but must be determined to get them all back on the job. Following the passage of Biller's motion, the delegates gave the fired workers a standing ovation, and later passed the hat at the convention center. A total of over $10,000 was collected.

In spite of Biller's move in favor of the fired workers, a leaflet circulated at the convention, reportedly written by members of his own local, described him as a "cornered eel," and charged him with a conspiracy to get rid of those "postal workers who dared expose Biller's no action policies." The leaflet continued: "After celebrating the removal of his opponents, grateful Biller shed crocodile tears all the way to the bank."[51]

All of this was in reference to Biller's failure to call a strike in support of the bulk workers. Few delegates appeared to take the leaflet seriously, but some condemned what they called Biller's "heavy-handed tactics."[52]

On August 23, the contract was rejected by members of the APWU by a vote of 94,400 to 78,487. Since the Letter Carriers and Mail Handlers had already rejected the contract, the unions demanded that the USPS return to the bargaining table, and Andrews made it clear that if the USPS refused, he would abide the mandate of the Denver convention and call a nationwide postal strike.

Bolger Balks

The three unions demanded that the USPS return to the bargaining table, but Bolger refused. "We have completed our negotiation as far as I am concerned," Bolger said on CBS's "Face the Nation" television program. Instead, Bolger insisted that the procedures called for in the Postal Reorganization Act be followed, that is, fact finding and binding arbitration. Eight hours before a midnight strike deadline, the Postal Service and the unions agreed to a compromise procedure. The agreement, drawn up by the chief federal mediator, Wayne Horvitz, combined the union's demand for negotiations and management's demand for arbitration by providing for the resumption of bargaining for fifteen days followed by binding arbitration if the two sides failed to reach an agreement. The Federal Mediation and Conciliation Service selected Professor James Healy from the Harvard Business School to serve as the mediator-arbitrator.

Moe Biller immediately blasted the compromise. On a network television show, Biller hinted that a spate of wildcat strikes might soon hit the postal service. Bolger, for his part, warned that strike action would not only hurt those workers who become involved, but would also damage the postal service.

The Healy Award

When further bargaining failed to produce an agreement, Healy imposed a binding settlement on September 15th. The cap on the COLA was removed, and wages were increased by 9.5 percent. However, the no–layoff clause, which was considered a strike issue by the unions, was weakened. Workers on the payroll as of September 15, 1978 were protected against layoffs, but those hired thereafter had to work six years to gain that protection.

On October 12, 86 percent of the APWU membership approved the modified contract. The "battle royal" was over, but its aftermath was felt for years to come. Later in 1978, Vincent R. Sombrotto defeated J. Joseph Vacca for the Presidency of the National Association of Letter Carriers, and in 1980, Moe Biller defeated Emmet Andrews for the Presidency of the APWU. James La Penta's "power brokers" became the "power wielders."

End of the First Decade

The first decade of the APWU ended with the union's fifth biennial convention in Detroit, Michigan in August 1980. Two months later, Moe Biller, running on a ticket with William Burrus and John Richards, was elected President of the APWU. From New Orleans to Detroit, the union participated in four historic collective bargaining sessions with the USPS, and obtained contracts that won major bread-and-butter gains for its 300,000 members. There were also improvements in work rules and working conditions, as well as major arbitration victories. APWU members, acting on their own, won over $156 million in Fair Labor Standards Act overtime suits against the USPS—all in all, a successful record.

On the legislative front, not one of the APWU's three legislative goals were realized. Hatch Act reform made it through both houses of Congress once, but was vetoed by President Ford. During the Carter Administration, Hatch Act reform passed in the House, but died when the Senate failed to act on the bill before adjournment. There was no action on the right to strike and union security.

A significant feature of the first decade was the emergence of Moe Biller as the strongest leader of the APWU. It was Biller and his attorney, O'Donnell, who shook up the union's first convention by staging the demonstration against the Farah Manufacturing Company. From that point on, Biller upstaged the APWU's national leaders by being the moving force behind every demonstration that occurred during the period. It was Biller who organized the picketing of Bolger's home and led the fight for rejection of the 1978 contract. He was conspicuous on major television programs and, when the APWU gathered for its fifth convention in Detroit, no one was surprised when an interview with Moe Biller, "Coordinator of the APWU," appeared on the front page of the *Detroit Free Press*. Where was Emmet Andrews, President of the union? According to Danny

Frank, "Andrews had no concept of public relations. He wouldn't know how to go about getting his name in the paper. By default, Moe would get...these media opportunities."[53]

As the period came to an end, it was quite apparent that the craft faction of the union was losing its power. Along with Biller, local leaders from the NPU faction, including William Burrus of Cleveland, John Richards of Pittsburgh and, later, Douglas Holbrook of Detroit would challenge craft candidates—and they would win.

The "kibitzers" would get a chance to "do it their way."

Chapter 7

ENTER MOE BILLER

As the APWU entered its second decade, the need for more aggressive leadership was apparent. The weakness of the national leaders during the 1978 negotiations was one factor, but looming in the future was a whole host of issues, including automation, privatization, health benefits, work rules, as well as the all important bread-and-butter issues, which would demand strong negotiators on the union side of the table. But as the election of 1980 approached, none of the declared candidates, including the incumbent, Emmet Andrews, appeared to have the strength and the "flair" that the times demanded.

Moe Biller was approaching his 65th birthday in 1980, and he had recently lost his wife of 38 years. As long as his wife, who had been seriously ill for several years, was alive, Biller would not run for national office because he would not consider moving her from New York to Washington, D.C. After Anne's death, Biller was undecided about what he wanted to do with the rest of his life, but he was certain that he did not want to stop working. He had been President of the New York Metropolitan local since 1959, and the officers of the Metro wanted him to challenge Andrews for the presidency in 1980. Ultimately, Biller decided that he would run, but didn't declare his candidacy immediately. Local elections were scheduled before the national's, and if he declared too early before the local elections, the dissident faction might make a move to gain control of the local. Biller had defeated Tyrone Monte, an Outlaw candidate, in 1978, winning 86 percent of the vote, but with Biller out of the way, and no one groomed to replace him, the dissident challenge could be a good deal more formidable.

Biller ran uncontested in the 1980 local elections and immediately thereafter announced his candidacy for President of the APWU.

The Man from the Lower East Side[1]

Moses Aaron Biller, the man who would lead the APWU in the 1980s and on into the nineties, was born on November 5, 1915, in a tenement apartment located behind a bakery at 104 Suffolk Street in Manhattan's Lower East Side, the heart of what was then known as the city's Jewish ghetto. Delivered by a midwife, he was the fourth of six children born to Sam and Minnie Biller, both immigrants from Eastern Europe. There has always been confusion about Biller's first name. "It took me sixty-four years to find out that the birth certificate says Moses Aaron, but they called me by my Hebrew name, Moshe, or its diminutive, Moshie, 'Little Moses'." Yet in all of the official records, he is listed as "Morris."

When Biller was four years old, Minnie Biller had five children and was also the janitor of the tenement in which they lived. She suffered from chronic illness and had enough to cope with without dealing with her energetic son. She told Biller's older sisters to register him in school and to tell the teachers that he was five years old, the mandatory age for entering kindergarten. His sisters thought that his name should be anglicized, so they decided to tell the teachers that his name was Murray. The teachers, all of whom were Irish, said that Murray would be confusing because it's an Irish surname. So, the teachers decided to register him as "Morris" Biller. Thus, Morris became his name.

Biller, however, had some other ideas. "If you were twelve years old and wanted to go with girls on the Lower East Side, you could be Moshe, but you couldn't be called Morris. That's not a name that was accepted on the streets, you know? So, I named myself Moe." And that is what he wants to be called—not Moshe, Moshie, Moses or Morris—but Moe. Moe Biller.

The Lower East Side of New York was a place of intense industry and political ferment. The Irish, who had occupied the area, were being replaced by Eastern European Jews who brought with them a culture steeped in a love of learning and intellectual curiosity. Sam Biller, a sewing machine operator on kneepants, or "knickers," may have been uneducated in

American secular schools, but he was quite educated in Hebrew and once aspired to be a Talmudic scholar. Minnie Biller learned to read and write English by listening to lessons on the radio. Biller says that her proudest moment came when she was able to read the comic strips in the Daily News.

Biller describes himself as a "sandwich child," the fourth of six, the child that has to fight for recognition. He says that he was always considered "wild, but not mean or anything like that," but rather "precocious, a royal pain in the ass, I suppose," a designation that often would be applied to him by future postmasters and rival union leaders. He was a pusher, he rushed everything, including his education. When he was twelve, he demanded that his parents take him out of public school and enroll him in Yeshiva, a Jewish parochial school. He became quite religious, wore the ringlets, and out-orthodoxed his very orthodox parents. Later, he completed Seward Park High School in three and a half years, was an honor student, and had a 100 percent grade average in mathematics. He haunted the Educational Alliance, a settlement house, where he played softball and basketball, and belonged to the Philo Club, a club named after Judaeus Philo, an ancient Hellenistic Jewish philosopher of Alexandria.

Despite the considerable socialistic and Communistic ferment on the Lower East Side, the Biller family, perhaps because of its religious orthodoxy, shunned the "radicals" and remained mainstream Democrats. Sam Biller was a great admirer of the graduate of the Fulton Fish Market, Al Smith, and felt sure that Smith would beat Hoover in 1928. Says Biller: "My first political recollection was in 1928 when my father told me that there was no question in his mind that Al Smith was going to be elected President. I really knew nothing then, but I was rooting for Al Smith. When he was defeated, I asked my father what happened. In his heavy accent, he said 'he lost because he was a Ketlick.' I remember crying and it gave me, perhaps, my first insight into being with the underdog."

While in high school, he obtained a job delivering summonses to the Commissioner of Deeds, a job that paid five dollars a week. However, after a week on the job, he heard that there was going to be a basketball tournament at the Educational Alliance. He appeared before Minnie with his head hung low and lied that he had lost the job. "I felt guilty about it, but I did it because it was more important to play basketball." His team did pretty well; they made the semifinals in the tournament.

Upon his graduation from high school, Biller was set to enter the City

College of New York (CCNY) Business School. Although he wanted to be a college-level math teacher, Minnie urged him to study to be an accountant. She said that the times were bad and that accountants made a good living. To please his mother, Biller agreed to enter CCNY, but he never did so, because Sam came home one night and informed him that he had found the boy a job.

The job was at Zatal's Bakery on Norfolk and Delancey Streets, a dairy restaurant with fancy cakes in the window, just around the corner from the famous Ratner's restaurant. Mr. Zatal told him that he would be paid a dollar a day and that his hours would be from seven in the morning until seven in the evening, and that he could eat his lunch at the restaurant. His job was to run day-old cookies through a machine that dripped warm chocolate, the idea being that the chocolate would freshen up the stale cookies. He was taken down to the basement, shown how to run the machine, and left on his own. Biller noted that every now and then, through no fault of his own, the machine would cast a cookie, laden with chocolate, on the sawdust-strewn floor. When this happened, Biller would throw the cookie in the garbage. A few hours later, Mr. Zatal came down to see how his new employee was doing and noticed several cookies in the garbage can and a few more on the floor. "What are you doing!" he screamed, "are you trying to ruin my business?" Biller replied that the cookies were spoiled, were dirty. Zatal said that he had never had a complaint yet. "The customers don't know," he exclaimed, "those cookies are delicious! Nobody has ever got sick on them." Biller, his stomach churning, had to pick up what was on the floor and run them through the machine again.

At lunch time, Mr. Zatal reappeared and offered him a restaurant meal, but Biller begged off, saying that he was not accustomed to eating out, and would rather go home. "It's up to you," Zatal said, "but be back here by one o'clock."

When Biller arrived home, he told his mother about the sawdust cookies. "My stomach is upset, I can't work in that place, I'm quitting." Minnie said, "Well, you can quit, but you must go back and get the day's pay." Biller protested that his pay wouldn't be that much, but Minnie insisted that he couldn't quit unless he went back and demanded whatever was coming to him. And, so he did. "Mr. Zatal," he said, "I think I'm going to be working somewhere else, so if you don't mind, could you give me my half day's pay?" Zatal looked at him, pounded the register, took out

(1) The National Postal Union stages a pay vigil outside the White House. August 31, 1967.

(2) Moe Biller, President of the Manhattan-Bronx Postal Union, surrounded by agitators, tried unsuccessfully to conduct a meeting at the Statler and was forced to escape through a kitchen and back door.

(3) Mania at the Statler: The members demanded a strike vote by hand NOW. Biller insisted on a vote by secret ballot supervised by the Honest Ballot Association. March 18, 1970.

(4) Moe Biller, together with Gustav Johnson, President of Branch 36 of the National Association of Letter Carriers, conduct a rally outside the New York City General Post Office. Also in the Picture are MBPU attorneys John O'Donnell (far left) and Eugene Victor (next to O'Donnell), and Tom Costigan, MBPU public relations man.

(5) Members of the MBPU vote at the Manhattan Center. March 21, 1970. The result was 8,242 "for" a strike and 940 "against."

(6) Moe Biller on the picket line gives a double V for victory sign.

(7) Biller and Johnson emerge from the New York City Federal Courthouse where fines were assessed on Branch 36 and Johnson by a Federal judge.

(8) Moe Biller, at a mass meeting outside the General Post Office, advised his members to return to work, March 25, 1970.

(9) The troops arrive in New York City, March 25, 1970.

(10) Military police and troops survey what appeared to be a hostile picket line.

(11) The mail rolls through a rural area in the South. The postal service subsidized every transportation system from the steam engine to the airplane.

(12) A typical railway post office car on the Hannibal-St. Joseph railroad, circa 1910. Between July, 1909 and July 1910, 98 postal clerks were seriously injured in train wrecks, and 27 were killed.

(13) Secretary of Labor George Shultz and Postmaster General Winton M. "Red" Blount announce memorandum of Agreement between postal unions and the U.S. Post Office Department, April 12, 1970. George Meany, President of the AFL-CIO is to the left of Shultz; Francis S. Filbey, President of the United Federation of Postal Clerks, is between Shultz and Blount; and James H. Rademacher, President of the National Association of Letter Carriers is third from right.

(14) President John F. Kennedy, surrounded by federal union and government officials, signs Executive Order 10988 granting recognition to federal unions and limited collective bargaining rights to seven postal unions, January 17, 1962.

(15) John MacKay, first president of the National Postal Union and leader of the rebellion against the National Federation of Post Office Clerks in 1958.

(16) Emmet Andrews, President of the APWU, lets the delegates know what he thinks of the two-hour demonstration against him at the 1978 convention.

(17) Francis S. Filbey, first President of the American Postal Workers Union.

(18) The Battle of the Bulk. Locked out workers at the mammoth New York Bulk and Foreign Mail Center in Jersey City, New Jersey, the site where Michael McDermott met his death.

(19) Biller accosts Postmaster General William Bolger after both appeared on Meet the Press. Biller is handing Bolger a copy of *The Washington Post* with a front page story regarding corruption on the Board of Governors, 1984.

(20) Moe Biller, President of the APWU, 1980 to the present.

(21) William Burrus, Executive Vice President of the APWU, 1980 to the present.

(22) Douglas Holbrook, Secretary-Treasurer of the APWU, 1981 to the present.

(23) Clark Kerr, Chairman of the 1984 Arbitration Board, announces the award.

(24) Scene from the 1984 arbitration hearings.

(25) The APWU, led by William Burrus, Moe Biller, Michael Benner, and Douglas Holbrook protest in front of the Merit System Protection Board. The MSPB charged Biller, Vincent Sombrotto, and Kenneth Blaylock with Hatch Act violations.

(26) The old APWU building in the middle of Washington D.C.'s "combat zone." The building was surrounded by porno shops, adult movies and topless bars.

(27) The present APWU Building Headquarters, since December, 1986.

(28) Moe Biller shakes hands with Administrative Law Judge Edward J. Reidy, after his oral hearing on Hatch Act violations. Reidy found Biller, Sombrotto, and Blaylock guilty as charged.

(30-31) Karen Atwood (above) and Barry Fichthal (below), deaf members of the APWU, who made history by participating in the 1987 and 1990 negotiations with the U.S. Postal Service.

(29) Moe Biller joins Gallaudet students in their strike against the school administration. The APWU was the only union to support the Gallaudet students.

(32) Women officers of the APWU. From left to right: Linda Coleman, Nilda Chock, Margaret Leaf, Barbara Prothro, Louise Yannuzzi, Elizabeth Powell, and Joyce Robinson.

(33) Vincent Sombrotto, President of the National Association of Letter Carriers, with members of the APWU 1990 bargaining team. From left to right: Sombrotto, Moe Biller, John O'Donnell, William Burrus, Doublas Holbrook, and Thomas Neill, Industrial Relations Director.

(34) The 1990-1991 Arbitration Board. From left to right: Bruce Simon, General Counsel of the NALC; Theodore W. Kheel; Chairman Richard Mittenthal; Joseph J. Mahon, Chief Negotiator for the USPS; and Peter G. Nash.

(35) Josie McMillian, president of the world's largest postal union local, the New York Metro.

a fifty-cent coin and slapped it down on the counter. Biller picked up the half-dollar and left without saying goodbye.

After the Zatal job, Biller was once again all set to go to college. His sister argued with him. She told him that he should forget college, find a job, and earn some money to help the family. The argument was resolved when Sam Biller came home one evening and told his son that he could go to work in the shop where he worked. The shop was a dirty, dismal looking room that housed about thirty sewing machine operators. His job was to sew buttons and buttonholes on the flies of boys' pants. At first, Biller tried to make certain that he would not become too competent at the job. "You stuck the button in, turned over the fly of the pants and sewed it. I made certain that the needle would hit the button so that it would break." When it became apparent, however, that his entrance into college would have to be delayed, he developed into a firstclass operator. He worked for two years alongside his father.

Biller finally did enter Brooklyn College to study Math, but his dream of becoming a college-level math teacher never was realized. He had grown up on the streets of the Lower East Side, an area that produced many famous and infamous people, including politicians, philosophers, entertainers, and gangsters. Senator Jacob Javits was born on the Lower East Side, as well as entertainers Eddie Cantor and Zero Mostel, dance instructor Arthur Murray (who was Biller's cousin), and the notorious gangsters, Little Augie and Red Levine, the latter a hit man for Lucky Luciano. But, something entirely different was in store for Moe Biller. He would combine elements of the philosopher, politician and, yes, entertainer, and become a labor leader.

The Postal Clerk

When Moe Biller entered Brooklyn College, he towered over Sam and Minnie, making them wonder what it was about the New York City atmosphere that turned children into giants. Not that Biller was a giant, but he must have seemed so to his 5'0" father who never weighed more than 100 pounds soaking wet, not to mention his mother who barely made it to the five foot mark. Biller grew to six feet and gradually attained a girth that made him look, if not fat, at least comfortable. When he was a little boy, the Irish teachers and even Mr. Zatal could not keep themselves from pinching his soft, round cheeks. He never lost that soft, round countenance, together with a disarming smile. But underneath it all was an aggressive, contentious nature that belied the soft, friendly appearance he showed the world.

While at Brooklyn College, Biller worked in the college bookstore, under the National Youth Administration (NYA), where he earned $15 a month. At one point, he had tried to join the Civilian Conservation Corps (CCC), the depression program designed to put unemployed youth to work in national parks and forests, but Sam put his foot down. When Biller told his father that he had enlisted in the CCC and that he would be going away soon, Sam rushed down to the CCC recruitment center and told the staffers that he didn't want his son to be in the CCC. When asked why, he replied in his very thick accent: "No kemps! I don't want kemps. No kemps for Moshe!" Many parents of the thirties were afraid that their children would meet and be affected by the dregs of American youth in CCC camps. For Jewish parents, the possiblity that anti–Semitism would make camp life extremely uncomfortable and perhaps dangerous for their sons was an additional cause for concern.

Income was more pressing than education. Moe's older brother, Seymour, knew somebody who worked in the Post Office and suggested to Biller that he take the test. "It's like chicken soup," Seymour said, "it pays $1,700 to $2,100 a year." Biller shrugged and thought why not? At that time in his life, according to Biller himself, he was "flighty," he jumped from one thing to another. "Later on I became a very probing individual, but in my youth I didn't investigate anything. If anybody suggested something, I was game to try it out"—even a job in the Post Office.

He and 400,000 other unemployed individuals took the test in the summer of 1936. On the Fourth of July, Biller had fallen asleep on the beach at Coney Island and had suffered a severe sunburn. When he took the test, his face was completely bandaged and he definitely was not feeling up to par. Nevertheless, he scored 95 on the examination, and on May 8, 1937 he was called to work by the Post Office.

The Sub

At that time, the stations were listed alphabetically rather than by location. Biller was assigned to Station B, located on Suffolk Street, just about a block and a half from where he was born and where he lived. "It was old, dumpy, the filthiest building ever. I wouldn't use the toilets there. I would sneak out and go home to my slum tenement apartment to go to the toilet."

Biller wanted to be assigned to part-time night work, about four hours a night, so that he could continue his education, but that definitely was not in the cards. As a substitute, he was on call all day, but worked only when work was available, or when regulars were absent or on leave. To make up for the lack of clerical postal work, and pay, he delivered special delivery letters on a piece work basis. A special delivery letter cost ten cents, nine cents of which was paid to the deliverer. He ran about twenty-seven specials a day, earning three dollars or less. "I was very disappointed...I cried, literally, I don't know why I stayed there. I just didn't know what the hell to do. And, you didn't get any real advice at home, you know? I had to buy a uniform and a bicycle. I paid $18.75 for the uniform and $5.00 for the bike. I borrowed the money." The substitutes did not have a shop steward, or station delegate, as stewards were called. All of them, including Biller, belonged to UNAPOC, but there was nobody available to handle their problems and grievances. As a result, the subs got together and agreed that Biller would become "the captain of the subs," or their informal station delegate. Surprisingly, Biller was advised to join UNAPOC by the station delegate of the National Federation of Post Office Clerks, a man who worked the money order window. He told Biller that the Federation was very weak at Station B, that he should join UNAPOC, because if he joined the Federation, he would end up on every supervisor's "S-list." Biller accepted his advice, but "discovered in a relatively short period of time that UNAPOC touted to the bosses, and it made a rebel out of me."

Biller worked at Station B for two-and-one-half years, or until he worked up the nerve to ask his local political club for help. Finally, with a little political pull, he was transferred to F Station, which eventually became known as Murray Hill, a business station located on 34th Street between 2nd and 3rd Avenues. At the time he was courting his wife-to-be, Anne Feifer, but he would not get married while he was a substitute. "That would cause too many problems—the indefinite income, the irregular hours—it would be too much."

In February 1940, close to three years after he entered the Postal Service, Biller became a regular, and on August 24, 1940, he and Anne Feifer were married. They remained married until Anne's death in 1978 and were the parents of two sons, Michael and Steven and the grandparents of two granddaughters. In 1984 Biller met Collee Ferris Brooks, an officer of the Oklahoma City local, at a convention of the Kansas State APWU. On January 4, 1987 they were married.

The Agitator

Biller's first three years in the Postal Service taught him that only through organization could the pay and working conditions of postal employees be improved. During the thirties, the industrial unions, after the initial sit-down strikes in the auto industry, were organizing aggressively throughout the country. Biller's sympathies were with the CIO, not with what he considered the ultra-conservative AFL. However, he belonged to a union that was not affiliated with either organization, and was, in his opinion, a stooge of the U.S. Post Office Department. The National Federation of Post Office Clerks may not have been a CIO-type organization, but it was affiliated with the AFL and, as such, was a part of the national labor movement. He therefore worked on an ad hoc committee whose purpose was to bring about a merger between UNAPOC and the National Federation. He became active and vocal at local meetings and began to gain a reputation as an agitator.

The leaders of UNAPOC were totally against merger and, therefore, did not appreciate Biller's activities. He was called in by the president of the local and was told that he "was a good guy with a lot of potential. Why do you resist us? What's this big merger deal?" But, Biller rejected the soft soap and continued to agitate for merger. He traveled to Washington to visit John Barrett, national President of UNAPOC, who gave him the same line as the local president. "You could go far, young man. Stop resisting and cooperate."

When the soft soap didn't work UNAPOC tried harsher tactics. At union meetings, when Biller got up to speak, people groaned and he was shouted down. Milt Rosner remembers that at one meeting when Biller took the floor somebody turned out the lights. Finally, in April 1943, he was told at a local meeting that he was expelled from UNAPOC. Biller nevertheless continued to speak. He was told to shut up and leave the hall. "You are no longer a member of this organization!" Biller replied that they would have to throw him out. Four burly members grabbed him and pushed him out of the hall and into the open arms of Local 10, National Federation of Post Office Clerks.

The Progressive

Immediately upon his expulsion from UNAPOC, Biller joined Local 10 of the National Federation, but attended only one meeting before he was drafted into the Army. He returned to work in February 1946, and was appointed Station Delegate, Murray Hill Station, in the summer of 1947. From that point on, his rise in the union was rapid. In 1949 local president, Patrick Fitzgerald—the same man who later brought security charges against him—appointed him Chairman of the Membership Committee. He was elected Guard in 1950, Vice President in 1951, and First Vice President in the same year. In 1954, he was appointed to the office of Executive Vice President, and in 1955, he was elected to that office.

Biller, of course, was very much a member of the Progressives, and was one of the delegates who walked out at the Boston Tea Party in 1958. Finally, in 1959 Moe Biller was elected President of the Manhattan-Bronx Postal Clerks Union, and it was Biller who was primarily responsible for dropping the word "Clerks" from the names of both the local and the national. He became the President of the "Manhattan-Bronx Postal Union" (MBPU), the first local of the first industrial post office union.

The man from the Lower East Side had finally found his place in the sun—that is, until 1980.

The 1980 Election

Ever since the formation of the National Federation of Post Office Clerks in 1906 (the parent organization of the United Federation and the APWU), not a single incumbent president had ever been defeated in an election; those who were replaced either retired or died in office. Emmet Andrews, the APWU incumbent in 1980, therefore, had every reason to believe that he would be reelected.

There were, however, several factors that worked against Andrews. The first was his own health which was not good. Andrews, perhaps bitter because of his repudiation by the rank-and-file in 1978, acted against medical advice and decided to seek reelection in order to redeem himself. He hoped to prove that the 1978 fiasco was engineered by the NPU dissidents, especially Moe Biller in New York, rather than by any real rank and file sentiment against him. Although Andrews' illness was not well known, his poor condition prevented him from waging a strong campaign.

Approximately one year later, he died of a heart attack.

The second obstacle to reelection was that two APWU officers decided to run against Andrews: David Johnson, Executive Vice President, and Ted Valliere, Director of Research and Education. The problem was not that Andrews could not defeat these candidates—he could and did outpoll both in the election—but that when Biller entered the race, they would split the incumbent vote away from Andrews.

The third and most important factor was that Moe Biller ran a formidable campaign. At a Presidents' Conference in April—a meeting of the presidents of all APWU locals—he announced his candidacy for President of the APWU. While his announcement did not by any means assure his victory, he went on to revolutionize the APWU election process by, first, putting together a slate of candidates, and, second, executing mass mailings to every member of the APWU.

Biller, Burrus, and Richards

Biller chose not to run alone, but to put together a slate of candidates for three of the union's highest offices. He would have liked to have had an even larger slate, but he made it mandatory that whoever ran on his team had to raise $10,000, funds which were needed for printing and mailing. William Burrus, President of the Cleveland local, wanted to run for a lesser position, but Biller convinced him to set his sights higher, to run for Executive Vice President, the union's second highest office. Burrus, who was born in Wheeling, West Virginia, attended West Virginia State College and served in the 101st Airborne Division, U. S. Army, between 1954-1957. He was employed by the Postal Service in 1958 and immediately became a union activist. Between 1958 and 1973, he was elected to a number of state and local union positions and in 1974 he became the first black president of the Cleveland local. Burrus is listed in *Who's Who in Black America* and has appeared in numerous publications, including *Business Week*, *Ebony*, *Jet*, and *Black Enterprise*. He serves on the National Board of the A. Philip Randolph Institute, is a member of the Board of Directors of the National Black College Alumni Hall of Fame and the Executive Board of the National Coalition of Black Voter Participation, and represents the APWU as an elected representative to the Postal Telegraph and Telephone International Organization.

John Richards, President of the Pittsburgh local, agreed to run for

Director of Industrial Relations. Both Burrus and Richards were former NPU members and both were considered militant advocates in the tradition of industrial unionism. Thus, the slate of Biller, Burrus, and Richards was born, and every member of the APWU would be bombarded with literature regarding their backgrounds and their program for the eighties.

Mass Mailings

Burrus and Richards raised the mandatory $10,000 and a good deal more than that was raised in New York. Biller hired Robert Armao, a public relations man, to design the brochures and other materials for the mass mailings. Robert Armao was not just any public relations man; he was Nelson Rockefeller's PR advisor. When Rockefeller, Kissinger, and Nixon were pressuring Carter to allow the cancer-stricken Shah of Iran into the country after Iran's Islamic Revolution, Armao was sent by Rockefeller "to improve the Shah's public relations internationally." According to James A. Bill: "...Armao served as a powerful and competent chief of staff for the Shah and was the main logistics man as the Shah traveled from port to port after leaving Iran."[2] Biller was not fooling around; his campaign would be designed and managed by the best flak in town.

The basic issue was leadership: Biller, Burrus, and Richards maintained that the APWU leadership historically had stood in awe of the millionaires who run the U.S. Postal Service. The Biller slate promised to deal with the Postmaster General on an equal basis, regardless of his wealth, strength, or position in government. They also promised to create a more efficient union, a union better prepared to deal with the USPS in negotiations, and capable of counteracting adverse public relations campaigns directed against union workers.

Both were persuasive issues. Postal union leaders had always had somewhat of an inferiority complex in dealing with the millionaires and kingmakers who ran the Post Office Department and the USPS. The Alabama Bourbon, Red Blount, for example, resisted meeting with postal union leaders at all, but when he was forced to grant their existence, he exhibited an air of grand condescension. After all, what were these so-called labor leaders? Nothing more than mere clerks and letter carriers. Francis Filbey once remarked that he was honored because Elmer Klassen spoke to him informally, whereas Blount would not even look him directly in the face. When Rademacher was called to the White House by Charles

Colson prior to the 1970 strike, other postal union leaders were more upset over the fact that they, too, weren't called than over the possible collusion between the Administration and the Republican, Rademacher. When the strike did break out the national leaders wrung their hands and protested to Blount that they had not called the strike, and immediately urged the strikers to return to work. The rank-and-file had become estranged from their leaders whom they considered gutless, scared rabbits in awe of the powerful.

Thus, when Biller, Burrus, and Richards insisted that they would deal with Postmasters General and other USPS officials as equals, and would not be afraid to attack when an attack was called for, they struck a deep and responsive chord. Their promise to create a professionalized union capable of matching or surpassing USPS expertise also was welcomed. But what made the major difference was the technique itself, the mass mailings to every member of the APWU. It had never been done before, but after Biller's 1980 campaign every future candidate for national office would use the same technique.

Mr. Biller Goes to Washington

The result was that the industrial faction swept aside the craft candidates. Biller, Burrus, and Richards, all former NPU members, were elected by a comfortable margin. Biller garnered 42 percent of the vote; Andrews 24 percent; Valliere 20 percent; and Johnson 13 percent. The slate, the mass mailings, and the efforts of Robert Armao were successful. Moe Biller, who had never lived more than one mile from where he was born on Manhattan's Lower East Side, moved 250 miles away to the nation's capital.

The New Regime

Biller, Burrus, and Richards arrived in Washington to assume their new positions in November 1980. The APWU offices were located in a dilapidated building at 817 14th Street between H and I Streets, the heart of the city's "combat zone." The union headquarters was surrounded by topless joints, porno shops, and prostitutes. Biller recalls that one day he walked into a shop that he thought was a newsstand and asked the man behind the counter for the New York Times. "The guy looked at me," Biller says, "as if I was putting him on. Then, I realized that I was in a porno shop and got out of there in a hurry."[3]

If the neighborhood was bad, the offices themselves were even worse. "The place was a total shambles. I couldn't figure out how to describe it. The only place that looked halfway decent was the second floor where the president sat. I realized that one of the first things that had to be done was to renovate the building."[4] That was done shortly after Douglas Holbrook replaced Chester Parrish, who retired, as Secretary-Treasurer in 1981.

A decrepit building located in a bad neighborhood might not be totally unacceptable if the organization, itself, were in good shape, if there existed a table of organization, or some sort of system for accomplishing the work of the union. What Biller found was that there were only two professionals on the staff, Bernard Cushman, who negotiated the first three APWU-USPS contracts, and an economist. The Communications Department consisted of a consultant who came in to cut and paste *The American Postal Worker*, the organization's monthly magazine. Biller also discovered that Emmet Andrews had resigned some time after the election and that David Johnson was Acting President. As for equipment, there was a word processor that nobody knew how to use. "They used it as a typewriter, like the same as an old fashioned typewriter!"[5]

Biller had his work cut out for him. For most of his life, he had been on the outside looking in, a vocal critic of those in charge. Now, he was in charge and the kibitzers couldn't wait to see him in action. In just four months he would meet his old foe, William F. Bolger, across the bargaining table and what did he have? A decrepit building, crumbling offices, inadequate staff, and the lack of any kind of a system for internal and external communication.

Preparation for an effective national collective bargaining negotiation requires a tremendous amount of work. The negotiators must understand economic trends, legal issues, the Consumer Price Index, inflation and productivity rates, the financial condition of the USPS, the economic condition of postal workers relative to similar workers in the private sector, the attitudes of the general public toward both the USPS and postal workers, trends in automation and electronic mail, and grievances regarding work rules and working conditions. Proposals must be drafted and each item must be backed up with supporting material, and a communications campaign must be launched to inform, promote, and defend the union position, as well as to attack, where necessary, the USPS position. All of this takes organization and professional help and expertise. Biller, Burrus, and Richards found that they had neither. They had to start from scratch and they had only four months to build a sound organization.

O'Donnell and Schwartz

One of Biller's first actions was to fire the law firm that represented the union and bring down from New York the law firm of O'Donnell and Schwartz. John O'Donnell, a native of County Donegal, Ireland, became the lawyer of the New York Metro at the end of the 1970 strike. Biller then had needed a lawyer who was experienced in dealing with illegal strikes and O'Donnell definitely had that experience. He had represented Mike Quill, a fellow Irishman and President of the Transport Workers Union, in the 1965-66 New York and Philadelphia transit strikes. As a youth in Donegal, O'Donnell had ties with the Irish Republican Army (IRA), was arrested for carrying a handgun, served a little time for his patriotism, and eventually put his bundle on his shoulder and set sail for New York. He was eighteen years old when he arrived and went to live with a relative in Brooklyn. Later he moved to Manhattan where, for a while, he worked as a teacher in a school for delinquent boys. Eventually, he worked his way through City College of New York and Fordham Law School and found his way into the field of labor law.

Of below average height, O'Donnell has the hands of a Donegal farmer and a voice that can be heard blocks away when he wants to make a point. He has never lost his soft, Donegal accent, his courtly manner, and his ironic sense of humor. At eighty-three, O'Donnell retains the same "thirst for justice" that led him to the IRA in his native country and to labor law in the United States, but, perhaps most important, O'Donnell is a "can do" lawyer, one who tells the client what is possible, rather than what is impossible.

O'Donnell, assisted by partners Asher Schwartz and, later, Darryl Anderson, and by associates Arthur Luby, Anton Hajjar, and Susan Catler, solved the union's legal representation problem. Biller now turned to another area of expertise—communications.

The Art of Public Relations

Nothing was more important to Biller than a mechanism for communicating with the membership and the general public. He was looking for a top-flight communications person, someone who knew his way around the media, could write good copy, and could put together a first-class Communications Department. He tried to fire the consultant who put together the monthly magazine, but discovered that Andrews had signed a multiyear contract with him just prior to the election. Biller wanted to take the matter to court because the contract was signed less than a month before he arrived on the scene, but O'Donnell advised him that court action would cost more and take more time than it would to reach a settlement. Ultimately, the consultant settled for a lump payment of eight months' salary and left the scene.

The search then began for a "Communications Director." There was no dearth of candidates. Ronald Reagan had won the Presidency in 1980, and for the first time in twenty-five years, the Republicans had wrested control of the Senate from the Democrats. Thus, many Democratic staff and committee members were thrown out of work and were looking for new jobs. Biller interviewed a number of former staff members of defeated Senators and Congressmen, among them Daniel Driscoll, former Administrative Assistant (AA) to Congressman Jerry Ambro of New York, who had been defeated in the Reagan landslide. Driscoll, who was recommended to Biller by Danny Frank, had been a reporter for the New York Daily News for nine years before he came to Washington to serve as Ambro's press secretary and, later, AA. Biller says that after interviewing Driscoll, he "put his name down."[6]

As for Driscoll, he says that he was contacted by Danny Frank and asked whether he would be interested in going to work for Biller. "I didn't have a job," says Driscoll, "my negotiating position was not all that strong, but I really didn't have much interest in the job, because, you know, it didn't sound that enticing to me." And, then, he met Biller:

I'm a media guy, a PR guy, and after talking to Moe for an hour, hour and a half, I quickly became intrigued with the possibilities of working with him. He was colorful, charismatic, interesting; I was

immediately attracted to him. He was kind of a PR guy's dream to
work with. I spotted that immediately and made the decision on the
spot that if he was interested in hiring me, I was interested in going
to work for him.[7]

Driscoll was hired and began immediately to build the Communications
Department. In December 1980 the first issue of "Communicating Directly
with You, the Member," Biller's monthly "letter" to the membership,
appeared in the magazine. Driscoll concentrated on both internal and
external communications. His goal was to keep the membership informed
of everything that was going on in the union, and to obtain media attention
for all union activities, especially for the union's position regarding contract
negotiations which were scheduled for April 1980. William F. Bolger must
have noticed the spate of APWU articles which appeared in the press and
understood that his old New York enemy had indeed arrived in Washington.

The Staff

Ted Valliere, one of the defeated candidates, had informed all members
of the staff that they would be fired when Biller took office. Valliere
admitted this to Biller because he really thought that Biller would do
exactly that. Biller met with the staff and assured the nonprofessional
members that they had nothing to fear. Bernard Cushman, who had done
an excellent job of documenting all previous negotiations, left in 1981 to
pursue his arbitration career. The only professional left from the old regime
was the economist.

Biller says that the economist drove him crazy; he could never
understand what he was talking about. "I remember asking Chester Parrish
about this and Chester said, 'let me tell you something: One of the reasons
he [the economist] is great at the bargaining table is we've got him talking
and management never knows what he's saying.' Well, that drove me
insane. I said, Chester, for God's sake!"[8] Ultimately, the economist, the
last professional from the old regime, was given his walking papers.

Biller began drawing on expertise from within the union, people like
Executive Vice President, William Burrus, attorney John O'Donnell,
Executive Assistant Mike Benner, Communications Director Daniel
Driscoll, and Larry Gervais of Minnesota, Douglas Holbrook of Detroit,
Tom Neill of Texas, and later, Driscoll's successor, Tom Fahey. Wherever

the expertise he needed was lacking, he hired experts on a consultant basis. Things were beginning to come together, but problems kept cropping up—fiscal problems and problems with the National Executive Board.

Fiscal Crisis

In February 1981, CPA Paul Gillis informed Biller that the APWU would face a $2.7 million deficit by the 1982 convention. Chester Parrish suggested that the union borrow a million dollars and then seek a per-capita increase at the 1982 convention. The loan, Parrish said, would prove to the members that there was a deficit. But, the whole idea of a loan was repugnant to Biller. There was only one answer and that was to seek an assessment of all members. Biller decided to wait until after what he hoped would be a successful 1981 collective bargaining agreement before seeking the assessment. However, when Bolger at first refused to come to the table, Biller decided to strike immediately. He asked the Executive Board to impose an assessment because of Bolger's "union busting" activities. "We rallied the members to it," thanks to Bolger, "but he probably never knew how much he helped me solve the union's financial problems in my first year as president."[9]

The members were assessed $2.05 per member per month, and at the 1982 convention, the $2.05 was added as per capita tax in the future. The per capita increase required a constitutional amendment, which, in turn, required a two-thirds majority vote. "In any free society," Biller says, "to get two out of three people to support anything, let alone an increase in taxes, is quite an achievement. I should have thanked the Postmaster General."[10]

The Cabal

At the 1980 convention, the union's National Executive Board was reduced from forty-eight to fourteen members and the officers' terms were extended to three years. One member of the Board was Kenneth Leiner, the fired worker and leader of The Outlaws, who was elected Vice President, Mail Handlers Division, in 1978. Emmet Andrews, who had no use for Leiner, waited until the young rebel lost his arbitration case, and then fired him as Vice President. Andrew's maintained that according to the APWU constitution, officers of the union had to be Post Office employees in good standing. Thus, when Leiner was fired, he was no longer a Post Office employee and could not, therefore, be an officer of the union. Moe Biller had no more use for Leiner than Andrews, but he protested Andrews' action on the grounds that an arbitrary action by management should not be allowed to abrogate the results of a union election. The members voted for Leiner; they, therefore, had the right to be represented by Leiner.

Leiner sought a restraining order in federal court to prevent his dismissal from union office, arguing that: (1) The New York Metro constitution provided that "no disciplinary action taken by the U.S. Postal Service which directly or indirectly resulted from a member's union activity shall diminish in any way such member's right to maintain full good standing membership and...he or she shall be deemed an employee of the Postal Service as long as good standing is retained"; and (2) that Andrews' action was not based on his dismissal from the Postal Service, but on Leiner's political activities in opposition to Andrews. The judge decided against Leiner, ruling that the APWU constitution, which does not contain the clause cited above, took precedence over the New York Metro constitution, and that the dismissal of Leiner was "based on reasonable interpretation of the constitution, not retaliation."[11] Regarding the latter, Leiner presented a good deal of material describing his anti–Andrews activities in an attempt to prove that his dismissal was politically motivated. After reading the material, the judge told Leiner that if he had been Andrews, he would have fired him a long time ago.[12]

Leiner pursued his case in the courts and received a favorable ruling from the Labor Department to the effect that as long as his case was pending, he had the right to run again for office in 1980. Despite the opposition of Biller, Leiner was reelected and became a member of the fourteen-person Executive Board. Biller, working with John O'Donnell, then sought and gained the approval of the Executive Board to pay Leiner $78,000 in back wages for the period of his suspension.

Biller's action on behalf of Leiner did nothing to soften Leiner's opposition to Biller. As a mail handler and a member of the APWU, Leiner asked the Executive Board to approve a resolution designed to decertify LIUNA as the bargaining agent for the Mail Handlers. Biller argued against the resolution. He maintained that the time was not right for such a campaign: "First, there wasn't a chance that the campaign would succeed, and second, we were in the process of building the union, preparing for negotiations, and, not only that, but we could not afford to spend money on a project that was doomed to failure."[13] But, Biller, who had appealed directly to the rank-and-file, ignoring the old power centers, had not yet consolidated his position within the Executive Board. The Board overruled him and voted for the Leiner resolution, and, to Biller's chagrin, John Richards voted with the majority. It was the first break in the Biller, Burrus, and Richards team, but it would not be the last. Richards and Leiner and, later, David Daniel of West Virginia, would become the not-so-loyal opposition to the Biller regime.

The $100,000 campaign to decertify LIUNA was a failure. Biller said "I told you so," and Richards and Leiner blamed the failure on the lack of commitment and support by the administration.

The 1981 Negotiations

Moe Biller's mettle would be tested in the 1981 negotiations. His election represented the final ascendancy of the NPU faction over the craft faction in the APWU. After years of being a sideline critic, he now assumed full responsibility for negotiating a contract that would not only be accepted by the rank-and-file, but would also realize his vision of what a good contract should contain. He was reunited with his New York colleague, Vincent Sombrotto, who also was negotiating his first contract since his victory over Joe Vacca for the Presidency of the Letter Carriers in 1978. They formed the Joint Bargaining Committee (JBC) of the APWU and NALC, which together represented 80 percent of all postal employees. Both Sombrotto and Biller were very much aware that they were on the spot, and that there were many in both unions who would not be unhappy if they failed.

The JBC was pitted against a formidable opponent, Postmaster General William F. Bolger. Bolger, a well-groomed, fastidious man with a high voice and a stubborn nature, was not an admirer of labor unions. He often said that there wasn't a manager alive who wouldn't like to see the demise of them all. Bolger never forgot that it was Biller who organized the picketing of his home in Virginia and, together with Sombrotto, led the fight against ratification of the 1978 contract. He was ready for Biller and Sombrotto, and he threw the first punch.

The Mail Handlers, who had defeated the APWU attempt at decertification, naturally decided to bargain separately with the USPS. Bolger, therefore, would have to negotiate with three separate union entities: the

Rural Carriers, the Mail Handlers, and the Joint Bargaining Committee of the APWU and Letter Carriers. In a last minute move, Bolger petitioned the National Labor Relations Board for an election to determine a single bargaining unit. On April 22 the negotiations were scheduled to begin, but the USPS did not show up. Bargaining did not begin until June when Bolger's petition was dismissed.

With the help of Dan Driscoll, Biller turned Bolger's maneuver against him. The press was bombarded with releases lambasting Bolger for insincerity, lack of good intentions, and unwillingness to engage in good faith collective bargaining. Danny Frank came down from New York and rented a room at the L'Enfant Plaza Hotel on the same level as, and facing, Bolger's L'Enfant Plaza office. He took a bedsheet and made a huge sign with the inscription: "BOLGER! WHY DO YOU REFUSE TO NEGOTI- ATE!" He hung the sheet out the window facing Bolger's office. "The thing was flying around," Frank says, "like something you would see at a college campus...All the people going to work in the morning saw it. It was enormous. The UPI came over and took a picture of it."[14]

The hotel people broke into Frank's room and removed the sheet. "I accused them of stealing stuff from my room, of breaking and entering. I had the doors double-locked. They told me I was breaking some law. I said, well, if that's the case, I'm going to file suit that you broke into my room and stole property. It sort of canceled itself out on that basis."[15]

By the time bargaining began, Bolger's punch and Biller's counterpunch more or less put the two antagonists on an even basis, but the negotiation time was cut by two months.

The Strike Threat

Moe Biller became an expert on using the threat of an illegal strike as a means to pressure management in contract negotiations. Prior to the start of negotiations he called a meeting of local presidents in Washington and asked them for the authorization to call a nationwide postal strike if it became impossible to reach an agreement with the USPS. Driscoll says, "We ballyhooed the hell out of that meeting. It was widely covered by the media—'Nation's Postal Workers Authorize Leaders To Call Nationwide Strike'—and all of that. We had to convince the nation that we were going to strike so that pressure would be exerted on the Postal Service to do everything possible to avoid a strike, because if management was convinced that we would not use the ultimate weapon, there would be no incentive for the USPS to grant concessions, to bargain in good faith."[16]

It was, however, a dangerous strategy, because if the union's bluff was called, the leaders either must actually call a strike or lose their credibility. The 1981 negotiations went right down to, and beyond, the wire. At midnight July 20th there was no agreement. At that point, as is customary when union-management negotiations reach the critical stage, Moe Biller and Vincent Sombrotto were the sole union spokesmen. They were meeting with Assistant Postmaster General Joe Morris. Driscoll was waiting in the press room, surrounded by reporters and television equipment, waiting for the word from Biller. At 12:15, he called Biller and asked, "What's going on?" Biller replied that the deadline was being extended hour by hour. He said that some progress was being made and that the talks would continue as long as there was hope for reaching agreement. If things should bog down, Biller would let Driscoll know and a strike call would go out.

At about 4:00 A.M., Biller called Driscoll and told him that he thought there may be an agreement. He said the USPS lawyers were putting it all down on paper for review by the JBC and USPS. Driscoll told Biller that time was running out, that if there was to be a strike, the news had to be released no later than 6:00 A.M. so that it could be carried by the morning news shows. There was no other way of notifying 600,000 postal workers that they were on strike.

When Biller left the bargaining room to report to the Rank and File Bargaining Advisory Committee, the scene was one of utter confusion. It was four in the morning, and the respective policy committees of the APWU and NALC were meeting in the same room, the APWU committee on one side, the NALC counterpart on the other. Not only were the media present in force, but also federal marshals, whose assignment apparently was to arrest Biller, Sombrotto, and other union leaders should a strike occur. Biller reported to the APWU Committee that a preliminary agreement had been reached with Joe Morris, chief negotiator for the Postal Service, which called for a $750 raise the first year and $600 raises in the second and third years. He did not say that the contract was definite, but that the agreement was being put down on paper by USPS attorneys. Considering the openness of the room in which the APWU and NALC committees were meeting, and the number of people involved, it is not surprising that news was leaked to the media that a contract calling for an $1,850 raise had been reached and, as a result, 600,000 postal workers who were poised to strike on the morning of July 21, 1981, went to work instead.

When Biller returned to the bargaining room, he found that the contract put down on paper was completely different from that to which the unions had agreed; it was, in fact, a "renege." At 5:00 A.M., Driscoll called Biller. Sounding dead tired, Biller said, "We have a renege, management reneged on the agreement." A few minutes later, Biller and Sombrotto came to Driscoll's room. According to Driscoll:

> At 5:15 in the morning, the two of them came into my room looking like death. By now, their nerves are frazzled and they're at each other, bickering about this or that. The three of us stood there and we knew, the three of us knew, that we have to make a decision, so we kind of went around checking each other out, you know, what do you think? Should we or shouldn't we? We came real close to calling a strike, but at the last moment, Moe and Vinnie decided to take one last shot at it, to go back into the room, sit down with Bolger, and make one last attempt.[17]

> At 7:17 A.M., Biller reported to the membership: ...I want to regret the pact I reported to you at 4:00 A.M. this morning. At that time, it was correct. We had agreed on a settlement, Sombrotto and I, which called for $750 the first year and $600 and $600. We had the approval of our various policy committees. When we went back with our lawyers, management presented us with a paper which was totally different from what we had agreed to. At that time, we insisted that we wouldn't sign anything like that and, therefore, there is no agreement presently....[18]

Biller's union opponents charged in the 1983 elections that he reported on an agreement before he had a signed contract in his hand and then caved in to the Postal Service by agreeing to wage raises half the size of those originally announced. In retrospect, that criticism seems rather harsh. It was management, not the unions, who reneged on the preliminary agreement, and Biller did not "cave in" to the Postal Service; the agreement eventually reached was a reasonably good one. And it was not Biller who leaked the news of the preliminary agreement to the media.

The major question raised by the 1981 negotiations was the use of the strike threat to pressure the USPS. It is highly doubtful that the media would have been present at four o'clock in the morning if the threat of a nationwide postal strike was not hanging in the balance. And, if the media was not present, the threat of news leaks would have been eliminated. Dan Driscoll speaks scornfully of "some local presidents who were hiding in their basements to avoid arrest when it seemed that a strike was imminent, and then became vociferous opponents of the contract after a strike was avoided."[19] Nevertheless, the question was raised: How often could the unions "cry wolf" and get away with it? The 1970 strike was becoming a memory, ancient history to new entrants into the Postal Service, and it was generally acknowledged that the strike succeeded only because of the special circumstances that existed at the time. It is highly doubtful that a strike could have succeeded in 1981. After all, had a postal strike occurred, the postal unions would have been only weeks ahead of the air traffic controllers and facing the same Administration. According to John O'Donnell:

I don't know if another postal strike is possible, not because it's against the law, but because postal workers don't have that same sense of being downtrodden. You've got to have a sense of injustice that is rankling the people, that they're being unfairly treated.[20]

In future negotiations, there would be less strike talk and the old slogan, "No Contract, No Work," would be heard far less frequently.

The Agreement

Twelve hours after Biller's announcement to the membership, an agreement was finally reached. It provided for three $300 annual salary increases; the same uncapped COLA of one cent for each 0.4 increase in the CPI; three $350 productivity cash bonuses, and an additional $150 cash bonus upon contract ratification; inclusion of $3,600 in previous COLA increases in the base pay for calculating pensions, shift differentials and other benefits; maintenance of the 1978 no–layoff provisions; and a limit on mandatory overtime to ten hours a day for five consecutive days in a service week.

Although both the Executive Board and Rank and File Bargaining Advisory Committee urged ratification of the contract, John Richards tried to organize a rank and file movement for nonratification. He was against the bonus provisions, which he considered a sop to make up for inadequate salary increases. He accused Biller of misleading the members and caving in at the last moment to the Postal Service. His break with Biller was now complete.

On August 27, 1981 the contract was approved by a four to one margin. Biller had survived his first test, but just barely. The negotiations had been concluded but while the members were still voting on the contract, PATCO led the air traffic controllers out on strike against the Federal Aviation Administration (FAA). Reagan's drastic response in firing 11,400 air traffic controllers may have had more to do with the lopsided 4–1 vote for ratification than rank-and-file postal worker satisfaction with the contract.

The Relevance of the PATCO Strike

Comparing the results of the only two nationwide strikes of federal employees in history may provide significant insights into the future of public sector collective bargaining. The personalities, politics, and economics of 1970 and 1981 were markedly different, but the lessons are still meaningful.

The Actors and Their Backgrounds

Neither Richard Nixon nor Ronald Reagan was a neophyte in collective bargaining, but their backgrounds were quite dissimilar. Richard Nixon had played a highly significant role, along with Secretary of Labor James P. Mitchell, in persuading the Eisenhower Administration not to intervene in the 1959 steel strike, allowing it to continue for 116 days, hurting both the union and the industry to such an extent that there was never a recurrence. Ronald Reagan, though long ago having been President of the Screen Actors Guild, had no such strike-favoring experience.

More important was ideology. Despite the personal paranoia displayed in 1972 and 1973, Nixon was a pragmatist in domestic affairs, more concerned with what works than ideological preconceptions. Already committed to postal reorganization and having publicly sided with the needs of postal workers for better pay and working conditions, the strike for Nixon was a positive political weapon. The national union leadership which had opposed postal reorganization was thereby neutralized. In 1981, on the other hand, months into an Administration characterized more by ideology than pragmatism, the PATCO strike gave Ronald Reagan an opportunity to impress his right-wing supporters, show contempt for unions, and raise the banner of law and order.

Of course, the hour-by-hour representation in both cases should have been from the Secretary of Labor. With the exception of one defeated politician, every Secretary of Labor of the postwar period, Democrat and Republican, until the Reagan-Bush era, brought expertise and relevant experience to the position—as labor leaders, management personnel representatives, or academic neutrals. All Reagan-Bush labor secretaries were amateurs. Secretary of Labor Donovan, for example, was Reagan's campaign manager in New Jersey and the vice president of a construction firm. By contrast, Secretary of Labor George Shultz was a mediator and arbitrator from the Massachusetts Institute of Technology and the University of Chicago. Shultz could have been expected to put strike settlement at the top of his agenda; Secretary of Labor Donovan could have been expected to wait for White House direction—direction that never came. Donovan had nothing to do with the PATCO strike. Reagan called on his Secretary of Transportation, Drew Lewis, for advice. It was Lewis who was behind Reagan's decision to fire the striking air controllers.

The Nature of the Strikes

Leaving aside the accidents of history, the 1970 walkout was a wildcat strike which spread against the national union leaders' will, whereas the PATCO strike was called as a calculated step in a collective bargaining strategy. The postal workers were striking as much against their union leaders as against their employer. The deciding body which could alleviate their grievances was neither; it was the U.S. Congress. The air traffic controllers were likewise aggrieved, considered their employer, the Federal Aviation Administration, unresponsive, but had not yet reached the point of spontaneous rebellion. Since no national union leader had called the 1970 postal strike, the government had no clear target for legal response. The leader of the 1981 air traffic controllers strike was clearly the PATCO President, Robert Poli. A back-to-work order could have little impact on the rebellious postal workers, whereas a substantial number of air traffic controllers returned to work when threatened with job loss.

Strike Effectiveness

The Postal Service is a massive organization with, at the time (1970), approximately 200,000 striking workers to replace. The Army tried to man the New York City post offices with little success. There was no way small military units could staff every post office across the land and perform door-to-door deliveries even if they knew how to do the job. The air controllers were a comparatively small group of workers at a limited number of sites. Management personnel and military air controllers, along with returning strikers, could keep a substantial number of planes flying. Of course, flights were delayed and there must have been safety risks until an emergency training course could provide replacements for the missing controllers. The flying public had to be inconvenienced and there is real doubt ten years later whether we have ever been as safe. Every home and business in the land was affected by the postal strike, whereas only a small percentage of the public are airline passengers in any given week. The householder knows the postal clerk and letter carrier. The householder and business person also know whether the mail is being delivered properly. Who knows how safe the airlines are unless and until crashes occur? Even then, who can identify air traffic controller availability and skills as a causal factor? Who knows the air controller? The postal worker wears a blue collar; the air traffic controller is perceived as a professional.

The Vietnam conflict had not generated the patriotism which might otherwise have made the 1970 strike anathema. By 1981, on the other hand, over a decade of inflation, reaching a virulent level after the 1979 oil price acceleration, combined with the rising unemployment of the 1981-1982 recession, focused the American public's attention on its own problems rather than those of an unfamiliar professional group. Declining union membership and the overwhelming election of a president who did, after he got in office, exactly what he had promised in his campaign, were all indicators that no union could expect much public support. It was a time for concession bargaining, not for challenging the power of the United States government. The postal unions might have had some advantages over the air traffic controllers in 1981, but not enough to win over a popular and anti-union President fresh from an overwhelming electoral victory.

The lessons are clear for federal sector collective bargaining. The illegal strike is a conceivable weapon only if the membership is united, aggrieved, and beyond restraint; the public perceives the strikers' demands as just; and the political powers would lose rather than gain by attacking the strike. Seldom is that constellation likely to be simultaneous in its essential order as it was in 1970.

The government, on the other hand, can put down an illegal strike only when the strikers are powerless to shut down an essential service, or the public is prepared to suffer inconvenience or forego service in order to see the lawbreakers punished. Which will prevail is a question of time, place, and circumstance. But, with electronic mail and private package services, the trends are probably against any repeat of the postal workers' 1970 success and, considering public attitudes, the PATCO experience is a more likely portent of the foreseeable future for all public employee unions.

The Health Plan Crisis

Health care protection has long been a major concern of the American labor union movement. Nineteenth–century unions formed and managed their own health and welfare plans based on membership contributions. Craft unions, by and large, lacked the continuing employment relationships with particular employers as well as the power to win employer-paid health care benefits. Industrial unions had the continuing relationships, but were generally confronted with employer intransigence until the U.S. Supreme Court ruled in 1949 that so-called fringe benefits were a form of pay and therefore a mandatory bargaining issue under the Taft-Hartley Act. For the unions, the existence of health care plans was important not only as an organizational device, but also for retaining membership in the absence of a union shop. Ben Evans, former director of the APWU health plan, puts it this way: "When you enroll a member of the union in a health plan, you also enroll the member's family. If a member's grievance is mishandled by the union, he may get angry, lose his cool and quit the union, but if he's a member of the health plan, he has to think about Mama and the kids, so he's far less likely to leave the union."[21]

When the merger took place in 1971, five different health plans were merged to form the APWU health plan. The plan operates under a Board of Directors (The National Executive Board), headed by the president of the union, and a Director who is elected. "The Director is elected by popular vote," says Evans, "he doesn't know a thing about health insurance or any other kind of insurance. Yet, the health plan is a big business, but back in 1981, it was being operated as a mom and pop operation."[22]

The health plan offices are located in the Francis S. Filbey building in Silver Spring, Maryland, a good distance from the national headquarters of the APWU. After their election, Biller, Burrus, and Richards soon learned that the health plan was in serious trouble. Whenever the three officers went out in the field to address members of local unions, they were bombarded with questions about unpaid claims. And at the home office, an inordinate number of telephone calls were received from members complaining that their claims were as much as six months or more in arrears. According to Darryl Anderson, the health center staff spent more time explaining to callers why claims hadn't been paid than in processing claims. When Moe Biller returned from a trip to Japan in September 1981 he learned that the health plan was $75 million in debt, and that Donald Devine, Director of the Office of Personnel Management, had decided to eliminate the APWU plan from the Federal Employees Health Benefits Program. If Devine was to get his way and the union was held responsible for the debt, the APWU would have been faced with bankruptcy, or at least the specter of a real financial disaster. In addition, the Reagan Administration was exercising its muscle against the air controllers at the time, and if the Administration was successful in canceling the APWU health plan, the prestige of the federal government's largest union would have suffered irreparable damage.

Rising Costs and Poor Management

There were two reasons why the APWU health plan was in trouble: rising costs and poor management. During the 1970s, health insurance costs were rising between 18 and 22 percent a year, compounded. The actuaries in the insurance industry badly underestimated rising costs; thus, all health plan carriers were "seeing red." In 1981, for example, Blue Cross/Blue Shield lost $200 million in the federal program alone. The APWU plan also was a victim of actuarial miscalculation, but the difference between the APWU and Blue Cross/Blue Shield was that Blue Cross/Blue Shield had the reserves to cover its underwriting loss; the APWU did not.

There are two ways that an actuary can measure liability—either through an analysis of a specific plan's past, present, and potential future liability, or through an analysis of industry trends. The APWU actuary had no way of estimating liability because of gross mismanagement at the Francis S. Filbey building in Silver Spring. When Biller visited the facility, he found that claims were being warehoused (stacked in large boxes). The staff not only couldn't pay the claims, they had no idea what was in the boxes. Thus, the actuary had no way of ascertaining the plan's liability. Biller was the first president of the union to visit the Silver Spring operation. When asked whether Andrews knew about the health plan problems, Ben Evans replied that Andrews received reports from the Health Plan Director, "that told the Board members what they wanted to hear. Filbey and Andrews never interfered with us out here. We did whatever the hell we wanted to do."[23]

Biller, with the help of Bill Burrus and Secretary-Treasurer, Doug Holbrook, lost no time in making sweeping changes in the entire operation. Biller gave Evans a deadline for eliminating the backlog and called in the consultant firm, Booz, Allen, and Hamilton to look over the operation and make recommendations. The staff was increased and trained in the processing of claims. Evans, with the backing of Biller, Burrus, and Holbrook, and a system introduced by Booz, Allen, was able to eliminate the backlog by the end of 1981. In the meantime, a battle to overrule Devine's decision to cancel the APWU plan was waged on two fronts—the judicial and the political.

The Federal Employees Health Benefits Program

The Federal Employees Health Benefits Act (FEHBA) was passed by Congress in 1959 and took effect in 1960. It provided that the federal government would pay 40 (later 60) percent of the costs of three types of health insurance programs: (1) Two governmentwide plans, a "fee for services" plan (Blue Cross/Blue Shield) and the other an "indemnity" plan (Aetna Insurance Company); (2) Health Management Organizations (HMOs), which feature preventive medicine; and (3) employee organization plans (e.g., the APWU and Letter Carriers plans). The latter were not included in the original act, but Senator Jacob Javits of New York was successful in amending the legislation to permit unions to participate in the FEHBA program.

Each year, the Office of Personnel Management (OPM) issues a request for proposals, calling on organizations to submit health insurance plans stipulating the proposed benefit package and costs. Successful bidders enter into negotiations with OPM to finalize the cost-benefit package. OPM then distributes brochures describing the approved plans to all federal employees. The employees can select whichever plan best suits their needs. Any federal employee can select any plan; in other words, postal employees are not limited to the APWU or Letter Carrier plans; they are free to choose Blue Cross/Blue Shield or an HMO if they so desire. Each year there is an "open season" when employees can either remain with their present plans, or switch to different plans.

Employees can choose between high-option and low-option plans, and plans which do or do not include deductibles and/or co-insurance (plans which require the employee to pay a percentage of the costs). The APWU plan was a high-option plan without a deductible or co-insurance and therefore a high-cost program. In addition, the federal contribution for postal workers was 75 percent, a gain which had been won in collective bargaining. The 60 percent employer contribution (or 75 percent for postal workers) was based upon the average cost of the so called "Big Six," or the two governmentwide plans, plus the two largest HMOs and employee organization plans. The APWU plan was one of the Big Six. Thus, if Devine could cancel the APWU plan, he could reduce considerably the basis upon which the federal contribution was calculated. Since the Reagan Administration was attempting to cut costs wherever possible, Devine could score a major point with the Administration if he could make his cancellation of the APWU plan stick.

Biller vs. Devine

In August 1981, after the APWU had submitted its plan to OPM and negotiated rates for 1982, Devine directed that major cuts be made in federal employee health benefits. He called a meeting of all providers and ordered that all plans be resubmitted with a $250 deductible and 75–25 percent co-insurance. The APWU balked. The union position was that it had fought through the years to obtain "first dollar" coverage for its members and it wasn't about to give it up. Devine responded with a whole series of ultimatums which the union ignored.

At a meeting with Biller and Darryl Anderson, Devine told Biller that he had no choice but to acquiesce. He called the APWU plan a "basket case," and said that the only way the APWU could stay in the program was to accept a low-option plan with a premium half the size of the APWU's then current premium ($60 per pay period). He told Anderson and Biller that the plan he was suggesting was the wave of the future and that he was offering the APWU its only opportunity to remain in the program.

Biller briefed the Executive Board on the Devine proposal and argued strongly against it. John Richards, however, introduced a motion that Devine's $30 low-option plan be accepted. Richards thought that the situation was hopeless and that the only way the union could avoid bankruptcy was to accept the Devine proposal. The Board backed Biller and rejected the Richards motion by a vote of eleven to one, with two abstentions.

While Biller was in Japan, Devine sent his last ultimatum: either accept the $30 low-option plan, or be dropped from the program. Bill Burrus, who was Acting President, was all ready to refuse Devine, but Anderson suggested that Biller be called in Tokyo. Biller, when reached, told Anderson to call Devine at home and tell him that Biller would meet with him upon his return from Japan. Devine, however, told Anderson that it was too late, that the APWU was no longer a part of the program. Anderson then worked all night to prepare a temporary restraining order (TRO) and was in court within two days. The judge denied the TRO, but under federal rules, when a judge denies a TRO, he must schedule a hearing ten days later on a preliminary injunction regarding the question of whether the plaintiff should be given emergency relief pending a trial of the case. Ten days later, the judge gave the APWU a preliminary injunction. Anderson successfully argued that Devine was discriminating against the APWU by not letting the union submit a plan with cuts, as he did with all other providers. Instead, Devine was demanding that the APWU accept his $30 low-option plan which, Anderson argued, would cut the Big Six average so much that the federal government would have paid $500 million less in health insurance in 1982 than in 1981. The judge ruled in favor of Anderson and ordered Devine to allow the APWU to submit its own plan.

When Biller returned from Tokyo, he immediately began a lobbying campaign to put pressure on Devine to back down. He saw Senator Howard Baker, then Senate Majority Leader, and Senator Ted Stevens and Congressman William Ford, Chairmen of the Senate Governmental Affairs and House Post Office and Civil Service Committees. At the White House, he met with Craig Fuller, Secretary of the Cabinet, and the White House labor liaison, Robert Bonatati. Senator Stevens held hearings on the FEHBP where it was revealed that OPM had a $446 million shortfall in its own budget—a good deal larger than the $75 million APWU deficit, and an indication as to why Devine was bearing down on all providers.

Biller hired the Stamford, Connecticut consulting firm of Johnson and Higgins to help draw up a new plan. The plan that emerged still did not contain a deductible or co-insurance for surgery, anesthesia, and ambulance services. Instead, the dollar impact on benefits was calculated as if $20 million were cut from a hypothetical $200 million in benefits paid during the previous year. In other words, OPM was told that the APWU would cut $20 million in benefits, but not by means of a deductible or co-insurance, but by cutting the benefits themselves. However, for supplemental benefits, the union agreed to a $150 deductible, rather than the $200 deductible sought by OPM, and 80-20 percent co-insurance instead of the 75–25 percent OPM wanted.

Perhaps because of the heat that was put on Devine through Biller's lobbying efforts, or because he just tired of the whole battle, Devine accepted the APWU plan, and the crisis was resolved. It was the second narrow escape for the new regime.

End of the Beginning

Moe Biller has his detractors both inside and outside of the labor movement. Certainly, Richards, Leiner, and Daniel are among his chief critics, maintaining that Biller stages vendettas against those who oppose him in good faith, and sometimes overemphasizes public relations to the detriment of dealing with real union issues. Across the negotiating table, USPS personnel believe that Biller is too strident and several of his labor union colleagues believe that Biller is a throwback to the thirties when industrial workers were really exploited and labor leaders had to be "tough." Some say that Biller is too pro-union, citing his defense of Jackie Presser, the discredited former President of the Teamsters. But not one of these critics would discount Biller's contributions to the APWU. He took a moribund organization and turned it into an efficient and well-managed advocate for its members. Today, the APWU has a first-class Communications Department, an exemplary library, a computerized communications system that links the national office with every local in the country, and a staff that is capable of providing all of the backup needed to present the union side of issues facing the USPS and the individual postal worker.

During its first term, the Biller administration had built up the union's professional staff, faced down a potentially devastating fiscal crisis, negotiated a controversial but nevertheless good contract with the USPS, and stood up to OPM Director Donald Devine and saved the union's health care plan, which today is in excellent shape, although its membership is well below the pre-1981 level—all in all, not a bad record. But, Biller and company would not be allowed to rest on their laurels; there would be fresh challenges to the leadership in the future, including internal opposition and even more difficult contract negotiations.

Chapter 8

THE REGIME SETTLES IN

With its first collective bargaining and external political challenges behind it, the Biller administration could now turn to overcoming a nascent internal opposition, strengthening its negotiating practices, and establishing an agenda of long-term objectives. As 1982 approached, in addition to the regular union agenda, preparations had to be made for the 6th Biennial Convention in Miami and, following that, for the 1983 elections. Regarding the latter, an organized opposition to the "Real Team," the sobriquet of the Biller slate, began to emerge. At the national level, the opposition was led by Biller's erstwhile running mate, John Richards, and included Michael Zullo, Director of Research and Education, Ben Zemsky, Director of Organization, and Kenneth Leiner, Director, Mail Handler Division. In the field, the center of opposition was the TRINE Council, a combination of the APWU-Tri State and Regional Councils, consisting of twelve eastern state organizations and four southern locals. The slate of candidates that would oppose the Real Team in 1983 was pretty much a creation of the TRINE Council.

The 1982 Convention

The Biller administration unveiled an eighteen-minute multimedia show, developed by the J. Walter Thompson Advertising Agency, that included thirty-second television commercials extolling the virtues of postal workers. The theme of the commercials was "We want to be letter perfect for you." Dan Driscoll describes the reaction of the delegates:

We put this thing on. I think it was a sixteen or eighteen projector slide show. There was dead silence. All the lights in the Grand Ballroom were killed. The screen was mammoth, huge. When the show ended, the ballroom erupted in applause, screaming, shouting, foot stomping...the delegates went crazy, they went berserk. Moe, standing there with boxing gloves on, brought the J. Walter Thompson people up to the podium. It was just a wonderful show.[1]

Not five minutes after the conclusion of the show, Biller moved to amend the constitution to increase the per-capita tax. According to Driscoll: "The emotion, the emotion played right off the...enthusiasm of the delegates, sailed right into the per-capita, slammed it home, overwhelming support on the per-capita increase."[2] The delegates had a right to cheer. They had been exposed to a Federal Express ad which portrayed postal clerks as lazy, sluggish, and rude, gossiping to one another about their future retirement, and ignoring the line waiting for service. The APWU had protested and had succeeded in getting all three networks and Federal Express to withdraw the ad. Now, they had an ad of their own showing postal clerks exactly the way they perceived themselves, smiling, happy, busy, eager to serve. The opposition accused Biller of "showmanship" to get his own way and cited his penchant for hiring expensive legal, consultant, and advertising firms, and ignoring the day-to-day problems faced by postal worker on-the-job. And, they showed some muscle during the 1982 convention by passing a resolution that supported the Mail Handler decertification campaign. Later, they would move in other ways to frustrate Biller programs.

The New Building

In the March, 1982 edition of The American Postal Worker, Secretary-Treasurer Doug Holbrook announced that the APWU was leaving D.C.'s "Peep Show Row":

In an unanimous vote by the Board's [National Executive Board] fourteen members, the NEB selected a site and building that will become the APWU's new home near Capitol Hill, probably by late 1983. The action means that APWU will be leaving Washington's sordid 14th Street area where the crowded APWU National Headquarters is surrounded by massage parlors, pornographic bookstores, "marital aids" shops, and bars featuring nude dancers.

The Board's decision came after hearing several hours of discussion on the proposal by realtors, developers, the best consultants in Washington, D.C., APWU's certified public accountants, and lawyers from the APWU's General Counsel's office....[3]

David Daniel, President of the West Virginia State APWU, sued in District Court to prevent the real estate deal. Daniel contended that the membership had not had sufficient time to consider the transaction and that the deal would put the union at risk. The District Judge ruled in favor of Daniel, thus preventing a move from Peep Show Row for at least two years. The union appealed the decision and in June, 1984, the District Court's decision was overruled by the Appeals Court. In its decision, the Appeals Court noted that the Labor Management Reporting and Disclosure Act does not give courts a license to interfere broadly in internal affairs. However, by the time the Appeals Court handed down its decision, the question had become moot. Time had proven the financial arrangements of the Capitol Hill site to be less than advantageous. A preferable site had become available at 13th and L Streets and in December 1986 the union moved into its present headquarters. As for Daniel, he would continue his opposition by challenging Biller for the presidency in 1983.

The 1983 Elections

The 1983 elections turned out to be something of a shock to the Biller slate. In his campaign statement contained in the August 1983 edition of *The American Postal Worker,* Biller merely said, "Our achievements—even with the conservative White House—are too numerous to list." And, he didn't do so. The remainder of his statement was a listing of the Real Team candidates.

The opposition forces would have preferred to have John P. Richards run against Biller. Richards was well known by the membership and had served for three years as the Director of Industrial Relations, but Richards decided not to run for either office. When Richards ran with Biller in 1980, he did not resign as President of the Pittsburgh local. He returned to Pittsburgh and became the Chairman of the "New Unity Committee," a pro-Daniel organization.

David Daniel was thirty-two years old in 1983, had a Master's Degree from West Virginia University in Legislative Politics and Statistics, was the President of the West Virginia State APWU, and Executive Vice President of the Huntington local. Although he was not well known nationally, he was extremely articulate and constructed an attractive platform. His theme was "Leadership, Not Showmanship," and his opening statement made clear what he meant:

> Showmanship has been substituted for leadership, rhetoric for action, lies for the truth. The membership has been insulted by the wasting of dues on high priced internal propaganda, consultants, and outside spoils system staffing. Zullo, Zemsky, Leiner and others have been censored, harassed, and insulted by the incumbent....[4]

Although Biller claims that he has never underestimated an election opponent, he nevertheless failed to exploit an impressive array of accomplishments. He had taken an organization that was in shambles and put it back together again, negotiated a pretty fair agreement under extremely difficult conditions, saved the health plan and the union from possible bankruptcy, computerized the entire administration of the APWU, forced Federal Express to retreat, and began a campaign to improve the public image of postal workers. These were legitimate accomplishments, but Biller did not see the need to articulate them.

Daniel surprised everyone by garnering 43 percent of the vote. Michael Zullo, a Biller foe, was defeated by Real Team candidate, James Adams, but Zemsky and Leiner were reelected as Director of Organization and Mail Handler Director, respectively.

The National Election Appeals Board ordered a new election for national Mail Handler Director, allegedly because of the incumbent's use of the Pittsburgh local's mailing lists. When the attempt was made to block this rerun, the Department of Labor broadened its investigation to include all races. The result was that the Labor Department found a number of improprieties, including:

1. Some of the funds for the Real Team slate came from employers and the union. Both are illegal sources in union elections. The Labor Department did not charge the Real Team with taking money from the Postal Service, but rather from smaller employers

not organized by the APWU, some of which did business with the union.

2. The Real Team benefitted from a dinner sponsored by the New York Metro which the Labor Department claimed was a part of the Real Team's campaign.
3. Some candidates were given access to postal facilities to campaign, while others were denied entrance.
4. Some locals made mailing lists available to candidates without informing other candidates that they could also use the lists. The New York Metro allowed the Real Team to use its list of retirees, while the Pittsburgh local allowed opponents of Biller to use their lists.

None of these complaints was particularly serious. There was no major skullduggery involved, but the Labor Department ordered the union to rerun the races for all top APWU officers except for a few who were unopposed in the original vote. Had the union refused, the Secretary of Labor would have taken the matter to court and thus caused a delay in determining who were the proper officers—a most unsettling situation. The officers decided, therefore, that the best interests of the union would be served by accepting the Labor Department's ruling. Consequently, ballots for the rerun, which would cost the union approximately $200,000, were mailed on October 12, 1984.

The results were the same. Daniel increased his percentage from 43 to 45 percent of the vote, but Biller was the clear winner. Daniel challenged Biller again in 1986 and gained 47.5 percent of the vote—close, but not enough. Moreover, in 1986, Zemsky and Leiner were defeated, thereby eliminating all opposition to the Biller regime at the national level. But Biller achieved his greatest victory in the 1989 elections—the entire Real Team slate was swept into office. Biller defeated Robert F. Caracciolo of the Springfield, Massachusetts area local, by a two-to-one margin, Elizabeth Powell upset the incumbent Regional Coordinator Lawrence Bocchiere, of the Stamford Connecticut Area Local, to become the first woman Regional Coordinator and member of the National Executive Board. Joyce B. Robinson, a Biller candidate, defeated Michael Zullo as Research and Education Director and, thus, became the first woman resident officer of the APWU.

Biller had finally neutralized the opposition. Daniel had proven to be a formidable candidate; he had a persuasive platform and articulated a significant case against Biller's policies, but he was up against a pro—at once dynamic, intelligent, and capable. No matter how hard Daniel tried to make his campaign a positive one, he ended up with negatives: Biller was undemocratic, he stifled dissent on the Executive Board, he was out to "get" those who opposed him, he caved in on the negotiations to the USPS, he spent union dues foolishly on lawyers, consultants, and advertising agencies, and, unlike his predecessors, he had not been selected as a Vice President of the AFL-CIO. (The latter charge would be put to rest on October 5, 1989, when Biller was sworn in as Vice President of the AFL-CIO Executive Council.) The Biller regime's accomplishments were real and could not be obfuscated by a negative campaign. Moreover, Biller as a spokesman for postal workers was constantly in the public eye—on "Meet the Press," the "Larry King Show," "Crossfire," and other top radio and television shows. He debated the conservatives and always performed well. He made the members proud of their union and he made them feel as if they had a strong and committed advocate in Washington.

The 1984 Negotiations

The central issue in 1984 was how to interpret the Postal Reorganization Act's requirement of pay comparability between postal workers and private sector employees. But what was comparable and with whom?

The USPS Board of Governors issued a statement on April 3, 1984 that postal pay and benefits exceeded the reward of private sector jobs and called for a "correction to this situation." The USPS introduced a "two-tier proposal" with a permanent scale that contained a 33 1/3 percent lower wage and benefit structure for new employees with no increase for incumbents. When the existing agreement expired on July 20, labor and management were at an impasse, approximately $13 billion apart in their proposals. On July 24 the Federal Mediation and Conciliation Service initiated fact-finding procedures. But on July 25 the Postal Service announced that it would unilaterally implement its two-tier proposal. The unions filed for an injunction in federal court. Postal management's plans to begin hiring new employees at 23 percent lower wages (rather than the 33 1/3 percent originally announced) was halted on August 10 when Congress voted in favor of a bill, introduced by Representative Silvio Conte of Massachusetts, to prohibit the action. Fact-finding, which recommended that the Postal Service abandon its two-tier proposal, and mediation both failed to produce an agreement.

The next step under the Postal Reorganization Act was arbitration. The parties agreed on a five-member arbitration panel with each union nominating one member and the USPS nominating two members. The panel then selected an impartial chairman, Dr. Clark Kerr, former President of the University of California.

The Battle of the Economists: Round I

Confronting the process of interest arbitration, of course, radically changed the strategies of both parties. For the union, collective bargaining negotiations had required convincing the Postal Service negotiators that the employees deserved all that was being demanded, that the service would not be irrevocably harmed by granting the concessions and might even gain through greater productivity and that failure to grant the union demands would cause great harm, even to the extent of a possible strike. The USPS had the equal and opposite case to make that any added labor costs would make the Postal Service vulnerable to competition and under greater pressure to automate—both threats to the job security of the employees—and that any strike action would not only result in a wage loss but also would face the consequences so forcefully demonstrated in the air traffic controllers strike.

None of those arguments would have more than peripheral persuasive power in an interest arbitration. The party representatives on the arbitration board would be there only to make certain that their party's arguments were clearly perceived by the neutral chair who would be the sole decisionmaker and to protect their respective parties against unforeseen consequences of any innovations discussed (though they might still reach informal compromises and propose them to the chairman for inclusion in his decision). The neutral chairman, Clark Kerr, was one of the most experienced labor arbitrators and mediators in the country. He was unlikely to be swayed by emotional appeals or aggressive language and could not be threatened. He would be searching for some basic principle, set of facts, or logic upon which to base and justify a nonpartisan decision. Factual presentations had occurred in the negotiation process to buttress each party's position in search of compromise and settlement. But now such presentations, and refutation of the opposite party's presentations, would be the whole of the proceeding. Hence the star performers would not be the party negotiators whose arguments would be heavily discounted, but lawyers, consultants, and expert witnesses whose persuasive powers would reside in their data. Enter therefore two economic consultants who would play key roles in both the 1984 and 1990 interest arbitrations between the JBC and the USPS: Michael Wachter, Professor of Economics, Law and Management at the University of Pennsylvania and Joel Popkin, President of Joel Popkin and Company, Economic Consultants and former Assistant Commissioner of the Bureau of Labor Statistics.

The first round of the Battle of the Economists was actually Round One-and-One-half. The USPS had employed Wachter to prepare data for argument during the 1981 negotiations and had him make a presentation to the parties during those negotiations. Popkin had also been an observer at the Wachter presentation as a consultant to the JBC. Wachter's point had been that the employees represented by the APWU and Letter Carriers were already overpaid by the standards established by the Congress under the Postal Reorganization Act of 1970, buttressing the USPS argument that the 1981 JBC demands were excessive. The crucial criterion was:

> It shall be the policy of the Postal Service to maintain compensation and benefits for all officers and employees on a standard of comparability to the compensation and benefits paid for comparable levels of work in the private sector of the economy of the United States.

The Congress had not bothered to explain what it meant by the phrase "comparable levels of work." It had used the same language without definition in the Federal Pay Act of 1970 covering all federal general schedule employees. That Act had required the Bureau of Labor Statistics to make an annual survey of private sector professional, administrative, technical, and clerical pay scales to test that comparability and recommend to the President and Congress the pay increases indicated. Consistently during the intervening years, the BLS had concluded that federal pay was lagging behind private sector wages, the gap identified as 14 percent in 1980 and 24 percent in 1986. Just as consistently, private economists had estimated a 10–20 percent gap in favor of federal employees, though private consultants, Hay Associates, would find a 10 percent lag in the federal general schedule in 1984. The Presidents involved, of course, ignored BLS and recommended far smaller federal pay increases, leaving it to Congress to resolve the issue.[5]

But as controversial as the comparability issue was for the primarily white collar general schedule employees, comparison was infinitely more difficult for the unique postal workers. The same issue would stymie the comparable worth movement in its pursuit of gender pay comparability in the broader economy. For generic jobs which exist across industries and firms—secretaries, truck drivers, custodians, for instance—even though what they do in a specific enterprise may differ substantially, there is still enough commonality in job content and requirements that a wage and salary survey can establish a norm. In a multifirm industry where each employer has essentially the same technology, intra-industry comparisons can be made. However, while the Postal Service may be perceived as part of a broader industry supplying message transmission and parcel delivery services, much of its service and most of its technology is unique. Who else does what postal workers do? There is some overlap with company mail rooms (at a very rudimentary level) and considerable overlap between parcel post and the United Parcel Service (UPS), but no general counterpart. Job evaluation is the standard device for determining comparability and establishing relative pay levels within an employing establishment characterized by firm-specific or industry-specific jobs. But that requires agreement on a baseline of benchmarks existing in other firms and industries, the few among many possible compensable factors to be analyzed, and the wage and salary differentials to be attached to each resulting score. It is a device never successfully used across industry lines.

Whether deliberately or inadvertently, Professor Wachter finessed the issue in his presentation during the 1981 negotiations in a way that shifted the basis of the entire comparability discussion during the two interest arbitrations to follow. He compared the compensation and benefits of "comparable workers" rather than "comparable levels of work." His data base was the monthly Current Population Survey of the U.S. Bureau of Census, a household survey in which the enumerator asks certain questions of whomever happens to answer the door during a nationwide sample of approximately 60,000 households. By its nature such a database contains little or no precision with reference to differentiating technicalities in categories such as occupations and pay provisions.

Using that source, then, Wachter compared the reported earnings of full-time postal workers with those of workers of the same race, gender, education, and work experience in various regions of the country for the economy as a whole and in the service and trade industries specifically. On that basis, he came to the conclusion that postal workers were being paid 21.1 percent more than comparable workers in the entire economy, 32.7 percent above than those in the service sector, and 32.3 percent above the trade sector.[6] In the only occupational comparison, Wachter used BLS Area Wage Surveys to show that postal wages were 21 percent above the average for materials handlers throughout the economy.[7] He also noted that the high application rates and low quit rates proved it unnecessary for the Postal Service to pay such wages in order to attract and retain employees.

After hearing the Wachter presentation, Popkin undertook a rebuttal study under the auspices of the Joint Bargaining Committee, even though the 1981 negotiations were concluded. Both Wachter's and Popkin's competing studies found publication three years later in a symposium of the Industrial and Labor Relations Review, sponsored by the New York State School of Labor and Industrial Relations at Cornell University.[8] Though the articles were not published until October 1984, they had to have been submitted for publication at least one year before that, and the source data they each used obviously had to have been concluded even earlier. Both studies, then, predated any testimony by these two authors during the 1984 interest arbitration.

Popkin used the same data as Wachter but subjected it to somewhat different statistical techniques, and came up with slightly different measures of the postal worker wage premium. As a result, Popkin drew conclusions that differed with Wachter's. He found no statistically significant differentials between the wages of white male postal workers as compared to those of other white males throughout the economy. The differential identified by Wachter, Popkin averred, occurred because the Postal Service did not discriminate in pay by race or sex as did most of the rest of the economy. Therefore, the appropriate comparison was between Postal Service wage rates and the national average for white males and on that ground, no postal worker differential existed.[9] Wachter responded that non-discrimination was the appropriate policy for the Postal Service, but that the normal market approach would have been to pay the women and minorities more and the white males less for the same overall average as the rest of the economy and that, therefore, his calculation of the postal wage premium was the correct one.[10]

The Wachter-Popkin debate proved to be the definitive exchange out of the 2,000 pages of oral testimony, 300 exhibits and 4,000 pages of documentation presented to the arbitration board. And Wachter won, determining the wage outcome not only of the 1984 arbitration but the 1990 arbitration as well. Without citing explicitly the two economists, Chairman Kerr stated:

> Congress said that wage rates should be comparable to the rates and type of compensation in the private sector of the economy. Had Congress not specified comparability, this Board would have been much concerned with it anyway, since it is a fundamental consideration in setting wages.
>
> Since July 1970, when the last increases mandated by Congress went into effect (presumably reflecting Congress's interpretation of comparability at that time), rates in the Postal Service have gone up substantially faster than rates in the private sector...
>
> ...Comparability, like beauty, is in the eye of the beholder...[The data presented] added up to the same conclusion as did the review of the historical record: discrepancies in comparability have emerged.
>
> This award interprets moderate restraint as a slowing of wage increases, as against the private sector, by 1 percent a year or for 3 percent in total over the life of this contract.
>
> ...This does not dispose of the problem. Moderate restraint may also be necessary in future years to approximate the guideline of comparability as established by Congress.[11]

Therefore, the decision was to restrict wage increases to 2.7 percent annually for the following three years plus whatever increases were dictated by the cost-of-living provisions. Nowhere in the arbitration proceedings nor the award was the shift from "work level comparability" to "worker comparability" noted.

The Award

Clark Kerr also remarked in his award:

> This arbitration is an unusual one. It involves directly half a million

people—the largest number ever covered by an arbitration in the history of the United States. It also involves $13 billion—the difference between what the union is demanding and what the USPS, on its side, is demanding...It also involves the prospective cost and quality of postal delivery that almost daily affects the lives and welfare of nearly every single resident of America and many living abroad.

With respect to interest arbitration, he issued a warning of future portent:

Arbitration of interests, as this arbitration is, sometimes may be necessary. It is never desirable. Arbitration of interests, if it becomes the practice rather than the occasional exception, can become lethal in the long run. It is far better for the parties and American society that the parties themselves write their own contracts.[12]

Kerr thus brought into bold relief the danger to collective bargaining if interest arbitration should become the rule rather than the exception, as subsequent experience may portend. Undismayed, Moe Biller has remarked that since two members of the arbitration panel are selected by the unions and two by the USPS, arbitration is really an extension of collective bargaining. This may be true, but the impartial chair is the person who eventually makes the decisions, thus relieving the parties themselves of the responsibility for establishing the rules which will govern their own industry.

The arbitration award, dated December 24, 1984, provided:

1. A 2.7 percent annual increase in wages for incumbent employees.
2. The maintenance of cost-of-living adjustments.
3. The addition of Martin Luther King Day as a paid holiday in 1986.
4. A ten percent increase in the uniform allowance.
5. The consideration by the Postal Service of human factors in the design and development of automated systems.
6. Lower starting wages and an elongation of the progression in grades (to reach the top of the scale would require thirteen years in grades 1-3 and ten-and-a-half years in grades 5-7, as opposed to eight years won as part of the 1970 Postal Reorganization Act).

7. Major improvements in working conditions, especially a reduction in mandatory overtime.

The improvements in working conditions were primarily due to the APWU's insistence on obtaining a Memorandum of Understanding with the USPS that reflected the union's position. The APWU's refusal to sign off on a less satisfactory agreement brought Biller and Sombrotto into conflict. Eventually, however, National Business Agent Lawrence Gervais, assisted by Darryl Anderson and Phillip Tabbita, drafted an APWU Memorandum that was accepted by both the USPS and the Letter Carriers. Biller considers the noneconomic improvement extremely important: "If it were not for the APWU, the contract would have had very few noneconomic improvements. This decision is of vital importance not just to government employees, but to the entire labor movement."[13]

The 1987 Negotiations

When Moe Biller entered the Postal Service in 1937, James A. Farley was the Postmaster General. Since that time, Biller has worked for and/or negotiated with sixteen additional Postmasters General. Between the 1984 and 1987 negotiations, three Postmasters General came and left before the appointment of Preston Robert Tisch in August, 1986. Paul N. Carlin had been named by the Board of Governors to replace William F. Bolger, who resigned to become Executive Director of the Air Transport Association. In February 1986 Carlin was replaced with an interim appointee, Albert V. Casey, who had been the Chief Executive Officer of American Airlines. Casey served until Tisch's appointment in October.

Tisch, a native of New York City, was (and is) a highly successful businessman. Together with his brother, Lawrence, he built a huge, diversified conglomerate with holdings in insurance, hotels, tobacco, and broadcasting. Biller praised the choice of Tisch: "He is a businessman who knows how to deal with people." Regarding the 1987 negotiations, Biller said: "If Mr. Tisch approaches next year's postal negotiations with a good-faith attitude, then perhaps we can avoid the time-consuming, expensive arbitration scenario brought on by management's refusal in 1984 to hammer out an agreement."[14]

In a meeting with the APWU National Executive Board, Tisch appeared optimistic: "Our first objective," he said, "is to reach a contract agreement that is fair to our employees, the Postal Service and the general public. We are looking forward to achieving a negotiated contract; and I believe that, working together, we can all achieve that. In no way do you go into negotiations expecting them to be easy, but we have every reason to believe they'll go smoothly. We're committed to an aboveboard approach."[15]

An agreement was reached on July 21, 1987 after a twenty-three-hour bargaining session that included the direct participation of the Postmaster General. Management had sought to double the number of casuals in the work force and extend the amount of time they could work per year, proposals that were completely unacceptable to the Joint Bargaining Committee. Eventually, the U.S. Postal Service agreed to withdraw the proposal. The length of the contract was extended from thirty-six to forty months.

The final agreement provided a 2 percent wage increase in the first year, two $250 increases in the second year, two $300 increases in the third year, and a $200 increase for the last four months of the agreement. Seven COLA adjustments were scheduled over the life of the contract, using the uncapped one cent for each 0.4 increase in the CPI. The agreement also provided for a reduction in the amount of time a Level 4 employee must wait before moving up in the pay progression, an increase in carryover annual leave from 240 to 320 hours a year, the purge of warning letters over six months old from employee files, and the establishment of a task force on child care to explore the demand for child care and related issues. The no–layoff provisions remained the same.

At about the same time the Joint Bargaining Committee was submitting its wage and benefits proposals to management, the Mail Handlers were signing an agreement with the Postal Service which contained a "Me Too" clause:

> If any of the subjects enumerated below, as set forth in the successor agreement to the 1984 APWU/NALC National Agreement, are more favorable to employees covered by the APWU/NALC National Agreement, with respect to the subjects enumerated below, than those set forth in the 1987 Mail Handlers National Agreement, such more favorable provisions shall be extended to the employees covered by the 1987 Mail Handlers National Agreement, on the same date that such provisions become effective for employees covered by the successor Agreement to the 1984 APWU/NALC National Agreement.[16]

What this meant, in effect, was that the Joint Bargaining Committee, which already comprised coalition bargaining by the APWU and Letter Carriers on behalf of their joint bargaining unit of 504,000, was also forced into negotiating for 50,000 Mail Handlers. When Biller was asked at a morning news conference what he thought of the "Me Too" deal, he ripped up a copy of the document and exclaimed, "They can shove it!" Biller added: "Even if the Mail Handlers ratify their contract, they still will have to live with the fact that their leaders gave back penalty overtime. And that's a major concession born of weakness." The Mail Handlers, a constant source of irritation to the APWU and Letter Carriers, would cause an even greater problem during the 1990 negotiations.

The 1980s Agenda

The 1980s were difficult years for all labor unions. There is nothing on the horizon to suggest that the coming years will be any easier. A repressive approach to public employee bargaining began with the election of Ronald Reagan in 1980 and his firing of the air traffic controllers when they struck a year later. That same spirit, perhaps already latent, was soon apparent in the private sector as well. According to Jo-Ann Mort, a spokeswoman for the Amalgamated Clothing and Textile Workers Union, "It [Reagan's firing of the air traffic controllers] marked a complete shift in public opinion...It was never considered a real option to just ignore the employees and hire new ones. Now, it's done all the time."[17] The idea that a strike prevents customers from patronizing a company is no longer true. Union drivers remained on strike at Greyhound month after month, but the buses kept rolling and the passengers did not seem to care who was driving. Eastern Airlines operated for two years despite a strike by the company's machinists, though it finally collapsed financially—an outcome that appears likely for Greyhound as well.

The new attitude was reflected at all levels of the Reagan Administration. The attempt was made to use the Hatch Act against union leaders. Reagan's OMB Director openly called for the privatization of the USPS, assaults were made on the health and retirement plans of all federal employees, and the Gramm-Rudman-Hollings Act threatened to place the USPS into an untenable fiscal position. The federal unions were constantly on the defensive, and the union agenda for the eighties was pretty much defined by the Administration's offensive.

Political Action

Prior to 1980, the amount of funds raised for the APWU's Committee on Political Action (COPA) never exceeded $34,000 in any year. If the union was going to reward its friends in Congress and fight its enemies, it had to do better than that. In January 1982, the APWU launched a COPA drive with a goal of $255,000. The amount raised was $385,000, $135,000 over the goal, and an 1,100 percent increase over the previous high. In 1984, COPA contributions rose to $532,000, and in 1990 to well over $800,000.

In September 1982, the APWU launched a "Voices in Politics" (VIP) program designed to encourage the union's 300,000 plus members to become politically active at the local level. The program stressed voter education on the issues and candidates in local areas, and other election activities. Particular emphasis was placed on voter registration and the limited types of political activities permitted under the Hatch Act. Patrick J. Nilan, APWU Legislative Director and Secretary-Treasurer of COPA, became the Chairman of the Program, assisted by Roy Braunstein, Legislative Aide and Letitia Chambers, Special Legislative Counsel to President Biller.

Braunstein described the COPA and VIP programs as examples of marvelous foresight and ingenuity. "These programs have united our membership in an extraordinary way," he said. "They have established goals, and the members are motivated to reach those goals."[18] COPA would be the APWU political arm at the national level and VIP at the local level.

Legislation

APWU battles in the legislative arena centered around protecting federal worker retirement benefits, protecting the USPS from fiscal problems due to deficit reduction legislation, and Hatch Act reform.

Retirement Benefits

On January 5, 1983 the President's Commission on Social Security proposed mandatory coverage under Social Security for federal new hires and recommended penalties for retirees receiving both Social Security and Civil Service Retirement. On February 12th the APWU conducted a massive seminar on Social Security—a teleconference for 10,000 participants in 47 sites coast-to-coast. The participants were trained on opposition to the merger of Social Security and Civil Service Retirement. In March a legislative rally involving 6,000 participants was conducted in Washington, D.C. The union put up a good fight, but this was one it could not and did not win. The Social Security Amendments of 1983, Public Law 98-21, required all federal employees hired after January 1, 1984 to be covered by Social Security. Incumbent employees could choose between Social Security and the Civil Service Retirement program.

Deficit Reduction

Congressman Mike Synar of Oklahoma filed suit in Federal Court charging that the Gramm-Rudman-Hollings Balanced Budget Act was unconstitutional on the grounds that the Act violated the balance of powers provisions of the Constitution by mingling the functions of the legislative and executive branches, and by requiring joint action on legal issues by the Congressional Budget Office and the Office of Management and Budget of the White House. The APWU submitted an amicus curiae brief in support of Synar's challenge.

On February 7, 1986 a special three-judge U.S. District Court ruled the Act unconstitutional. Under the law, the Congress had attempted to give the head of the Government Accounting Office (GAO), a nonelected official, enormous power to slash federal programs. The court held that the attempt to delegate this power to the Comptroller General, who is not an officer of the Executive Branch, violated the principle of separation of powers under the Constitution. The District Court's decision was upheld by the Supreme Court.

The deficit reduction bill finally passed by the Congress in December, 1987, would have forced a $1.7 billion cut in the Postal Service budget. The unions, together with the USPS, launched a campaign to take the USPS off-budget. Their December 2, 1989 success marked the only time during the 1980s that the APWU and the USPS acted in concert.

The Hatch Act

The battle of the Hatch Act was fought on two fronts: legislative and judicial. The Special Counsel of the Merit Systems Protection Board (MSPB) accused Biller, Sombrotto, and Kenneth Blaylock, President of the American Federation of Government Employees (AFGE), of engaging in campaign activity in support of the Presidential candidate, Walter Mondale, and against the reelection of Ronald Reagan. The basis of the accusation involved endorsement of Mondale in union publications and the collection of funds from union members to be used for political purposes (for example the APWU's COPA fund). In letters to the three union leaders, the Special Counsel said: "In certain circumstances, in order to avoid the time and expense of litigation...we provide employees with the opportunity to avoid prosecution of Hatch Act violations by resigning or retiring from covered employment...This offer will be available to you until February 26, 1985."[19] All three refused this "golden opportunity." Said Biller, "I will not resign. I will not retire. I will fight this anti-union harassment all the way."[20]

An oral hearing for Biller was set for Wednesday, May 8, 1985 before Administrative Law Judge, Edward J. Reidy, representing the MSPB. Judge Reidy's order also consolidated, for the purposes of the hearing, the cases of Biller, Sombrotto, and Blaylock. When the hearing was completed, the parties submitted briefs on the case and the Judge made a recommended decision to the full MSPB. The MSPB, a three-member panel made up of Administration appointees, then acted on Judge Reidy's recommendation. Biller had argued that he was not covered by the Hatch Act while on leave to serve as APWU President. He also asserted that application of the Hatch Act to him would deprive him, APWU members, and the union itself of their rights of free speech, association, and participation as free citizens in the political process.

On October 22, 1985, Reidy handed down his recommended decision: Guilty of Violation of the Hatch Act. In stating that Biller's endorsement of Mondale violated the Hatch Act, Reidy said:

> Who can doubt that these unions, having as they do extensive membership, pose a major force toward influencing political action?...Respondents assimilate enormous political clout in their position as leaders of national unions.

He recommended that the three union leaders be suspended from their jobs for a period of sixty days. Biller appealed the decision before the full MSPB. On February 5, 1986 the MSPB acted on the Reidy recommendation and ordered the suspensions.

Well over two years later, on August 10, 1988, the Eleventh Circuit Court of Appeals acquitted Blaylock of Hatch Act charges, and in December 1988, the Second Circuit Court of Appeals declared Biller and Sombrotto innocent of Hatch Act violations. In the Biller-Sombrotto case, the judge stated:

Finding "partisan activity" implicitly requires a nexus between the government employee and the effort to promote the political party or elect its candidate. It is not enough that the federal employee and the candidate pursue the same political goals independently; the two must work in tandem or be linked together for there to be a violation of the Hatch Act...Although the plain purpose of the challenged writings was to raise funds, it cannot be demonstrated that the funds were solicited for use by a partisan political campaign or organization...The funds were "not designated for any political campaign, party, committee or candidate at the time they were made."[21]

The Justice Department eventually decided not to appeal the Circuit Court's decision to the Supreme Court. The case had involved an inordinate investment of time and effort, but it was a major victory for all federal workers.

The unions had a good deal less success on the legislative front. On November 17, 1987 the House passed a Hatch Act Reform Bill (HR 3400) by a vote of 304-112, but in October, the Senate adjourned without acting on the bill. In 1990, both Houses passed a Hatch Act Reform Bill. Bush's veto was overridden in the House, but the Senate failed by one vote to override the President's veto.

Privatization

The greatest assault on the private express statutes, which give the U.S. Postal Service a monopoly on first class mail, took place during the 1980s. President Reagan's Privatization Council came out for repeal of the private express statutes, as did Reagan's Director of the Office of Management and Budget, James C. Miller, III. "The Last Dinosaur: The U.S. Postal Service," a paper by the Cato Institute's James Bovard, provided a rationale for the campaign, and several firms took advantage of the favorable atmosphere by attempting to circumvent the USPS monopoly. The whole question of privatization will be discussed in more detail in Chapter 9; below are brief descriptions of APWU actions to thwart privatization attempts during the 1980s.

The Case of React Postal Service

In 1982, React Postal Service, a Salt Lake City presort letter mailing firm, placed collection boxes in 114 Seven-Eleven (7-11) stores where they sold decals (a substitute for stamps) at less than Postal Service rates. A special business discount was offered for Mountain Bell Telephone bill payments that React collected and delivered directly to the utility. React collected other letters, aggregated and presorted them at the presort first class rate (seventeen cents per piece), or the carrier sort rate (sixteen cents), and pocketed the difference. Of course, React paid its collection, distribution, and delivery personnel at wage rates far below Postal Service rates, and their personnel received no benefits.

The 7-11 Corporation eventually withdrew from the program. React then put its boxes in twenty-six Smith Food King Stores and some other outlets in the Salt Lake City area.

The APWU sued in federal court arguing that the postal monopoly covers all carrying of unstamped letters over postal routes. The only exception to this rule is where the Postal Service receives the same revenue that it would have received without this handling. The USPS argued in favor of React, contrary to its own survival interest, but in keeping with Administration policy.

In August 1984, after two years of litigation, the U.S. District Court in Salt Lake City ruled that the APWU "is entitled to an order permanently enjoining React from continuing to operate in violation of the private express statutes." In his opinion, Judge Bruce Jenkins said: "The Private Express Statutes are designed to bolster the United States Postal Service's monopoly by preserving its revenue base. Private companies whose operations deprive the USPS of revenue violate the Private Express Statutes...."[22]

React appealed and the USPS filed a brief in its behalf in which Judge Jenkins' decision was termed "crabbed and pointless." The APWU, in turn, filed a brief in support of the Jenkins decision.

In October 1985, the Court of Appeals overturned the Jenkins decision. Although granting that presort results in taking away sortation work from postal workers, the Court ruled, "To this extent, a portion of the USPS monopoly has been turned over to those in the private sector who wish to compete with the USPS." The Court found enough leeway in the private express statutes to permit the USPS to interpret the rules in favor of React.[23] React, meanwhile, had won the legal battle, but lost the economic war; whether because of legal costs or lack of adequate profits, the firm had already gone out of business before the final favorable decision.

The Sears Roebuck Story

The USPS entered into an agreement with Sears Roebuck and Company to conduct a pilot program at ten Sears stores in Chicago and one in Madison, Wisconsin to sell Postal Service products. Under the contract, the USPS would train Sears employees on the use of postal equipment and the sale of its products. When the unions were informed by the USPS of the Sears program in November 1988, Executive Vice President Bill Burrus informed postal officials that "the APWU opposes this type of operation and will do everything in its power to stop it." President Biller took the APWU complaint directly to the new Postmaster General, Anthony Frank. "The Postmaster General has to understand that there is a major obstacle to improved relations with the APWU when he is in the business of replacing unionized workers with nonunion, low-wage workers doing work that belongs to our members."

Postal officials denied that the Sears contract would have any effect on postal employees, claiming that such projects are an effort by postal management to slow the growth of, rather than reduce, postal employment. The USPS not only initiated the project, but began to study the feasibility of installing similar operations in shopping malls throughout the country.

The APWU launched a massive campaign against the project. It began with a letter from Biller to Edward A. Brennan, Sears' Chairman of the Board, in which he concluded: "I have previously written to you expressing the concern of postal employees. You referred my letter to your Labor Relations specialist indicating your lack of serious consideration of these concerns. Postal employees intend to fight for their jobs so brace yourself, Mr. Brennan, 'we're mad as hell and we're not going to take it anymore.'"

Members of the APWU Chicago local picketed the Sears Tower and all eleven of the pilot stores. The press picked up the APWU challenge, and major stories appeared in newspapers across the country. The USPS fought back with a news release of its own, including a statement by Assistant Postmaster General Gordon C. Morison:

> We are dismayed that the leaders of the APWU oppose a program that is clearly desired by our customers. The contract units were introduced at Sears to provide greater convenience to the mailing public. Their locations and hours of operation augmented service available at the Post Office. The convenience centers were never a threat to postal employees' job security. In fact, the revenue generated through the sale of additional Express Mail, Priority Mail, and Parcel Post shipments helped create more job opportunities in delivery mail and mail processing.[24]

Biller responded with a proposal of his own: "First, the USPS should expand the business hours of its own post offices. In addition, it should ask America's malls to donate a modest amount of space in each mall where the USPS could establish Postal Service retail windows, staffed by APWU members and open every hour of every day the malls are open." When asked about the Biller proposal, Postmaster General Frank responded: "They're open twelve hours a day and seven days a week. I can't afford to have people staffing those—overtime, double time, and all the rest." Assistant PMG Morison made a similar statement: "Staffing the postal contract stations with APWU members...would be too expensive." The APWU concluded that the "convenience" argument was a smokescreen to hide the USPS' real goals—union avoidance and privatization.

Chairman of the Board Brennan received thousands of letters from APWU members which ended with the following statement: "If you do not shut down your pilot operations we will have no choice but to cut up our Sears and Sears Discover credit cards, return them to you, and never patronize your stores or purchase Sears merchandise again."

Within a month, the project was abandoned. On June 30, 1989 the USPS announced that the Sears venture would be terminated by October 1st. However, in the same announcement the Postal Service stated: "The Postal Service has begun negotiating with retailers locally to establish convenience centers in large shopping malls across the nation...Union opposition will not stop us from establishing a presence in the majority of the nation's shopping malls."[25] Today, consumers can buy stamps in supermarkets and postal services at such franchise operations as Mail Boxes, Etc., Parcel Plus, and a host of other comercial outfits—another battle the postal unions appear to have lost.

The APWU won the Sears campaign, but has not been victorious in the battle against privatization. The USPS goal apparently is to sell more products without having to pay for the labor involved, in the long run reducing its labor requirements per unit of output. The question is whether the APWU will be able to block this trend in the future. To be successful, the APWU would need the support of a public that to date has shown neither reluctance to buy its stamps at the supermarket nor willingness to boycott the franchise operations.

International Remailers

International remailing companies collect mail bound for overseas, fly it to foreign countries, and mail it there, paying foreign postage. Ordinarily, customers would pay U.S. postage and the mail would be delivered by foreign post offices in accord with an existing international agreement. The USPS, in a move that was not popular with many career USPS officials, changed its rules to permit the remail operation. It was said that powerful individuals within the Administration, including one Cabinet member, put pressure on the Board of Governors and the Postmaster General to change the rules in favor of the international remailers.

The APWU and the Letter Carriers sued in Federal Court to prevent the remailing operation, charging that it was a blatant violation of the private express statutes, and would result in an $883 million give away in postal revenues to the private sector. On December 19, 1989 the U.S. Court of Appeals ruled for the unions, but in January 1991, the Supreme Court overturned the Appeals Court decision and ruled in favor of the defendants, another loss in the battle against privatization.

Employee Involvement

Like many large U.S. employers, the USPS finds itself enamored with "quality circles" and other forms of "employee involvement." When Postmaster General Bolger assumed office in 1978, he indicated that employee involvement (EI) would be the centerpiece of his labor relations policy. Early in his incumbency he explained the idea to the union leaders and managed to gain the cooperation of all the postal unions except the APWU.

The APWU's position was (and remains to this day) that to establish an Employee Involvement Program there must first be a measure of trust between the worker, union, and management; and a climate in which the parties feel free to exchange ideas and concepts without fear of repercussions and retribution. "It is inconceivable to the [APWU] leadership that an employer who attempts to lower the wages of all employees, reduces the pay levels of distribution positions until reversed by an arbitrator, bars the use of radio headsets, and endorses the total lack of respect displayed to postal workers—has any sincere intent to respond to the concerns of workers."[26]

Biller has been criticized for his hard line on EI, but he has not deviated from his belief that the program is, in essence, an attempt to establish company unions, and on July 26, 1985 his opinion was reinforced by an action of the NLRB. The Board accused the USPS of setting up a company-dominated union when it established an Employee Involvement Committee in Santa Ana, California. In a formal complaint, the Board charged that the USPS, through the Management Sectional Center Manager/Postmaster, committed an unfair labor practice by forming an Employee Involvement Committee whose "function and purpose...was and is to discuss collective bargaining topics and to make recommendations which will affect the terms and conditions of employees in the unit...." Since that time, the APWU has filed unfair labor practice charges against Employee Involvement Committees in many areas of the country. According to the union, Postmasters are not only guilty of establishing company-dominated unions, but also of discriminating against APWU members who refuse to participate in the program.

On June 7, 1991 the NLRB General Counsel issued an eighty-one-page complaint alleging that the Postal Service's employee involvement program often was in violation of the National Labor Relations Act. The General Counsel charged that EI Committees are "dominated and assisted" labor organizations, and that several committees violated the Act by interfering with and undermining the APWU as the representative of bargaining-unit employees. The complaint involves post offices in every geographic area of the country.[27]

The Postal Worker Image

Public relations has been one of Moe Biller's specialties throughout his career. He was often in the headlines before he was elected president and since his election he has appeared on almost every major radio and television news and political talk show. He has served as the Labor Chairman of the March of Dimes Executive Council, Vice President of the Muscular Dystrophy Association, and was a recipient of the Americans for Democratic Action's Walter Reuther Award. Biller also is a member of the Executive committee of the Postal Telegraph and Telephone International, a world-wide federation of unions in the communications industry. There were times when Biller's bluntness got in the way of his community work. For example, in 1981 he was named Vice Chair of the Combined Federal Campaign under the Chairmanship of Drew Lewis, Secretary of the Department of Transportation—the man who allegedly advised Reagan to fire 11,400 air controllers during the PATCO strike. At a party for all the federal volunteers, a man approached Biller and said, "Well, Moe, how do you think we're going to do this year?" Biller responded, "Well, if we could get rid of that jerk, Lewis, we might do all right." The man he was speaking to was Drew Lewis. Lewis, however, did not take offense. Instead, he told Biller that the only mistake he made during the PATCO strike was in giving the striking air controllers only 48 hours to return to work. He said that if the deadline had been set at one week, the mass firings might not have occurred.

He and the APWU were not content to strike back at television commercials which attacked postal workers; they created their own commercials designed to improve the image of postal workers. The "Letter Perfect" commercial appeared right after the Federal Express ad was withdrawn in 1982, and the "Rain of Letters" television commercial was run in 1984. And when Biller and the APWU believed that government workers (not just postal workers but all federal workers) were being attacked from the extreme right, they fought back.

One example was the counterattack directed against J. Peter Grace, Chairman of President Reagan's Commission to Eliminate Waste in Government and founder of "Citizens Against Waste," an offshoot of the Grace Commission. The Grace Commission had recommended slashes in all federal benefit programs and numerous other federal agency changes, including regressive reductions in the Civil Service Retirement System.

J. Peter Grace was personally vulnerable as a target for Biller's counterattack campaign. In Buffalo, New York, the bankruptcy of a Grace plant left a nuclear waste dump and $400 million in cleanup costs to be paid for by the government. The dumping of chemicals by another Grace plant contaminated the water in Woburn, Massachusetts, allegedly causing leukemia in thirty children living in the area. That scandal made the W.R. Grace Company the subject of the television program "60 Minutes." Finally, the Grace Company could be tagged as a recipient of "corporate welfare." Between 1981 and 1983, the W. R. Grace Company earned $684 million in corporate profits and not only paid no taxes, but actually made more money by selling excess income tax credits for $12.5 million.

These situations made J. Peter Grace an excellent target for Moe Biller's publicity and media campaign. Wherever Grace was scheduled to speak, he was greeted outside by APWU pickets. Inside, Danny Frank was waiting to surprise Mr. Grace with an award of his own or with questions that put the waste cutter czar on the defensive. In Erie, Pennsylvania, the hotel at which Grace was speaking called the police to break up the demonstration. The police arrived with dogs, but after talking to the pickets, they put on APWU buttons, told the dogs to lie down, and allowed the demonstration to continue. The hotel people put on the sprinklers, drenching the pickets, but the pickets carried on in good humor, soaking wet. Inside, Danny Frank and Roy Braunstein took over the microphones during the question-and-answer period and peppered Grace with questions about his company's income tax and his company's negligence in Woburn, Massachusetts.

In Memphis, Frank rented a room through which Grace's guests had to pass in order to get to the room where Grace would be speaking. He installed a television set and ran the "60 Minutes" show that concerned the Grace company's alleged negligence in Woburn. Thus, everyone who came to hear Peter Grace also learned about his company's indictment on water pollution charges. The company not only pleaded guilty, but agreed to pay reparations to the families of the children who had contracted leukemia. APWU representatives attended the affair and watched eagerly when Roy Braunstein stepped up to the dais and presented Grace with a bottle of contaminated water taken from the Woburn, Massachusetts chemical dump. The cause and effect is not provable, but none of the Grace Commission's recommendations regarding postal and federal workers has ever been signed into law.

The Remainder of the Agenda

The agenda of the APWU's second decade may have been defined primarily by reactions to the programs of two conservative Administrations, but it was by no means limited to that. The APWU was active in support of its minority and female members, the hearing impaired, and in the arbitration process.

Minorities in the APWU

The experience of minorities in the American labor movement, especially black Americans, has been subject to the same racism that tainted most other American institutions. As late as the 1950s, blacks were either barred from many craft unions or were segregated in black-only locals. Segregationist policies began to crumble with the rise of industrial unionism in the 1930s, but as late as 1962, when President Kennedy issued Executive Order 10988, it was still necessary to specify that recognition be extended only to unions "which are free of practices denying membership because of race, color, creed, or national origin...." Clearly, discrimination still existed.

Black Americans were barred outright from the Railway Mail Association, which for sixty years was the "aristocrat" of postal unions. The establishment of the all-black National Alliance of Postal and Federal Workers (Alliance), was the direct result of the RMA's racism. But, an all-black union, as necessary as it was at the time, fostered rather than eliminated segregation. Dual black and white locals existed in the National Federation of Post Office Clerks and its successor, the United Federation, until the late 1950s. The formation of the Progressive-Feds within the National Federation of Post Office Clerks in the mid-1940s resulted in a determined effort to end racial discrimination in postal unions. When the Progressives broke from the Federation in 1958 and formed the National Postal Union, one of the major goals of the new organization was the complete elimination of racial discrimination, including dual black and white unions. As a result, blacks, especially in the big cities, deserted the Federation and even the Alliance in favor of the NPU. By 1971 black NPU members had moved into leadership positions at both the national and local levels, and after the formation of the APWU their upward movement continued.

Today, black Americans comprise about 30 percent of the APWU membership. Seven members of the union's fourteen-person National Executive Board are black, including Executive Vice President Bill Burrus; Norman L. Steward, Director, Mail Handlers Division; Donald A. Ross, Director, Motor Vehicle Division; George N. McKeithen, Director, Special Delivery Messengers Division; Elizabeth Powell, Northeast Regional Coordinator; Raydell Moore, Western Regional Coordinator; and Philip C. Flemming, Jr., Eastern Regional Coordinator.

The APWU had been in the forefront of the fight for civil rights legislation and the elimination of apartheid in South Africa, but perhaps its most important contribution to civil rights has been its active promotion of equal opportunity in the USPS and in its own organization. The century-plus story of the black American battle for equal rights in the Postal Service could be the subject of a book in itself, but the Progressive-Fed-NPU-APWU contribution to the elimination of racial discrimination in postal unions is one of the major accomplishments of the postal union movement.

Women in the APWU

Women now constitute 44 percent of the APWU membership. Prior to the 1970s, female participation generally was limited to volunteer work and employment in lower-level union positions. As the number of women in postal jobs grew, however, a movement was initiated to increase the amount and level of female participation in union affairs. When the industrial faction of the APWU took over the union's leadership in 1980, it became the policy of the union to promote increased participation by women in leadership positions, a policy which has been highly successful.

Moe Biller immediately set the tone of the new policy by appointing Dorothy Campbell as his Executive Assistant in 1980. Prior to coming to Washington, Biller groomed Josie McMillian to replace him as the President of the largest postal union local in the world, the New York Metro. Biller, along with McMillian, was also responsible for the first APWU's women's meeting which was held in New York City in 1974. As noted in Chapter 6, this led to the formation of POWER in April 1979, a women's action group within the APWU. In 1983 three women, along with Biller, Burrus, and Holbrook, were elected National Business Agents (NBA's): Nilda Chock (the first to be elected in a special election early in the year), Liz Powell and Barbara Prothro. In 1984 Sonyia Legget became the first woman to chair a session of an APWU convention. Margaret Leaf joined Chock, Powell and Prothro as an NBA in 1986. Two more "firsts" occurred in 1989, when Liz Powell was elected Northeast Regional Coordinator and the first female member of the National Executive Board, and Joyce Robinson became Director of Research and Education, the first woman resident national officer. The 1989 elections also added two new NBA's, Linda Coleman and Louise Yannuzzi, for a total of seven national officers, five of whom are members of minority groups.

Currently, five state organizations are headed by women, and the chair of the conference of APWU local and state presidents is Linda Reidy Williams, President of the Indianapolis local. At the local level the presidents of eighty-two locals with fifty or more members are women, and in locals with less than fifty members, women holding the top office can be found in nearly every state.

Nilda Chock of Hawaii, who was the first woman to be elected full-time national officer of the APWU in 1983, said the following about her victory:

> I can honestly say that in my years of service within the American Postal Workers Union, I have always been treated without discrimination. Many women today do not realize the opportunities available especially in the field of labor. Of course, it takes a lot of dedication, determination and utilization of talent to the fullest extent....[28]

Since Ms. Chock's election, six additional women have joined her as national officers, and the number of women in leadership positions at the state and local levels has doubled, a truly impressive record.

The Hearing-Impaired

Over 4,000 deaf or seriously hearing-impaired individuals are employed by the Postal Service. In July 1987 the APWU established a Task Force on the Hearing-Impaired, and made history when deaf representatives participated directly in contract negotiations. The result was a Memorandum of Understanding which set forth management's responsibility to "reasonably accommodate hearing-impaired applicants who request assistance in communicating with or understanding others in work related situations...."[29]

Building on this foundation, two Hearing-Impaired Task Force Leaders,

Karen Atwood (Seattle) and Barry Fischthal (San Fernando Valley, California) presented proposals for strengthening the Memorandum of Understanding at the 1990 negotiations. Atwood and Fischthal spoke in sign language which was translated by a certified interpreter. Both emphasized the need for interpreters certified in American Sign Language. They said that volunteer interpreters, finger spellers and even written communication are often totally inadequate. Atwood concluded:

> I still see a long road ahead to educate others about our deafness, deaf culture, and our language, American Sign Language. But the questions from management after our presentation showed some small signs of improved understanding.[30]

The Atwood-Fischthal presentation resulted in new language in the national agreement to provide staff training on the use of special telecommunications devices, visual alarms on moving powered industrial equipment, and visual fire alarms in all new postal facilities.

The APWU also has conducted national conferences on the hearing-impaired, and in March 1988 the APWU demonstrated its solidarity with its deaf members by providing financial and moral support for striking students at Gallaudet University, the nation's leading education institution for the deaf. The APWU was the only union to participate in the student strike, even though Biller was warned off by various advisors because Gallaudet is not a unionized installation.

The IRS vs. APWU

Sometime in 1987, the Internal Revenue Service (IRS) performed an audit of the APWU's 1984 income tax return. Although the APWU, like all unions, is exempt from the payment of federal corporate income tax, it must nevertheless file an annual return. Nonpostal workers who select the APWU health plan pay $35 to become "Associate Members" of the union. The IRS maintained that the APWU was liable for taxes on all of its Associate Member fees and on a portion of its Health Plan services fee. The IRS billed the union for $730,550 in back taxes and interest for the years 1982 and 1983. The union paid the bill but appealed the ruling in federal court.

On December 19, 1989 the U.S. District Court Judge Royce C. Lamberth ruled that the IRS must refund $731,240 for improper taxation of dues from associate members. Once again, however, the lower court decision was reversed by the Supreme Court, a decision which will adversely affect not only the APWU, but all unions which enroll associate members.

Grievance Arbitration

The APWU was consistently successful in arbitration cases arising out of contract interpretation disputes, although less so in the compromise-prone process of interest arbitration in pursuit of contract negotiations. Important victories were won regarding the unilateral reclassification of postal worker positions by the USPS, annual and incidental leave, overtime, work schedules, maintenance of the 90 percent–10 percent ratio of regular workers to "part-time flexibles" (PTFs), and holding down the hiring of "casuals" to the 5 percent limit. The reclassification arbitration award resulted in 57,000 clerks gaining approximately $45 million a year in salary increases, and the payment of $5 million in back pay. The 90/10 award resulted in the payment of $8.5 million to PTFs in twenty of the largest post offices, plus millions more to those in 420 other facilities.

The 1990 Negotiations

As the 1990 negotiations approached, both sides seemed to be heading on a direct collision course. The Postal Service implemented its "Reduced Delivery Service Standards" initiative despite Congressional, Postal Rate Commission, and union opposition. Delivery standards on first class mail were reduced from a one- and two-day standard to three or more days. The new Postmaster General, Anthony M. Frank, implemented the reduced standards at the same time he asked for a rate increase from the Postal Rate Commission. The crowning blow came when, after months of procrastination, the Postmaster General announced the contracting out of a new Remote Bar Code System which would result in the replacement of 17,000 postal workers with low-wage, nonunion workers. Biller and the delegates to the American Postal Worker Union's Tenth Biennial Convention in Las Vegas, called for Frank's resignation. Frank dismissed the demand with the offhand comment, "That's Biller's crapshoot out there." Later, the Board of Governors issued a statement defending Frank and condemning "one union figure's...irresponsible, unwarranted, and undeserved personal attack" on the Postmaster General. Biller responded by citing a host of headlines regarding what he termed "Frank's Follies," noting particularly the idea of reducing delivery service standards in order to achieve "consistency" and combining a request for a rate increase with lower service standards—in other words, telling the public that we're going to provide you with worse service and make you pay more for it.

Anthony M. Frank was appointed sixty-ninth Postmaster General of the United States on February 2, 1988. He replaced Preston Robert Tisch who resigned to return to private business. Frank joined the Postal Service from the First Nationwide Bank, a subsidiary of the Ford Motor Company, where he was Chairman of the Board and Chief Executive Officer. Under his leadership the bank became the second largest savings institution in the United States, growing almost 100-fold from assets of $400 million in 1971 to $34 billion in 1988.

At a Washington, D.C. news conference, Frank spoke of his desire to serve his country: "The courtesy this country gave to my family and myself when we arrived from Nazi Germany in 1937 is not forgotten and I would like to return some of that."[31]

As a banker Frank had very little experience dealing with unions or with the collective bargaining process and this weakness soon became apparent in his dealings with postal unions. In the past the most successful postal negotiations were conducted with Postmasters General who were experienced in private-sector collective bargaining, men like Elmer Klassen, Benjamin Bailar, and Robert Tisch. Klassen and Tisch had participated personally in the negotiations and, thus, were able to avoid interest arbitration. Frank appeared at the ceremonial opening session, but never reappeared at the bargaining table, even after the two sides found themselves at an impasse. Interest arbitration occurred twice under the career Postmaster General, William Bolger, and again under Frank in 1990.

In the early bargaining sessions, despite a show of civility on both sides of the table, animosity quickly rose to the surface. The Joint Bargaining Committee (JBC) of the APWU and Letter Carriers, which had delivered a whole host of written proposals, or "talking points" to management, complained continuously that management had delivered nothing in writing to the unions. Management had, in fact, presented a nine-page position paper which stated in part:

We have deliberately elected to state our negotiation position in the form of objectives, interests, and concerns rather than demands or proposals that the contract be modified in a variety of specific provisions. We do this to emphasize our desire that this negotiation period be spent in a joint effort to find solutions which satisfy the mutual needs of the U.S. Postal Service, its customers, and employees.[32]

Management's broad objectives included (1) Incentives to Increase Employee Commitment; (2) Changes in the Work Rules to Improve Service; and (3) Cost Restraint. The JBC demanded more specific proposals and, at times, tempers flared. At one point, Joseph J. Mahon, chief negotiator for the USPS and a personable man who seldom lost his cool, responded to an anti-Frank remark by asking Biller what he expected to accomplish by demanding the resignation of the Postmaster General. "By what set of mental gymnastics do you think that such a demand will help smooth the bargaining process?" Biller replied: "I am not here to shove vaseline up his [Frank's] rear in order to make him feel good. That's not my job." After the laughter on the union side had died down, Mahon, whose expression was one of amused incredulity, said that he had to go to the bathroom. "Well, go," Biller replied, "You're excused. You'd better go. You've got a new suit on. You don't want to have an accident." And, so, the collective bargaining process continued...after a fashion.

The Impasse

The general feeling on both sides of the table right from the beginning of negotiations was that there would be no negotiated settlement in 1990. Does this mean that neither side entered into the bargaining sessions in good faith? It means that the USPS was determined to present radical solutions to what management considered severe problems and was not about to back away from the principles underlying its proposals, and it means that the JBC was not ready to accept those "underlying principles."

The Management Position

Management sought radical changes in the wage and postal work force structure. Specifically, it sought to retain the basic wage negotiated in 1987, provide lower starting wages for new employees, develop a new COLA formula that would deny COLA increases until the CPI had risen by 4 percent in a given year, and change the composition of the work force to allow management to hire more part-time workers. Management argued that these changes were needed in order to bring the wages and benefits of postal workers more in line with the wages and benefits paid for comparable work in the private sector, and to provide management with increased efficiency and flexibility in dealing with the transition to an automated work structure. In addition, the USPS proposed an overhaul of the present medical insurance system.

The JBC Position

The JBC proposed substantial increases over a three-year period in basic postal salaries, revision of the COLA formula to yield one cent per hour for each 0.26 rise in the CPI, thus replacing nearly all of the real wage loss from inflation (the previous formula was one cent for each 0.4 rise, replacing only 50–60 percent of the inflation wage loss), no "two-tier" wage system for new hires, no change in the structure of the work force to permit the increased employment of part-time help, and no change in the present health insurance system. Underlying the union position was a denial of the management contention that postal workers were paid a premium over the private sector, and conviction that the USPS already had all the flexibility it needed to operate efficiently.

After the JBC presented its economic demands four days before the breakdown in negotiations, management never returned to the table. Instead, the press was told that the union's proposal would cost $50 billion and lead to a forty-three-cent stamp. Biller was reminded of the 1981 negotiations when the USPS claimed that the JBC's pay proposal would lead to a fifty-cent stamp, and management created a mockup of what they called the Biller-Sombrotto 50-cent commemorative stamp. Nine years later, Biller pointed out that the price of a stamp was only twenty-nine cents.

Collective Bargaining Fails

Collective bargaining began on August 28, 1990 and terminated on November 20, 1990 with the parties at an impasse. The APWU and NALC mutually agreed to waive fact-finding and go directly to the formation of a five-member arbitration board consisting of one member appointed by each of the unions, two members appointed by the Postal Service, and a fifth neutral arbitrator selected jointly by the JBC/Postal Service board members, and formally appointed by the Director of the Federal Mediation and Conciliation Service. The union appointees were Bruce Simon, General Counsel of the NALC, and Theodore W. Kheel, a nationally noted New York arbitrator. The Postal Service appointees were Joseph J. Mahon, chief negotiator for the Postal Service, and Peter G. Nash, former General Counsel of the National Labor Relations Board in the Nixon Administration. All four had participated in the 1984 Kerr panel. The parties then agreed to the selection of Richard Mittenthal as chairman of the five-member board.

When negotiations broke off, the key unresolved contract issues were:

1. Wages: The JBC proposed a three-year agreement with a base wage increase of 8 percent the first year and 7 percent in each of the last two years. The Postal Service proposed a two-year contract with no increase in the basic rate of pay, but lump sum bonus payments to union employees of $2,000 in four increments over the two-year period.

2. Cost-of-Living Adjustments (COLA): The JBC proposed that the present COLA (one cent per hour for each 0.4 rise in the CPI) be revised to yield one cent per hour for each 0.26 rise in the CPI. Management proposed that no COLA payments be made until a 4 percent rise in the CPI triggered payment of one cent for each 0.4 rise in the CPI (the existing formula).

3. New Hires: The USPS proposed a new hire schedule which reduced starting salaries in all grades; the unions opposed any so-called "two-tier" wage proposal.

4. Incentive Payments: The USPS proposed an incentive program which guaranteed each full-time employee a lump sum payment of $200 the first year of the program as well as additional potential payments over two years of up to a total of $1,190 per year. The unions objected to incentive programs in general, particularly in lieu of general wage increases.

5. Work Rules: The USPS proposed to change the part-time complement from 10 percent, under the 1987 agreement, to 30 percent. In addition, the USPS proposed an additional category of employee called the "transitional employee," a noncareer

position which would be used to fill positions impacted by the introduction of automation and to fill vacant withheld positions. The unions objected to any changes in the historic structure of the work force and argued that no such changes are required, particularly because the USPS had not utilized the flexibility already available under the present 90/10 ratio of full-time to part-time employees.

6. Medical Insurance: The Postal Service proposed to cap the dollar amount of the Postal Service's contribution to medical insurance and provide payments to employees who waive insurance coverage or select less expensive coverage. The JBC objected to any change in the existing medical insurance system.

These were not minor issues; they were issues which had the potential of altering the historic Postal Service collective bargaining process and the structure of the Postal Service work force. Lump sum payments in lieu of an increase in the basic salary rate would adversely affect the union position in future negotiations as well as the basis upon which postal worker retirement annuities would be determined. At the end of the contract period the basic salary rate would be no more than it was in 1987 and COLA payments would be substantially reduced. As for the structure of the work force, a 30 percent complement of part-time workers would constitute a severe blow to the historic union demand that the work force be composed predominately of regular, full-time employees.

It was obvious that the USPS was basing its proposals on private sector trends where lump sum bonus payments, in lieu of raises in basic salary rates, were becoming increasingly common, but the precedent that the Postal Service cited in an attempt to influence the JBC/Postal Service Board of Arbitrators came from an entirely different source and, once again, it was the Mail Handler leadership that caused the problem.

The Mail Handler Deal

Just prior to the start of interest arbitration hearings, the Mail Handlers Union reached agreement with the Postal Service on a tentative three-year contract that provided:

1. Lump sum bonus payments instead of pay increases—$900 in each of the first two years and $600 in the third year. This money would not count for the purposes of COLA calculation, overtime, premium pay, promotion, or retirement.
2. Entry-level mail handlers hired in the future would be paid at a special lower grade. Their compensation would be 20 percent below regular employees, and there would be no pay raises at this new rate for the life of the contract.
3. Newly hired mail handlers would remain at the new level for ninety-six weeks.
4. Incentive payments would be made on the basis of worker productivity.

One unresolved issue was taken to arbitration. An arbitration panel ruled that newly hired mail handlers would receive no COLAs for one year. The USPS had proposed a two-year moratorium on COLAs for new hires.

Thus, the Mail Handlers accepted the entire Postal Service package. But there was more to it than that. Theoretically, "tentative agreements" must be ratified by the membership. However, the Mail Handler membership never got the opportunity to vote on the tentative agreements. The Mail Handler negotiators agreed to a proposal made by Joseph Mahon of the Postal Service that in the arbitration procedure regarding the one unresolved issue, all tentative agreements would be approved by the arbitrators and incorporated in the arbitration award. The arbitrators would decide the one outstanding issue, make the tentative agreements final and binding, and, thus, eliminate the ratification process. According to Mahon:

I inquired as to whether ratification by the NPMHU would nonetheless be expected in the event that the parties agreed to this approach (i.e., the interest arbitration award would be comprised of all tentative agreements as well as the single remaining...issue). Either Mr. Coia [Secretary-Treasurer of LIUNA] or Mr. La Penta [chief Mail Handler negotiator] shook his head, signifying a negative response. During the course of the conversation that followed on this issue, it was apparent that no ratification vote would be needed in the event that they consented to my proposal. Later...Marion Wright

[Secretary-Treasurer of the Mail Handlers] approached me in my office and told me that the union needed to reflect upon my suggestion. At that point, I said to Mr. Wright, in words or substance, that you know your membership and if your membership anticipated a ratification of a complete and total National Agreement, then the union should not agree to the Postal Service's suggestion. Mr. Wright promised to contact me the next day with his answer, which he did...Mr. Wright agreed with the Postal Service's proposal and said that the parties should proceed in the manner which had been discussed....[33]

To the JBC, this smacked of a sweetheart contract, and a deliberate attempt on the part of the Postal Service to use the Mail Handlers contract, affecting 50,000 members, as a "pattern" to influence the JBC arbitration procedure, affecting 600,000 postal workers. Bill Burrus termed the capitulation of the Mail Handler negotiators "conscious and deliberate deception...The [Mail Handler] leadership was unwilling to inform its members that they had agreed to a 20 percent reduction in starting salary and no COLA for the first year of the contract. They agreed to this further reduction in mail handler salaries and then attempted to obtain political cover by requesting an arbitrator to bless the decision as though it was his own."[34]

Led by the largest Mail Handler local, Local 300 of New York City, thirteen local presidents, representing over one-half of the entire Mail Handler membership, sought an injunction to prohibit management from handing out the first of the lump sum bonus payments. "In their classic sneaky style," Moe Biller said, "postal officials couldn't wait to distribute the bonus payoffs to mail handlers throughout the country. Management did this apparently knowing that the sham ratification of the 'tentative agreement' was being held up in court by Mail Handler locals. Management was seemingly confident that the arbitrator's decision could nonetheless be used to trample the democratic rights of Mail Handler Union members."[35] The attempt by Local 300 and other dissident Mail Handler locals to negate the national agreement was not successful, but the JBC participants continued to perceive the Mail Handler's agreement as both a sweetheart contract and an obstacle to their own pending arbitration.

When the interest arbitration hearings opened on March 5, 1991 John O'Donnell, in his opening remarks, went on the offensive: "I notice [management's] reference to an 'alleged contract' they have as a result of arbitration with the Mail Handlers Union. So that there be no question about it...I am now demanding that if they're going to refer to that so-called arbitration, that they produce the transcript of the record made before that arbitrator!" Despite all-out JBC efforts to discredit the Mail Handler agreement and, therefore, prevent its use as a precedent, the question as to whether the Mail Handler capitulation had an adverse effect on the Mittenthal award remains very much open.

The Hearings

The interest arbitration hearings began on March 5th and ended on June 5, 1991. A total of nineteen days of hearings were conducted, tens of thousands of pages of testimony and exhibits were received, and expert opinion was heard from a vast array of economists, statisticians, engineers, lawyers, and management and union officials (both past and present). The cost to both sides was in excess of $4 million,[36] and the results were predictable: The unions would get a pay raise, less than they demanded, but more than was offered, and management would get more flexibility. If both sides knew the results before interest arbitration began, why weren't they able to reach an agreement and avoid the cost of arbitration? The answer has to be that one or the other of the parties believed that it had more to gain through interest arbitration than through collective bargaining, and in this case, the party that had the most to gain appears to have been management.

The Battle of the Economists: Round II

The same two union and two management appointees to the arbitration board were carried over from 1984 to 1990 and the approaches and decisions of the prestigious 1984 chairman clearly hung over the 1990 chairman, Richard Mittenthal, veteran of many Postal Service grievance arbitrations. Wachter and Popkin played their former roles by updating their previous studies and repeating essentially the same arguments.

Wachter now concluded the average postal worker to be receiving 128.8 percent of the pay received by the average private sector worker of the same race-sex-education-work experience characteristics and that, although the gap had narrowed after the 1984 award, it had actually widened again since the 1987 settlement.[37] A COLA reimbursing postal workers approximately 60 percent of inflation losses whereas most workers had no automatic protection against cost-of-living increases was an important factor, along with the wage and salary improvements of the 1984 and 1987 agreements. Noting that most new entrants to postal employment had been previously employed in the service industry, Wachter pointed out that, on the average, their starting salaries in the Postal Service resulted in a 53.6 percent increase over their previous earnings, support for the USPS proposal for a "two-tiered" system with lower pay for new entrants. Continuation of the trend, he warned, would threaten the competitive position of the USPS and, therefore, the employment security of postal workers.[38]

Popkin responded again that to bind postal workers to a demographically-based pay comparison was to allow, and even require, the Postal Service to replicate the race and gender pay discrimination still too evident in the private sector. A white male comparison was the proper one and on that basis there was no wage premium. Since postal workers should have the advantage of their decision to unionize, a comparison with white male union workers would be more appropriate, but he identified no significant union/nonunion differential, despite persistent AFL-CIO advertisements of the substantial wage and benefit advantages of union membership.[39] However, most of his testimony was directed to the need to strengthen the COLA and to the argument that productivity improvements were achieving a persistent decline in Postal Service labor costs. Work level comparability again was not mentioned by either economic witness.

The only comparable unionized activity with similar job content is the work performed by UPS employees. Full-time UPS workers reach the top of the company's wage scale in only two years. Their 1991 hourly wage rate was $17.50, or $36,418 a year—$2.83 an hour above what APWU workers with four years' experience will earn in 1994 and $1.76 an hour above the top APWU 1994 grade. In 1992, the UPS hourly wage rate will increase to $18.50, or $2.76 above the top APWU grade. The trade–off, however, is that 50 percent of the UPS work force is part-time; only the drivers and a few other personnel work full-time. Under the 1991 arbitration agreement, 20 percent (up from a previous 10 percent) of APWU employees are part-time.

Other than the perpetuated shift in the comparability standard, it is not as readily apparent in 1991 as it was in 1984 who won the battle of the economists. Chairman Mittenthal accepted the existence and persistence of a postal worker premium, cited and reiterated Chairman Kerr's call for "moderate restraint" and lowered the annual increments to 1.2, 1.5, 1.5, and 1.6 percent for the retroactive one and subsequent three years. However, he rejected the USPS request to forego any general wage increase and allow only three subsequent $500 lump sum bonuses which would not be perpetuated in the wage schedule nor pyramided into the employee benefit structure, and would not tamper with the COLA to reduce its impact, though he would not increase it either.[40] Comparability, however defined, was still the guiding criterion, but no wrenching changes were to be directed toward its accomplishment.

Coda

The 1990 negotiation/interest arbitration proceedings ended on as sour a note as they began. The Postmaster General made a surprise appearance on the last day of the hearings to present management's closing statement. Frank proceeded to characterize Biller and Sombrotto as "intractable," praised the Mail Handler contract and asked the Board not "to punish the Mail Handlers," and cited the need to penalize "union leadership for the failure of negotiations." Biller, who was not scheduled to speak, took five minutes out of the union's half-hour allotted for closing legal argument to respond to Frank. "Why is Tony Frank here today?" Biller asked. "Does he really think that he or his title can intimidate this panel?" Biller then challenged Frank directly: "It's still not too late. There is still time. I challenge General Frank to sit down with me and President Sombrotto —now, not later, as he suggested—to resolve the outstanding issues." Before Biller spoke, Sombrotto also made a statement that was videotaped by an NALC crew. Thomas Fahey, APWU Communications Director, approached his NALC counterpart and requested that the NALC crew tape Biller's statement. The answer was "sure." But when Biller took his place in front of the microphone, the video lights went out. For just a moment Biller was reminded of that evening many years before when the lights were deliberately turned off while he was speaking before a UNAPOC meeting. But this time it was his brethren at the NALC who turned off the lights. When Fahey asked why Biller wasn't taped, the answer was "orders from above." At any rate, Frank did not accept Biller's challenge.

The Award

In his comments regarding the award, Chairman Mittenthal said:

> The impasse was the product of Management's belief that major changes are needed at this time in the wage structure and the work force structure...The JBC resisted such structural changes. Its position essentially was that the Postal Service's present situation did not warrant such a dramatic departure from twenty years of bargaining history and that a contract fair to everyone's interest could be reached through the use of the conventional bargaining model...Given these positions, strongly felt, it is hardly surprising that the negotiations failed and the parties invoked the interest arbitration procedures of the Postal Reorganization Act....[41]

The award was pretty much what everybody predicted: The traditional wage structure and COLA were maintained, and changes were made in the work structure to permit greater management flexibility. The major awards were as follows:

Basic Salary Increases
—A one-time cash payment of $351 on June 15, 1991 in lieu of retroactive salary increases and COLA and,
—General salary increases of 1.2 percent on June 15, 1991, 1.5 percent on November 16, 1991, 1.5 percent on November 28, 1992, and 1.6 percent on November 27, 1993.

COLA
—Continuation of the current COLA formula on a semiannual basis without any cap or floor; and
—COLA roll-in to be handled as before and counted in calculating overtime, premium pay and retirement.

Entry Level Pay
—New entry level pay steps, Grades 1 through 10;
—10 percent lower starting rates for Grades 1 through 7; and
—6.5 percent lower starting rates for Grades 8 through 10.

Work Rules
—Reduction in the 90/10 formula for full- and part-time employees to 80/20 for employees represented by the APWU and 88/12 for

employees represented by the NALC.
—The establishment of a noncareer "transitional" job classification
to fill anticipated impacted positions as a result of automation. All
aspects pertaining to the transitional employee classification to be
decided jointly by representatives of the USPS and the JBC. If the
parties fail to reach agreement, referral of the dispute to a Panel
composed of the Chairman, one USPS interest arbitrator and one JBC
arbitrator for a final and binding decision.

Benefits
—The establishment of a Task Force to study ways to limit USPS
exposure to increasing health care costs. If the Task Force is unable
to reach agreement, the arbitration panel will reconvene to render
a final and binding decision on the issue.

The panel rejected the USPS proposal for incentive pay bonuses, and,
by granting increases in the basic salary rates, rejected the USPS lump sum
pay proposals. The Panel refused to take a position on the USPS "preliminary" decision to contract out work related to the initiation of the Remote
Bar Code System. The APWU and the Letter Carriers split on whether this
issue should be considered by the Panel (the issue is now the subject of
rights arbitration). The split led Theodore Kheel to release a separate
statement in which he "reluctantly" concurred with the Panel's decision:

> As the U.S. Postal Service has acknowledged, the jobs at issue are
> core bargaining unit jobs performed by Postal Service employees.
> The sole reason for the Postal Service's preliminary decision to
> subcontract is the low-cost of the nonunion employees who will be
> doing the work...
>
> ...While the two unions of the JBC raised this issue during
> negotiations, only one of the two unions thought it desirable to
> pursue the issue here, rather than in a rights arbitration forum...
>
> I, therefore, reluctantly concur in the Panel's decision to omit this
> issue from our deliberations. I am concerned, however, that the issue
> will continue to divide these parties. No matter which party prevails
> in the pending rights case...I predict that the pending rights arbitration
> forum will not serve to accommodate the interests of both parties.
> To fully accommodate the parties' interests, a negotiated settlement
> of future interest arbitration will be necessary.[42]

In a separate opinion Kheel also expressed "grave reservations" regarding the USPS positions on "flexibility" and the need for a transitional work force, and the Panel's decision "to vest final jurisdiction over task forces on the transitional workforce to Chairman Mittenthal...it will be extremely difficult for the Chairman properly to maintain jurisdiction over the work of these two task forces, which are rife with potential conflicts of interest." Finally, Kheel expressed his disappointment that the issue of remote bar coding was not assigned to a task force on the transitional workforce.[43]

Union and Management Reaction

In a memorandum to USPS employees, Postmaster General Frank expressed guarded satisfaction with the award: "We believe that this is a decision our customers can live with, although the total cost of the package will exceed what we factored into our rate case. We believe the new contracts provide the moderate cost restraint we sought and, therefore, give us a fighting chance to meet our Strategic Plan."[44] Certainly, the USPS had conceded less and won more from the arbitration process than the unions would have agreed to without bruising negotiations, negative publicity, and persistent strike threats.

Moe Biller, in a letter to APWU local, state, and national officers, said: "It is important to understand that the Mail Handler Agreement, which the Postal Service wanted to be the pattern, was not forced upon us. In addition, our annual increases will be regular wage increases and not phony lump sum bonuses...Our COLA clause still remains intact."[45] In statements to the press, Biller emphasized that by defeating USPS proposals regarding incentive payments and lump sum bonuses, and by maintaining the present COLA, the APWU/NALC reversed a trend in current labor-management negotiations and, by doing so, made an important contribution to the labor movement at large. He admitted, however, that the APWU "took an unnecessary and unfair hit on the flexibility issue." Biller believes that Mittenthal made a serious mistake when he allowed the USPS to raise the question of a transitional work force at the arbitration hearings. He claims that the question never was raised during the negotiations and therefore should not have been considered in interest arbitration. Only those proposals which were made during negotiations should be part of an interest arbitration procedure. He also faults Mittenthal for his statement, "a poorly negotiated agreement is better than an arbitrated agreement." Without the right to strike or some other method of rewarding or penalizing the parties, there is no way that interest arbitration can be avoided.

The estimated total cost of the award to the Postal Service, not counting the lower step wage rates and the effect of the 80/20 decision, and assuming an average inflation rate of 3.9 percent over the four-year period, would be $6.1 billion. Over a twenty-year period, the average APWU member and letter carrier would earn approximately $15,000 more than the average mail handler. In comparison to earlier contracts, however, the rate of wage increases appeared to be declining. The increase was 5.3 percent in the 1984–1987 contract, 4.4 percent in the 1987–1990 contract, and an anticipated 3.9 percent increase in the 1990–1994 contract. The parties could both live with the results, but they were grants from a third party decisionmaker, not the fruits of give-and-take collective bargaining.

* * *

When the delegates gathered for the 10th Biennial Convention of the APWU at the Las Vegas Hilton on July 30, 1990 Moe Biller was approaching his 75th birthday. He had taken a union which was in disarray and made it into an effective advocate for the membership, and not only had survived a serious challenge to his leadership, but neutralized the opposition in the process. During a conservative political Administration, the union had maintained its aggressive posture and considering the opposition it faced, had scored some impressive victories. Now, at the beginning of a new decade, the union remained as feisty as ever. The delegates demanded the resignation of Postmaster General Anthony Frank, and created a traffic jam in downtown Las Vegas when they joined hotel workers on the picket line. For reasons of his own, not in response to the APWU demand, Frank actually did resign in February 1992.

At the same time, some critics were charging that Biller and the APWU were anachronistic—a throw-back to the thirties, and that the techniques of the thirties would not work in the nineties. Howard Evans, who supported Biller in 1980, but opposed him in 1986, wrote:

...Moe Biller grew and matured in the environment of an industry without real unions. Strikes, tough talk, and power plays—yesterday's tools—created unions in the Postal Service, in fact, created the Postal Service itself. Moe's National Postal Union was midwife, if not parent to that creation. But, like many a prizefighter who can't make the transition from brawler to boxer, Biller could not make the transition from guerrilla to statesman. Ironically, Moe could take a 300,000 member union to the nineties, but couldn't extricate himself from the 1960s....[46]

Evans' article was written in the middle of a hotly contested union election and was meant to influence members to vote for Biller's opponent, David Daniel, but it nevertheless summed up the feeling that many, both inside and outside the union, had about Biller. However, the fact of the matter is that Biller did appear to extricate himself from the 1960s. During the eighties, there was a significant change in the way the APWU operated. For example, there was very little strike talk during the 1984, 1987, and 1990 negotiations, and Biller, a high school graduate with two years of college, comported himself well in television debates with some of the more sophisticated conservatives of our time, including William F. Buckley, Jr., James C. Miller, III, Patrick Buchanan, John McLaughlin, and others, all of whom played a role in the Reagan Administration postal and labor policies.

An English actor/director, Basil Langton, after listening to a colleague criticize the ability of one of the most noted actors of the English stage, said: "I cannot discount success." As of 1991, that comment appears appropriate to Biller and the APWU. Whether that success is likely to continue is the subject of the final chapter.

Chapter 9

THE FUTURE

The APWU's third decade coincides with the last ten years of the twentieth century, a ten-year period that, according to many prognosticators, will see the continued weakening of labor unions as a powerful force in the nation's economy. Commenting on the bitter 1990 New York Daily News strike, Leo Troy, Professor of Economics at Rutgers University, said: "The recent past for private sector unions in New York was bad. But the future will certainly be worse. By some time in the next century, the private sector unions that once ruled the city will be extinct."[1] According to Michael Specter, "that refrain has been repeated in working-class cities nationwide as manufacturing jobs fled such highly organized, expensive, and inflexible northern urban centers as Buffalo, Pittsburgh, Detroit, and Chicago, and headed to the South or to other countries where labor is cheap."[2]

It is significant that the major support for the Daily News strikers came from public sector unions. Over 10,000 municipal and postal workers joined the strikers in a November 1990 rally outside the Daily News headquarters. Other than the building trades and communication workers, the public sector labor organizations were the only unions left in the city with large memberships and a certain amount of political clout. If, as Professor Troy predicts, private sector unions will become extinct in the next century, what about public sector unions? Are they, too, destined for extinction? Many of the issues underlying the 1990 negotiations between the USPS and the postal unions were indirectly concerned with that question—issues regarding the contracting out of technological innovations, changes in the work rules to allow an increase in part-time help and corresponding decrease in regular full-time employees, and policy regarding privatization of the 215-year-old institution founded by Benjamin Franklin as a service to the American people. It wasn't until 1962 that federal unions were recognized as legitimate agents of government employees, and 1971 that collective bargaining was instituted in the Postal Service. Now, after twenty years of collective bargaining, questions regarding the survival of both the USPS and its unions were being raised.

State of the USPS

Before discussing the future of the APWU and its relationship with the USPS, a discussion of the present state of the Postal Service (circa 1991) is in order. What follows, therefore, is a discussion of the fiscal condition of the USPS, the demand for postal services, the effect of inflation on the cost of the stamp, and a comparison of the rates charged by the USPS with those charged by other industrialized nations.

Fiscal Condition

The Government Accounting Office (GAO) predicted that the USPS would run a $1.6 billion deficit in fiscal year 1990. Postmaster General Frank, in his fiscal year 1989 annual report, accepted that prediction, although by the time negotiations began in August 1990, the projected deficit was reduced to $730 million. During the ten-year period 1981–1991, the Postal Service had five surpluses and five deficits. Over the decade, Postal Service revenues were within one-quarter of 1 percent of expenses.[3] Thus, the USPS has been able to meet its legal mandate to break even over time.

Postal Service Demand

Total mail volume increased by 2.9 percent between fiscal years 1989 and 1990, from 161 billion to 166 billion pieces. All classes of mail increased during the year, offsetting decreases in four classes experienced in 1989. The largest increase was in first-class mail which grew by 4 percent over the previous fiscal year (1989). The second largest segment of the mail—third class mail—increased by 1.5 percent, recovering from a slight decline in 1989. All told, the volume handled by the USPS represents 40 percent of the world's mail volume.[4]

The Effect of Inflation

The cost of the first class stamp rose at approximately the same rate as inflation, remaining constant in real dollars. It has risen faster than the total Consumer Price Index, but substantially less than the index of all service costs.[5] If, however, direct taxpayer subsidies are taken into account, the cost in real dollars of sending a letter actually declined from 28.1 cents (the real value of an eight-cent stamp in 1971) to 27.6 cents (the real value of a twenty-nine-cent stamp in 1991).[6] Direct taxpayer subsidies were eliminated completely in 1983.

In comparison to other consumer goods and services, postage rates have risen less than utilities, most daily newspapers, weekly magazines, automobiles, housing, and entertainment.[7]

U.S. vs. Foreign Postal Rates

U.S. first class rates are the lowest in the industrialized world. It costs over twice as much to send a letter in Germany and Italy, and over one-and-one-half times as much in Norway, Austria, Japan, Belgium, France, Holland, and Sweden. The closest to U.S. rates are Australia (33 cents), Canada (34.5 cents), Switzerland (39.3 cents), and Great Britain (42.5 cents).[8]

Pressure on the USPS

The foregoing appears to indicate a relatively healthy organization, but there are immediate problems facing the Postal Service, and still others that loom on the horizon. The effect of the most recent rate increase, especially on third class mail, has yet to be determined. Third class mail accounts for 38 percent of total Postal Service volume; thus, a decline in business bulk mail, or even a flattening out of first class volume as a result of the rate increase, as well as an expected increase in the use of electronic mail, could have a significant negative effect on future Postal Service revenues.

The Omnibus Budget Reconciliation Act of 1990 (OBRA) requires the USPS to pay up to $4.7 billion in new costs over the next five years to fund the health care benefits and cost-of-living adjustments for postal workers who retired from service between 1971 and 1986. When asked about the effect of OBRA on the U.S. Postal Service, Postmaster General Frank responded:

> It's a bitter body blow. When you end up $730 million better than budget and then get hit with $4.7 billion over five years in additional costs imposed on you by legislation, that makes it hard. You take a step forward and a step back. We are concerned because eventually the American people will pay that. It's just a stamp tax. And when we raise postage rates to accommodate that, people say, "Oh, this idiotic, inefficient, unfeeling, bureaucratic Postal Service!" We can't go out and teach civics to 250 million people. In 1991, our budget was to make $1.2 billion. Now with this legislation we lose $1 billion. For the next rate increase it means more, sooner.[9]

These factors, plus soaring health care costs, which affect not just the Postal Service but society at large, will assure a hard bargaining posture by the USPS in future negotiations.

The APWU and the Nineties

Moe Biller, who was born in 1915, has participated in the struggle for union recognition, seen unions reach their peak of influence in the U.S. economy after World War II, and begin a decline which would accelerate during the Administration of Ronald Reagan in the 1980s. Biller once remarked ironically that you had to look to Poland and the U.S.S.R. to find vibrant labor movements today. In Poland, the labor movement unseated an entrenched Communist regime, much to the glee of anti-union conservatives in the United States, and in the era of glasnost, unions were striking against the Soviet government whether they had the right to or not—and they were getting away with it. Yet in the United States the once-powerful trade union movement was on the defensive and its economic and political influence was on the decline.

The APWU, however, survived the eighties in good condition. There has been no significant decline in its membership, and its collective bargaining achievements have been impressive. The wages of APWU members have kept ahead of inflation and have risen at a greater rate than all workers in the private sector and at a much higher rate than Federal General

Schedule (GS) employees. But looming in the future are two issues which could cause major problems for the APWU and all postal unions: Automation and Privatization.

Automation

The USPS has embarked on an ambitious program to automate its entire operation by 1995. A total of $5.2 billion is to be invested for automation and mechanization, an investment that is expected to eliminate almost 100,000 workyears (read: jobs) by the end of 1995. No one expects an immediate decline in APWU membership, but by the year 2000, few doubt that automation and an expected increase in the use of electronic mail will result in a significant decline in the USPS work force. The decline in union membership, if it occurs, could tip the scale in favor of management.

An article in the October 7, 1991 edition of *Business Week* called attention to the labor reduction goal of the USPS:

The USPS is about to undergo some big league belt tightening. Postmaster General Anthony Frank plans to announce shortly that he wants the Postal Service's 700,000 strong workforce to shrink 47,000 by 1995. The cuts, which will save an estimated $4.5 billion annually, come on top of the loss of 37,000 slots since 1989. Frank expects that attrition will account for most of the job losses. But, he says, "layoffs may be necessary if mail volume doesn't pick up." It shows no signs of doing so.[10]

The APWU has insisted that it is not against automation or any policy which will help strengthen the USPS, but it has not hesitated to call attention to the Postal Service's questionable record in the field of automation, including the billion dollar plus failure of the 1970 bulk mail centers. The union also has accused the USPS of trying to bypass Article Four of the national agreement which states:

Any new job or jobs created by technological or mechanization changes shall be offered to present employees capable of being trained to perform the new or changed job and the employer will provide such training.

The Postal Service's preliminary decision to contract out the Remote Video Encoding program is held by the APWU to be a violation of Article Four, and is now the subject of rights arbitration. In an appearance before the Board of Governors on January 8, 1990 Moe Biller said, "It is our considered judgment that the Postal Service would do better to consolidate and implement existing automation programs, and to invest in improvements in service, before attempting another expensive change through automation." He went on to say:

> Rather than take on the burden of financing a big, new program, I recommend investing in one of the Postal Service's best, old-fashioned products, namely, retail services...If the Postal Service loses sight of its mission to provide retail postal services, it will be reduced from a basic and fundamental public service to just another delivery company, or will become a provider of last resort of services that no one else is willing to provide. That is a ticket to the destruction of this great institution. I strongly urge you to reject this regressive approach and lead the Postal Service to a higher, rather than a lower goal.[11]

Biller's plea was ignored and the automation program is scheduled for implementation. When the USPS and the JBC renew negotiations in 1994, the APWU probably will remain at full strength. Whatever reductions occur will be the result of attrition rather than mass layoffs, but the future result of automation in reducing the membership of the APWU no doubt will have an adverse effect on its bargaining position. Lower membership means reduced resources and a good deal less clout at the bargaining table.

However, automating post office functions is only half of the technological threat. The Post Office exists to carry the mail. To the extent that communication occurs through other forms of transmission, e.g., telephone, telex, fax, etc., the role and function of the USPS is reduced and, therefore, so is employment. Such electronic mail has been and will continue to multiply. The only questions are, how far? and how fast?

Privatization

When asked why he took the job of Postmaster General, Anthony M. Frank replied that it is "the biggest management challenge in the United

States....plus I wasn't born in this country, and I thought I could pay back a little of what I owe it."[12] Frank refused a salary raise in 1990 and as a result his postal salary is less than the salaries of his Deputy and two of his Assistant Postmasters General. Notwithstanding Frank's generosity in refusing a raise, the unions believe that the Postmaster General's goal "to pay back a little" actually means "giveaways" to the private sector of some of the Postal Service's most profitable activities. The USPS, under Frank, engineered the abortive Sears program, gave its blessing to franchise and packaging operations, and decided to contract out the Remote Bar Coding operation. Thus, to the unions, Frank's "patriotism" is heavily loaded in favor of the private entrepreneur and pretty much indifferent to the men and women who work for wages on an hourly basis. In addition, Frank's decision to lower service standards at the same time he asked for a rate increase appears to be an open invitation to competition from the private sector.

Frank denies that he is a privatizer. When he was asked by Time Magazine whether "we actually need a Postal Service...Couldn't private operators like Federal Express do a better job?" he replied:

> They wouldn't take it if you offered it to them. The revenue per piece for Federal Express is $17. Ours is 28.4 cents. Federal Express has 12 percent of our number of employees. Their employees deliver two-tenths of 1 percent of our volume. We deliver in any morning what they deliver in a year. They're a different business. The Postal Service is not a business. It's a business-like public service. I could cut out $5 billion in one day. But our charter is to provide universal, uniform service to the American people, which means everybody gets the same service at the same rate. Compared to almost any other country, we are certainly the cheapest postal service and probably the best and getting better. People don't seem to understand. Would companies compete for Manhattan? Yes. Would they compete for the Bronx? I don't think so.[13]

Despite Frank's remarks, criticism of his policies emerged not only from the APWU and other postal unions, but also from the National Association of Post Office Supervisors (NAPS). Rubin Handelman, NAPS President, cited several policy decisions by the Postal Service which "can only be considered privatization and have me very concerned about the direction in which we're going." Handelman continued:

> It seems I and my officers are unpatriotic if we take exception with
> newly established postal policies, if we don't march in lock step with
> Headquarter's decisions, if we don't go along to get along.
>   Well, that's too bad. If they want somebody to sit back and watch
> over the contracting out of the entire Postal Service, it won't be done
> by me...You want to call us a union, go right ahead and call us
> whatever you wish....[14]

Handelman's remarks came as a welcome surprise to postal union leaders
and the fact that his speech was delivered before the National Association
of Postmasters of the United States and circulated to the National League
of Postmasters assured that "creeping privatization" would become a
concern not only of union workers, but of management personnel as well.

Pressure for Privatization

Since its beginning, the Postal Service has stimulated the building of roads
and highways, subsidized every major transportation system from the steam
engine to the airplane, and made possible mail order marketing and mer-
chandising. Montgomery Ward and Sears owe their existence to the USPS,
to say nothing of the hundreds of firms that today market their merchandise
by means of third class mail. Yet today, the very institution that has been
a major stimulant to private enterprise is the target of privatization. The
issue as to whether the private express statutes should be eliminated in
order to permit private entrepreneurs to compete with the USPS has been
argued in the newspapers, on major television public policy forums, and
in such prestigious think tanks as the Brookings Institution. Top Reagan
and Bush Administration officials have taken the affirmative on this
question, and have based their position on the "abuse of a federal
monopoly."[15]

James Bovard, sounding very much like the postal union leader, wrote:

> ...In the past fifteen years, the USPS has intentionally slowed mail
> delivery, cut back on mail collection pickups, shortened the target
> zone for overnight delivery, reduced business deliveries, and imposed

strict requirements on the size of letters it will accept, and begun the abolition of home delivery...[16]

This is a criticism of USPS management, one that has been echoed by postal unions, and appears to be more of an indictment of the giants of American industry who have served as Postmasters General over the past twenty years than of the Postal Service itself. It is true that services have declined and the price of the stamp has risen slightly over the rate of inflation, but it is also true that the Postal Service has not received direct taxpayer subsidies since 1983, and that the price of the stamp in real dollars has declined since 1970 when the Postal Service did receive substantial direct taxpayer subsidies. Bovard's complaint about reduced services sounds very much like the testimony Moe Biller presented before the Board of Governors on January 8, 1990.

However, Bovard has a different explanation for that result. He charged that the increase in postal rates has been the direct result of "out of control" postal wage rates. He quotes Postal Rate Commissioner John Crutcher who called postal workers the "highest paid semi-skilled workers in the world."[17] Crutcher's standard of comparison appeared to be the $5 to $6 an hour paid to minorities and women in private mail-sorting operations, rather than the nearly $3 per hour premium paid to full-time UPS workers with only two years' experience, compared to APWU workers with eight or more years of experience. The gains won by postal workers through collective bargaining—a process adopted from the private sector—have resulted in wages slightly above the inflation rate, while the real wages of most nonunion and many union workers have fallen behind. Should the small gains or the substantial losses be the most decried? And, can postal unions take credit with their members for keeping their wages ahead of inflation and still argue before future arbitration boards that those wages have not exceeded private sector comparability?

The major question, however, is whether a universal, uniform service to the American people can be maintained if the private express statutes are eliminated. The supporters of the private express statutes maintain that if the postal monopoly is eliminated, private sector entrepreneurs would skim off the most profitable routes—in other words, they would choose Manhattan but not the Bronx—and leave the rest to a subsidized Postal Service. The proponents of privatization do not address this problem.

Creeping Privatization

The 1980s assault on the private express statutes was not successful. Bills were introduced in Congress, but they went nowhere. Congress was no doubt cognizant that polls showed that overall favorability toward the Postal Service was at an all time high in 1990,[18] and that the perception was widespread that the breakup of the American Telephone and Telegraph monopoly resulted in worse services and higher rates to the American public. The privatizers were in no position to guarantee that the same wouldn't occur if the private express statutes were abolished, and the popularity of the Postal Service with the general public offset the often strident criticism of the proponents of privatization. However, a climate was created within the Reagan and Bush Administrations that made possible creeping privatization, or a change in the rules to permit firms such as React and the international remailers to operate in competition with the Postal Service, and the courts have ruled in favor of these changes. The USPS also announced its intention to contract out work once performed by postal workers, gave its blessing to franchise operations, and attempted to install postal retail installations (staffed by nonpostal workers) in stores, malls, and supermarkets throughout the country. There is no doubt that these efforts will continue in the future, and that they could have an adverse effect on the bargaining position of the APWU.

The Future of Postal Service Collective Bargaining

The APWU largely accomplished a necessary transition from craft to industrial unionism in the Postal Service. It reduced postal unions from a divisive eight to a more cohesive four, never being able to achieve the long advocated single union of postal workers, but engaging in generally united coalition bargaining with the Letter Carriers (a persisting craft union). Although they divide when their interests divide, as in the controversy over the contracting out of the Remote Video Encoding program, they do not publicly fight with or undercut each other. However, they both suffer from failure to incorporate or control the maverick Mail Handlers, and the Mail Handlers also suffer from the lack of access to the superior bargaining power of the more skilled workers in the other unions.

The APWU, operating under the Postal Reorganization Act of 1970, has achieved a transition from relatively ineffective selective lobbying (begging) before the Congress to effective collective bargaining with the Postal Service. It has been able to achieve wage increases over time above those of the average American worker, far greater than the average nonpostal federal employee (who depends on the President and the Congress for wage increases), and at least equal to the average private sector union worker. It has manifested that collective bargaining success by keeping its members' incomes slightly ahead of inflation, whereas the wages of most other American workers have been falling behind the inflation rate.

That APWU collective bargaining success is also marred by the growing reliance on interest arbitration, probably an inevitable result of the absence of the right to strike. Employers and employees have inherent areas of commonality and conflicts of interest. Wages and benefits, unless directly tied to productivity, are in the conflict arena. Any bargaining exercise terminates successfully because both have more to gain (or less to lose) by agreeing than by failure to agree. At the final hour of a private sector collective bargaining session, the union asks itself, "Can we gain more by means of a strike (despite the pain) than by compromising now?" Management asks the same question about its ability to weather a strike. But, if there is an additional step to be taken to postpone the moment of truth, one or the other will see an advantage in taking it. Only if the expected neutral decision is less palatable than the available compromise will the arbitration step be avoided.

Three of five postal negotiations from 1978 to 1990 have ended in arbitration. The 1981 negotiation might have been added to the list had it not been for the alleged management renege which robbed union militancy of its momentum. The negotiated 1987 settlement was clearly more favorable to the union under the prevailing circumstances than either of the 1984 and 1991 arbitration decisions, perhaps explaining management's obvious intent to arrive at the arbitration step as expeditiously as possible in the latter year. The temptation to do so again will be strong in 1994 if union strength continues. And if the shoe were on the other foot, there is no assurance that the unions would not become the advocates of arbitration.

Arbitration also tends to postpone compromises and encourage extreme positions. "Last offer" arbitration, which limits the arbitrator to an either/or decision, can force the parties toward more reasonable positions, but does not end the temptation to go for arbitration rather than accept the available compromise. Legalization of federal strikes is unlikely. Only California, Pennsylvania, Montana, and a few other states have chosen to allow strikes by nonessential public employees, and the Congress has manifested no such permissiveness, though it is difficult to assign greater essentiality to most federal services than to many private ones. Without the right to strike or some other substitute through which the parties can penalize or reward each other without resort to a third party escape hatch, true collective bargaining will inevitably atrophy. Negotiated settlements may still occur when the differences between the parties are not major, but significant compromises are unlikely as long as the alternative is so readily available and tempting. The situation will still be better than resort to Congressional lobbying. At least the parties will have an opportunity to present evidence before an expert and neutral third party rather than politically elected generalists.

Have we gone from selective lobbying through collective bargaining to expert rule-making in only twenty years?

Wage Criteria

Apparently, private sector comparability is the given criterion for arbitration guidance. But, that always raises the question of what is comparable? The comparable worker criterion accepted by the 1984 and 1991 arbitration boards has neither a legal nor an economic rationale. On the other hand, the comparable level of work criterion is admittedly difficult to apply when the tasks in question have few counterparts. The Postal Service employs some workers with generic skills (such as clerical workers and truck drivers) but most of its employees are performing unique tasks, though not necessarily highly skilled ones (such as the sorting of mail either by hand or machine). Even UPS and Federal Express do not sort mail; their jobs may be comparable to parcel post, but have little comparability to the distribution of mail of any class. The work of company mail room employees may be comparable in some ways to the work performed by APWU members, but not in automated and mechanized mail facilities, where most APWU members are employed. A UPS comparison would undoubtedly be a boost for the APWU, but the actual jobs performed by UPS employees are more like those performed by mail handlers and letter carriers than those of APWU members. Thus, private sector comparability may be impossible to measure, and expert testimony regarding whether postal employees are or are not paid a premium over the private sector are, at best, highly speculative. Without a selection of jobs of comparable content, it is impossible to make a legitimate comparison. And even that would leave the questions of whether private sector race-gender discrimination should be perpetuated in the public sector, and whether those who choose to organize should have the advantage of their enhanced bargaining power.

The Struggle Continues

The APWU is an "enterprise union," much like Japanese unions whose members are generally employed by one individual company. As a result, the APWU's future is directly tied to the future of the USPS. Since the USPS is vulnerable to electronic mail and to privatization, so is the APWU; the union cannot spread its risks over other employers.

Moe Biller is very much aware of the APWU's dependence on the USPS:

> Our constitution gives us the right to organize outside the Postal Service. While we will fight attempts to privatize the USPS, if privatization should occur, we are prepared to organize those nonunion workers who take over our jobs. It's just a question of union vs. nonunion. Perhaps the time has come for the APWU to reach out into the private sector. If that's what we must do, rest assured that that is what we will do. I don't underestimate the power of those large corporations that are poised to take over USPS functions, or the bite of the United States Government, but where there are low wages and poor working conditions, there is a rich opportunity for union organization. We are now giving serious thought to outside organization, serious planning, and at the approporiate time, it will be undertaken.[19]

Regardless of the degree to which the privatization of the USPS succeeds, the USPS will be with us for a long period of time as the residual mailer. But it must inevitably shrink before the onslaught of electronic mail that eliminates the necessity for physical transmission of the letter. Since the USPS has not been successful in competing with the private overnight carriers (even though postal overnight rates are cheaper), and parcel post has lost ground to UPS, the future role of the USPS may change radically in the twenty-first century, and the role of the APWU will necessarily change with it.

The APWU, however, has proved to be a democratic, well-organized, well-managed advocate for its members. It faces, along with its employer, severe challenges in the future, but it has the capacity to see to it that the rights of its members will be respected as change occurs. Moe Biller's constant theme is, "The Struggle Continues," and so it will during the last decade of the twentieth century, and on into the twenty-first century. Regardless of what may happen in the future, the APWU has scored some impressive victories, not only in the field of collective bargaining, but in rights arbitration, the promotion of equal opportunity for minorities, women, and the handicapped, and in the battle against privatization. The APWU celebrated its Twentieth Anniversary in July 1991, beyond question the most propitious twenty years in postal labor union history. The solid presence of the Postal Service's only industrial union was in no small measure responsible for the impressive victories won by postal workers, victories that were won in spite of the conservative administrations during at least half of that twenty-year period.

As to the future, the challenges facing both the USPS and its unions are formidable, and much of what may happen is beyond the control of either. But the presence of the federal government's largest union, the APWU, will assure that as change occurs the interests and rights of its members will be observed and protected.

NOTES

Chapter 1

1. David Whitman, "Selling the Reorganization of the Post Office," Center for Press, Politics and Public Policy, Kennedy School of Government, Harvard University, 1984, p. 1.

2. *History of the U.S. Postal Service 1775-1984*, United States Postal Service, Washington, D.C., Publication 100, p.1, 1985.

3. *Newsweek*, "The Day the Mail Stopped," March 30, 1970, p. 14.

4. Joseph Modzelewski, "Strachan Tours Postal Dungeon," *New York Daily News*, March 31, p. 2.

5. One of the many letters which were circulated to post offices in the New York area prior to the strike (APWU files).

6. Remarks made by President Richard M. Nixon during a visit to the Post Office Department, February 10, 1969.

7. *The Union Mail*, Jan.-Feb., 1970, front page.

8. Ibid.

9. Murray B. Nesbitt, *Labor Relations in the Federal Government Service*, Bureau of National Affairs, Inc., Washington, DC, 1976, pp. 373–374.

10. Sidney A. Goodman, President, National Postal Union, Remarks to Federal Bar Association, Seminar on Collective Bargaining in Federal Service, Washington, April 18, 1967, p. 10.

Chapter 2

1. Based on anecdotes contained in the March 30, 1970 edition of *Newsweek*, p. 16.
2. Lawrence F. O'Brien, "How the Post Office Plotted Suicide," *Washington Post*, August 18, 1968, p. B4.
3. Murray B. Nesbitt, *Labor Relations in the Federal Government Service*, Bureau of National Affairs, Inc., Washington, DC, 1976, p. 336.
4. *Carriers' Flash*, New York Letter Carriers Organization Committee, Branch 36, NALC, December 31, 1969 (signed by Herman Sandbank, Executive Vice President).
5. Interview with Phillip Seligman, July 12, 1990.
6. Branch 36 Outlook, December 1969.
7. *Carriers' Flash*, March 12, 1970 (signed by Gustav J. Johnson, President, and all Branch 36 officers).
8. "Chronology of Events Leading Up To and Through the Postal Strike," unpublished diary of Moe Biller, March 12–March 26, 1970.
9. Ibid.
10. Ibid.
11. Interview with Milton Rosner, July 10, 1990.
12. "Chronology of Events," op. cit.
13. Interview with Douglas Holbrook, June 28, 1990.
14. *Newsweek*, "The Day the Mail Stopped," March 30, 1970, p. 14.
15. Interview with John O'Donnell, August 1, 1990.
16. *Army Magazine*, "Remember Moe Biller," September 1975, p. 27.

Chapter 3

1. Sterling Denhard Spero, *The Labor Movement in a Government Industry*, Macmillan Company, 1927, Reprint Edition 1971 by Arno Press, p. 13.
2. *Business Week*, "Federal Workers March to a New Drummer," March 28, 1970, p. 10.
3. *New York Times*, March 22, 1970, p. 40C.
4. Memorandum of Agreement between Postmaster General Winton M. Blount and the Seven Exclusive Postal Unions, April 2, 1971.
5. *Congressional Record—Senate*, June 18, 1970, p. 20328.

6. Public Law 91-375, 91st Congress, August 12, 1970.

7. Murray B. Nesbitt, *Labor Relations in the Federal Government Service*, Bureau of National Affairs, Inc., Washington, DC, 1976, p. 345.

8. Interview with Moe Biller, August 14 and August 24, 1990.

9. Ibid.

10. Ibid.

11. United Federation of Postal Clerks, AFL-CIO, Proceedings, Special Convention, Cleveland, OH, April 1966, p. 1.

12. Interview with David Silvergleid, July 11, 1990.

Chapter 4

1. Murray B. Nesbitt, *Labor Relations in the Federal Government Service*, Bureau of National Affairs, Inc., Washington, DC, 1976, p. 6.

2. *History of the U.S. Postal Service 1775-1984*, U.S. Postal Service, Publication 100, April 1985, p. 1.

3. Ibid., p. 1.

4. Ibid., p. 2.

5. Comdr. Karl Baarslag, U.S.N.R., History of the National Federation of Post Office Clerks, National Federation of Post Office Clerks, 1945, p. 15.

6. Ibid., p. 15.

7. Ibid., p. 15.

8. Ibid., p. 17.

9. Ibid., p. 17.

10. Sterling Denhard Spero, *The Labor Movement in a Government Industry*, Macmillan Company, 1927, Reprint Edition 1971 by Arno Press, Inc., p. 114.

11. Ibid., p. 114.

12. Ibid., p. 126.

13. Ibid., p. 128.

14. Ibid., p. 129.

15. *Harpoon*, September, 1909, p. 12.

16. Murray B. Nesbitt, *Labor Relations in the Federal Government Service*, Bureau of National Affairs, Inc., Washington, DC, 1976, p. 36.

17. Ibid., p. 36.

18. Ibid., p. 37.

19. Sterling Denhard Spero, *The Labor Movement in a Government Industry*, Macmillan Company, 1927, Reprint Edition 1971 by Arno Press, Inc., p. 80.

20. Ibid., p. 80.

21. Comdr. Karl Baarslag, U.S.N.R., *History of the National Federation of Post Office Clerks*, National Federation of Post Office Clerks, 1945, p. 6.

22. *The Labor Movement in a Government Industry*, op. cit., pp. 111-112.

23. "These Are The Men," pamphlet published by the National Postal Clerks Union (Undated, circa 1959).

24. Interview with Phillip Seligman, July 12, 1990.

25. Interview with Moe Biller, August 14 and August 24, 1990.

26. "Excerpts from Supreme Court's Ruling and the Dissent in Security Ouster Case," *New York Times*, June 12, 1956, p. 22L.

27. Ibid.

28. Interview with Moe Biller, August 14 and August 24, 1990, verified by interview with Walter Noreen, February 28, 1991.

29. Ibid.

30. See Official Transcript of Proceedings before the Post Office Department, Docket 32893, PS in the Matter of Morris Biller, New York, New York, May 28, 1956.

31. "Excerpts from Supreme Court's Ruling and the Dissent in Security Ouster Case," *New York Times*, June 12, 1956, p. 22L.

32. "These Are The Men," pamphlet published by the National Postal Clerks Union (Undated, circa 1959).

33. Ibid.

34. Interview with Moe Biller, August 14 and August 24, 1990.

35. *Progressive Fed*, November–December, 1958, p. 4.

36. Ibid., July, 1958, p. 1.

37. Ibid., September, 1958, p. 3.

38. Thirtieth Convention of the National Federation of Post Office Clerks, *Proceedings*, Boston, MA, August 25–30, 1958, p. 99.

39. Ibid., p. 28.

40. Ibid., p. 115.

41. Ibid., p. 117.

42. "The Postal Strike," *Biennial Report*, National Convention of United

Federation of Postal Clerks, Los Angeles, CA, August 10-15, 1970, pp. 7-8.

Chapter 5

1. Sterling Denhard Spero, *The Labor Movement in a Government Industry*, The Macmillan Co., 1927, Reprint Edition, Arno Press, Inc., 1971, p. 9.

2. Ibid., p. 10.

3. *Congressional Record* (66th Congress, 2nd Session), p. 5132.

4. *New York Sun*, May 18, 1909.

5. Sterling Denhard Spero, *The Labor Movement in a Government Industry*, The Macmillan Co., 1927, Reprint Edition, Arno Press, Inc., 1971, p. 20.

6. Joseph Stewart, "How Can Government Employees Secure Redress of Grievances Without Striking?" *National Civic Federation: Proceedings*, 1912, pp. 74–75.

7. Order by Postmaster General, William L. Wilson, 1895.

8. Executive Order by President Theodore Roosevelt, January 31, 1902.

9. Sterling Denhard Spero, *The Labor Movement in a Government Industry*, p. 112.

10. Ibid., p. 112.

11. Executive Order of President Theodore Roosevelt, January 25, 1906.

12. *The Labor Movement in a Government Industry*, op. cit., p. 113.

13. Executive Order of President William Howard Taft, November 26, 1909.

14. *New York Sun*, December 1, 1909.

15. Sterling Denhard Spero, *The Labor Movement in a Government Industry*, p. 131.

16. Ibid., p. 140.

17. Ibid., p. 124.

18. Ibid., p. 125.

19. Senate Doc. 866 (62nd Congress, 2nd Session), p. 47-48.

20. *The Labor Movement in a Government Industry*, Op. Cit., p. 168.

21. *Union Postal Clerk*, March 4, 1921.

22. *Postal Bulletin*, March 11, 1921.

23. Murray B. Nesbitt, *Labor Relations in the Federal Government Service*, Bureau of National Affairs, 1976, p. 45.

24. Ibid., p. 45.

25. Ibid., p. 45.

26. Ibid., p. 10.

27. Ibid., p. 10.

28. Letter dated August 16, 1937, as cited in Nesbitt, pp. 10–11.

29. *Labor Relations in the Federal Government Service,* op. cit., p. 11

30. Floyd W. Reeves and Paul T. David, Personnel Administration in the Federal Service, 1937, p. 54.

31. Op. cit., p. 12.

32. Taft-Hartley Act, Public Law 101.

33. Order by Postmaster General Arthur E. Summerfield, 1953.

34. National Civil Service League, Employee Organization in the Public Service, 1946, p. 16.

35. U.S. Commission on Organization of the Executive Branch of the Government, *Report on the Task Force on Personnel and Civil Service,* 1955, p. 110.

36. Murray B. Nesbitt, *Labor Relations in the Federal Government Service,* p. 15.

37. U.S. House of Representatives, H.R. 12, 87th Congress, 1st Session, 1961, Sec. 201 (b) (1).

38. Letter from John F. Kennedy to John W. Ames, Publicity Director, Illinois Federation of Postal Clerks, October 31, 1960.

39. Murray B. Nesbitt, *Labor Relations in the Federal Government Service,* p. 19.

40. President's Task Force on Employee-Management Relations in the Federal Service, November 30, 1961; Executive Order 10988, January 17, 1962.

41. Wilson R. Hart, "The U.S. Civil Service Learns to Live with Executive Order 10988: An Interim Appraisal," *Industrial and Labor Relations Review,* January, 1964, p. 205.

42. Proceedings of the Institute on Employee-Management Cooperation, U.S. Department of Labor, Office of Employee-Management Relations, March 8, 1963, p. 33.

Chapter 6

1. Telephone interview with Robert Kephart, March 4, 1991.

2. Telephone interview with Chester Parrish, March 7, 1991.

3. Interview with Owen Schoon, December 10, 1990.

4. First Biennial Convention of the American Postal Workers Union, AFL-CIO, August 12–16, 1972, Proceedings, pp. 391-392.

5. James H. Rademacher, President, NALC, *The Postal Record*, April, 1971, pp. 4–5.

6. Telephone interview with Chester Parrish, March 7, 1991.

7. Interview with William Burrus, June 21, 1990.

8. Interview with Michael Benner, June 5, 1990.

9. First Biennial Convention of the American Postal Workers Union, AFL-CIO, August 12–16, 1972, Proceedings.

10. Interview with Moe Biller, August 14 and August 24, 1990.

11. Interview with Moe Biller, August 14 and August 24, 1990.

12. Interview with Moe Biller, August 14 and August 24, 1990.

13. Ibid.

14. Interview with John O'Donnell, August 1, 1990.

15. *The Union Postal Clerk*, May, 1971, p. 4.

16. Ibid., p. 4.

17. Interview with Bernard Cushman, January 29, 1991.

18. Ibid.

19. Damon Stetson, "Postal Workers' Rally Becomes Melee," *New York Times*, July 27, 1971.

20. Interview with Josie McMillian, December 11, 1990.

21. *News Flash*, Joint Organization of Mail Handlers, MBPU and Local 1, Jan. 4, 1972 (Signed by Sam Mason, Local 1, LIUNA and Moe Biller, President, MBPU).

22. Jeffrey Keefe, "Collective Bargaining in the Postal Service," IMLR Rutgers University, May 2, 1990, p. 4.

23. George Meany, Statement, AFL-CIO, Washington, D.C., November, 1974.

24. Interview with Josie McMillian, December 11, 1990.

25. *Time Magazine*, March 4, 1991, "Interview," p. 12.

26. William F. Bolger, Address before USPS Managers Meeting, Cleveland, Ohio, March 15, 1978.

27. Bob Williams, *Federal Times*, July 31, 1978, p. 5.

28. Mike Causey, *Washington Post*, "A Civil Service Contrast," p. C2.

29. Op. cit.

30. Ibid.

31. Interview with Moe Biller, August 14 and August 24, 1990.

32. *Signed, Sealed and Delivered: Labor Struggle in the Post Office*, Documentary Film by Tamerik Productions, funded by North Star Fund Cultural Council Foundation, Artists Project, CETA Title IX, 1980.

33. Ibid.

34. Interview with Josie McMillian, December 11, 1990.

35. Ibid.

36. Interview with Danny Frank, August 3, 1990.

37. Ibid.

38. Ibid.

39. David Neustadt, "Post Mortem: Did Mike McDermott Die in Vain," *The Village Voice*, Jan. 7, 1980, p. 11.

40. Ibid.

41. Ibid.

42. Ibid., p. 12.

43. Morris Biller, Coordinator, Northeast Region, American Postal Workers Union, AFL-CIO, "Update on NYB/FMC Story Re: Michael McDermott," January 11, 1980.

44. Moe Biller, Testimony Before Joint Congressional Committee on Safety Conditions in the Post Office, January 7–8, 1980.

45. *Signed, Sealed and Delivered: Labor Struggle in the Post Office*, Documentary Film by Tamerik Productions, funded by North Star Fund Cultural Council Foundation, Artists Project, CETA Title IX, 1980.

46. Interview with Moe Biller, August 14 and August 24, 1990.

47. Ibid.

48. Bob Williams, *Federal Times*, September 4, 1978, p. 5.

49. Ibid.

50. Fourth Biennial Convention of the American Postal Workers Union, Denver, CO, August 14–19, 1978, Proceedings, p. 18.

51. *Federal Times*, August 28, 1978, p. 6.

52. Ibid.

53. Interview with Danny Frank, August 3, 1990.

Chapter 7

1. All the material in this section is based on interviews with Moe Biller on August 14 and August 24, 1990. All quotes were obtained from those interviews.

2. James A. Bill, *The Eagle and the Lion*, Yale University Press, New Haven and London, 1988, p. 333.

3. Interview with Moe Biller, August 14 and August 24, 1990.

4. Ibid.

5. Ibid.

6. Ibid.

7. Interview with Daniel Driscoll, January 28, 1991.

8. Interview with Moe Biller, August 14 and August 24, 1990.

9. Ibid.

10. Ibid.

11. LRRM, Leiner v. Andrews, U.S. District Court, District of Columbia, July 6, 1979, p. 2820.

12. Interview with Kenneth Leiner, March 22, 1991.

13. Interview with Moe Biller, August 14 and August 24, 1990.

14. Interview with Danny Frank, August 3, 1990.

15. Ibid.

16. Interview with Daniel Driscoll, January 28, 1991.

17. Ibid.

18. Videotape, *1983 Elections American Postal Workers Union*, Dave Daniel for President, 28th Street Video, Inc., New York, New York, 1983.

19. Interview with Daniel Driscoll, January 28, 1991.

20. Interview with John O'Donnell, August 1, 1990.

21. Interview with Ben Evans, December 21, 1990.

22. Ibid.

23. Ibid.

Chapter 8

1. Interview with Daniel Driscoll, January 28, 1991.

2. Ibid.

3. Douglas C. Holbrook, "APWU Leaving Peep Show Row," *The American Postal Worker*, March, 1982, p. 10.

4. David E. Daniel, "Statement," *The American Postal Worker*, August 1983, p. 50.

5. Alan B. Krueger, "Are Public Sector Workers Paid More Than Their Alternative Wages? Evidence from Longitudinal Data and Job Queues," in Richard B. Freeman and Casey Ichniowski (eds.), *When Public Sector*

Workers Organize, The University of Chicago Press, Chicago, 1988, pp. 217–220.

6. Jeffrey M. Perloff and Michael L. Wachter, "Wage Comparability in the U.S. Postal Service," *Industrial and Labor Relations Review*, Vol. 38, No. 1, (October 1984), p. 28.

7. Ibid., p. 31.

8. Ibid., pp. 26–38 and Martin Asher and Joel Popkin, "The Effect of Gender and Race Differentials on Public-Private Comparisons: A Study of Postal Workers," *Industrial and Labor Relations Review*, Vol. 38, No. 1 (October 1984), pp. 16–25.

9. Asher and Popkin, op. cit., p. 18.

10. Perloff and Wachter, op. cit., p. 35.

11. Arbitration Proceedings, United States Postal Service and National Association of Letter Carriers and American Postal Workers Union, AFL-CIO, Opinion and Award, Washington, DC, Dec., 1984, pp. 21–22.

12. *The American Postal Worker*, Feb., 1985, p. 3.

13. "Chronology of Meetings at Federal Mediation and Conciliation Service and Continuing Update Through Interest Arbitration," unpublished diary of Moe Biller, Dec., 1984, p. 12.

14. *The American Postal Worker*, Oct., 1986, p. 7.

15. Ibid.

16. Ibid., August, 1987, pp. 8–9.

17. Washington Post, Nov. 3, 1990, p. A10.

18. *The American Postal Worker*, Sept., 1982, p. 5.

19. Ibid., March, 1985, pp. 2–3.

20. Ibid.

21. Ibid., Jan., 1989, p. 3.

22. Ibid., Sept., 1984, pp. 4-5.

23. Ibid., Oct., 1985, p. 10.

24. Ibid., July, 1989, p. 2.

25. Ibid.

26. Ibid., May, 1985, p. 6.

27. "NLRB Issues Complaint Against USPS Over Employee Involvement Programs," *Employee Relations Weekly*, Bureau of National Affairs, Volume 9 (July 8, 1991), p. 751.

28. *The American Postal Worker*, Sept. 1983, p. 4.

29. Collective Bargaining Agreement Between American Postal Workers

Union, AFL-CIO, and U.S. Postal Service, July 21, 1987–November 20, 1990, p. 183.

30. Op. cit., "Focus on Hearing Impaired Issues," Nov., 1990, p. 6.

31. *Time Magazine*, "Interview—Neither Rain Nor Sleet Nor 29 Cent Stamps," March 4, 1991, p. 12.

32. 1990 Negotiations U.S. Postal Service, American Postal Workers Union, AFL-CIO, and the National Association of Letter Carriers, AFL-CIO, Position of U.S. Postal Service, p. 3.

33. Joseph J. Mahon, Jr., Declaration, United States District Court for the District of Columbia, Civil Action No. 91-0479 (LFO), pp. 11-12.

34. William Burrus, Viewpoint—"Conscious and Deliberate Deception," *The American Postal Worker*, April, 1991, pp. 4-5.

35. Moe Biller, "Communicating Directly With You, The Member," *The American Postal Worker*, April, 1991, p. 2.

36. According to APWU Secretary-Treasurer Douglas Holbrook, the APWU's arbitration costs were $1,360,000. Assuming that the costs were the same for the NALC and the USPS, the total cost of the arbitration procedure would have been over $4,000,000.

37. Michael L. Wachter and James W. Gillula, "Wage Comparability in the U.S. Postal Service: The Total Pay Premium, New Hire Results, and Changes in Product Market Competition," Testimony to USPS-JBC Interest Arbitration, March 21, 1991, p. 1.

38. Ibid., p. 8.

39. See AFL-CIO News, "Unionized Workers Profit From Decided Advantage," July 8, 1991, p. 6.

40. Arbitration Proceedings, United States Postal Service and National Association of Letter Carriers and American Postal Workers Union, Opinion and Award, Washington, DC, June 12, 1991, pp. 16–18.

41. Ibid.

42. Statement by Theodore W. Kheel, Member of the Board of Arbitrators, appended to Arbitration Proceedings, June 12, 1991.

43. Ibid.

44. Anthony M. Frank, "Memorandum For All Officers, Field Division General Managers, Postmasters," June 12, 1991, p. 1.

45. Moe Biller, Letter to Local, State and National Officers, June 12, 1991.

46. Howard Evans, *Salt Lake City Post*, Feb., 1986, p. 1.

Chapter 9

1. Michael Specter, "New York News Strike: Unions Still Bark, But Some Doubt They Can Bite," *Washington Post*, November 3, 1990, p. A10.

2. Ibid.

3. Annual Report of the Postmaster General Fiscal Year 1990, p. 21.

4. Ibid., p. 53.

5. Arbitration Proceedings, United States Postal Service and the National Association of Letter Carriers and the American Postal Workers Union, June 12, 1981, Exhibit #86.

6. Ibid., Exhibit 89.

7. Ibid., Exhibit 87.

8. Ibid., Exhibit 92.

9. *Time Magazine*, Interview—"Neither Rain, Nor Sleet, Nor 29 Cent Stamps," March 14, 1991, p. 10.

10. *Business Week*, "More Downsizing at the Post Office," October 7, 1991, p. 42.

11. Moe Biller, Remarks before the Board of Governors United States Postal Service, Washington, DC, January 8, 1990, pp. 13-14.

12. Interview with Moe Biller, October 28, 1991.

13. Ibid.

14. Rubin Handelman, "A Controversial Speech?" *The Postal Supervisor*, December 1990, p. 3.

15. James Bovard, "The Last Dinosaur: The U.S. Postal Service," Cato Institute Policy Analysis, No. 47, February 12, 1985, p. 1.

16. Ibid.

17. Ibid., p. 13.

18. Arbitration Proceedings, United States Postal Service and the National Association of Letter Carriers and the American Postal Workers Union, June 12, 1981, Exhibit #94.

19. Interview with Moe Biller, October 28, 1991.

INDEX OF PEOPLE

SUBJECT INDEX

APPENDIX

ORIGINAL EXECUTIVE BOARD
AMERICAN POSTAL WORKERS UNION AFL–CIO

Francis S. Filbey
General President

Patrick J. Nilan
Legislative Director

David Silvergleid
General Executive Vice President

Owen H. Schoon
General Secretary Treasurer

Philip E. Dooley
President, Clerk Craft

Monroe Crable
President, Maintenance Craft

Chester Parrish
President, Motor Vehicle Craft

Michael Cullen
President, Special Delivery Craft

Don E. Dunn
Director, Industrial Relations

Edward L. Bowley
Legislative Aide

Joseph F. Thomas
Organization Director

Ted Valliere
Research & Education Director

Jack Love
Hospital Plans Director

John R. Dubay
Assistant Hospital Plans
Director

Ben Evans
Assistant Hospital Plans
Director

Robert P. Kephart
Administrator of Finance &
Records

Zoltan Grossman
National Representative at Large

John R. Smith
Mail Handler Vice President

CLERK CRAFT

John F. McClelland
Administrative Vice President

Emmet Andrews
Administrative Aide

John A. Morgen
Executive Aide

NATIONAL VICE PRESIDENTS—CLERK CRAFT

John Held

Willis Cadman

Carroll Rohr

Donald Silvestri

Clinton C. Gross

Bernard A. Schultz

Hugo Monkkonen

Thomas J. Coffey

Robert P. Whitman

James W. (Bucky) Walter

Robert L. (Bob) Soule

Thomas MacDonald

H.O. Wright

Walter T. Kenney

James P. Williams

NATIONAL REPRESENTATIVES—CLERK CRAFT

James M. Murphy

Bernard Schwartz

Thomas L. Thompson

Dominick R. Prosperi

Lawrence J. (Larry) Gervais

Raydell R. Moore

MAINTENANCE CRAFT

Richard I. Wevodau
Administrative Aide

William J. Kaczor
Administrative Assistant

MOTOR VEHICLE CRAFT

Leon S. Hawkins
Administrative Vice President

NATIONAL FIELD REPRESENTATIVES
MOTOR VEHICLE CRAFT

Leon W. Hopton

Ernest J. Romano

Moe Biller
Member-at-Large
National Executive Board

PRESENT EXECUTIVE BOARD
National Executive Board

Moe Biller
President

William Burrus
Executive Vice President

Douglas C. Holbrook
Secretary-Treasurer

Thomas A. Neill
Industrial Relations Director

Kenneth D. Wilson
Director, Clerk Division

Thomas K. Freeman, Jr.
Director, Maintenance Division

Donald A. Ross
Director, MVS Division

George N. McKeithen
Director, SDM Division

Norman L. Steward
Director, Mail Handler
Division

Regional Coordinators

James P. Williams
Central Region

Philip C. Flemming, Jr.
Eastern Region

Elizabeth "Liz" Powell
Northeast Region

Archie Salisbury
Southern Region

Raydell R. Moore
Western Region